TWENTIETH-CENTURY GERMAN POLITICAL THOUGHT

TWENTIETH-CENTURY GERMAN POLITICAL THOUGHT

Peter M. R. Stirk

EDINBURGH UNIVERSITY PRESS

Peter M. R. Stirk, 2006

Edinburgh University Press Ltd
22 George Square, Edinburgh

Transferred to digital print, 2007

Typeset in Linotype Sabon by
Iolaire Typesetting, Newtonmore, and
Printed and bound by CPI Antony Rowe, Eastbourne

A CIP record for this book is available from the British Library

ISBN-10 0 7486 2290 X (hardback)
ISBN-13 978 0 7486 2290 0 (hardback)
ISBN-10 0 7486 2291 8 (paperback)
ISBN-13 978 0 7486 2291 7 (paperback)

Contents

Preface

This book is intended to convey a sense of the diversity and richness of German political thought in the twentieth century and to introduce English-speaking readers to a wider range of German political theorists than they are likely to find in other volumes. It makes no claim to be comprehensive, and eminent figures whom some readers might expect to find have been neglected. In a work of this size and range, that is inevitable. The omission of political thought in the German Democratic Republic might seem more surprising. However, the political thought of that part of Germany, while interesting in its own right, has had limited impact upon the understanding of the development of German political thought. Nor did the Democratic Republic present the same conceptual challenge as the Third Reich.

I am grateful to the School of Government and International Affairs at the University of Durham for research leave that enabled me to complete this book.

Introduction

Any attempt to survey German political thought in the twentieth century is bound to be influenced by awareness of the turbulence of German political history and especially by the shadow of the Third Reich, the crisis and collapse of the Weimar Republic that preceded it and the division of Germany that followed it for almost half a century. If one considers the historical context of German political thought a little more widely, that impression of turbulence is enhanced, at least for the first half of the century. At the beginning of the twentieth century, German political theorists inhabited not only the recently formed German *Reich* to the north but also the multi-national Habsburg Empire to the south. Many of the theorists prominent in the early chapters of this account were born in or influenced by the peculiar nature of that empire. Its collapse at the end of the First World War left behind a largely homogeneous German Austria that was subsequently incorporated into the Third Reich and then re-established as an independent state at the end of the Second World War. Not surprisingly, this political discontinuity is reflected in many accounts of the development of German political thought.

According to Wilhelm Hennis, despite what he described as the 'German misery' of the preceding centuries, the German lands had not seen anything comparable to the crisis of legitimacy experienced in France and England in the religious wars of the sixteenth and seventeenth centuries until 1933. Only in the twentieth century did Germany, the 'belated nation', experience an analogous crisis 'with all that goes with it: exile on a massive scale, "internal emigration", fanaticism, collapse of civil order, finally ethically motivated resistance'.[1] The sense of rupture has been expressed even more starkly by Jürgen Habermas, who was influenced by the Frankfurt School theorists who formed part of that massive exile. According to Habermas:

> Unfortunately, in the cultural nation of the Germans, a connection to universalist constitutional principles that was anchored in convictions

could be formed only after – and through – Auschwitz. Anyone who wants to dispel our shame about this fact with an empty phrase like 'obsession with guilt' . . . anyone who wants to recall the Germans to a conventional form of their national identity, is destroying the only reliable basis for our tie to the West.[2]

Many people do not agree with Habermas's concern that there could be a plausible threat to Germany's tie to the west, but there is general agreement that German political thought was distinctive, that there was a specifically German tradition of political thought and that this distinctiveness has either evaporated as part of a wider process of westernisation or has at least diminished. Exactly when and how this process took place, and exactly how complete it is, is highly disputed. It is notable that those suspected of clinging to elements of the old tradition are often criticised by invoking their supposed proximity to discredited theorists of the past. A prime example of this is the use of Carl Schmitt, a political theorist who was highly critical of the democratic system of the Weimar Republic and was tainted by his association with the Third Reich. To identify someone's ideas with those of Schmitt is often to imply, and sometimes to explicitly assert, that those ideas are not only misguided but also politically dangerous. Even those who take a more favourable view of Schmitt often take care to mark out their distance from him in key respects. To that extent, the shadow of the failure of Weimar and the Third Reich extends to contemporary German political thought. Similarly, consideration of the German tradition of political thought prior to the Third Reich, and even prior to the Weimar Republic, is inevitably accompanied by knowledge of what was to follow. Sometimes the same critical strategy is deployed. The description of Carl Schmitt as the legitimate heir of Max Weber by Habermas was rightly perceived as a damning indictment of Weber.[3] More typically, theorists are accused of an inability to comprehend the true nature of modern parliamentary democracy precisely because of their entrapment within a tradition of political thought hostile to it. The picture is not a wholly monochrome one, though usually those exempt from the general judgement are presented as isolated figures whose exceptional status proves the general rule. One example of this is the interest in Hugo Preuss, who drafted the Weimar constitution but who was relatively neglected until recently.[4]

The prism of Weimar's failure and the Third Reich is difficult to avoid, not least because of the persistent reference to those traumas by later political theorists. Yet it is also distorting. It is so, in the first place, because theorists at the beginning of the century, and many on the eve of the advent of Third Reich, had no conception of a political system like the Third Reich. This statement is more than a trivial and obvious observation about our inability to predict the future. One of the difficulties that political theorists had, and still have, in dealing with the Third Reich is its novelty and inconsistency. The difficulty posed by the nature of the regime has been well put by a recent commentator: 'The quest for a system seems to me a wrong approach to begin with, since no system existed and none was supposed to'.[5] Of course, many did seek to define a system, including those who remained within Germany and more or less enthusiastically supported the regime. As will be shown in Chapter 3, however, their efforts were frustrated and they were far from agreed on what the nature of the regime was. The exiles were also confronted with the elusive quality of the regime. The sheer novelty of the Third Reich and its possible resemblance to Stalinist Russia induced a search for the roots of this strange phenomenon which some, like Helmuth Plessner, found in the 'belated nation' of the Germans while others, like the Frankfurt School members Theodor Adorno and Max Horkheimer, went back to the beginnings of western civilisation in an attempt to explain how something like this regime was possible at all.[6]

The prism of the Third Reich is distorting in the second place simply because the twelve years of political thought within that regime cannot throw sufficient light on the almost half-century of subsequent political thought within the Federal Republic of Germany. More illumination can be had from reference to the debates within the Weimar Republic, which have continued to be an important point of reference, even for those keen to mark out the difference between the Weimar Republic and the Federal Republic, whether the latter is identified as the pre-reunification Bonn Republic or the post-unification Berlin Republic. That Bonn is not Weimar, nor is Berlin, does make a great deal of difference. The possible connotations of Carl Schmitt's ideas at the end of the twentieth century are not the same as during the final years of Weimar or at the height of the power of the Third Reich. Context makes a difference. Again, this observation may sound obvious and even trivial. It may be obvious but it is not trivial, as will be shown below. It is worth making another apparently obvious point. Almost fifty years of political thought in the Federal Republic has not taken place solely in the form of a debate with Weimar or Wilhelmine political thought. Thus, after Habermas published his *Between Facts and Norms*, one of the criticisms he responded to was the charge that he had unduly neglected certain figures in the German political tradition. His response was that in part their ideas were so familiar to him that he had simply taken them for granted.[7] Equally important, however, is the fact that Habermas has been engaged in a long-standing trans-Atlantic debate that provides a biographical illustration of the process of westernisation.[8]

It is also worth noting that, as the case of Hugo Preuss illustrates, a tradition of political thought is something that has to be constantly appropriated, reassessed and reshaped. An even more striking illustration of this is provided by two books. The first, on anti-democratic thought in the Weimar Republic, by Kurt Sontheimer, was published in 1962, was reissued in an abbreviated version in 1968 and became a standard reference point for the study of Weimar political thought.[9] The second, on democratic thought in the Weimar Republic, was published almost forty years after the first edition of Sontheimer's book. Its editor, Christoph Gusy, noted the long, and continuing, influence of Sontheimer's text and then added in bold text: 'About democratic thought in the [Weimar] Republic we know, now as before, almost nothing'.[10] That was an exaggeration, but there was more than enough truth in it to demonstrate how the German political tradition is being reshaped.

The prism of the Third Reich is distorting in the third place insofar as it is associated with the presumption of the existence of a political tradition, either one that perniciously persists or one that had thankfully now been abandoned. This presumption is distorting not because of a lack of change but because it draws attention away from the fact that the German tradition of political thought has been a contested one and, crucially, because the very idea of a German political tradition has been a polemical weapon in disputes about the nature of the state, politics, the nation and much else. It has been deployed by those who have wished to put forward certain ideas as distinctive and positive values to which Germans should subscribe. It has also been deployed by those who have put forward certain ideas as distinctive but negative values which Germans should abandon. It is this aspect of German political discourse which will be emphasised in the following account. There is a broader issue here as well. With reference to the historian Ernst Troeltsch, George Iggers wrote that

> Every culture appears to consist rather of a conglomerate of contradictory
> forces, visions and ideas that logically cannot be brought under a single

roof. Troeltsch did not deny this, but did not want to concede that thereby the possibility of scientifically understanding the essence of a specific culture, and working out its ideal from its objective substance, is lost.[11]

This is arguably a problem that can be found in any national political tradition, though this cannot be pursued here. Given the political turbulence of the first half of the twentieth century, including defeat in the First World War, the failure of Weimar and the first Austrian Republic, the Third Reich and its long shadow, and the division of Germany for much of the second half of the twentieth century, it is not surprising that the idea of a German tradition of political thought has been contentious.

This does not mean that it is impossible to discern recurrent themes and concepts. Polemical disputes presume that there are sufficient common reference points about which disagreement is possible, even if the disagreement is carried to the point where the concept at issue is deemed by some to be one that should be abandoned. The most obvious starting point in the history of twentieth-century German political thought is that of the state. Many accounts that identify a German tradition of political thought place the concept of the state at the centre. According to some, for example Kenneth Dyson, the German tradition is based on a broader continental tradition of 'state' societies, where the 'term "state society" refers to societies which have a historical and intellectual tradition of the state as an institution that embodies the "public power"'.[12] In contrast, the Anglo-Saxon tradition is one of 'stateless' societies, that is societies that lack this experience. Others, for example Christoph Möllers, insist that the German approach to the state is distinctive from the French approach.[13] There is indeed a tradition whereby legal scholars produce texts with the title *Allgemeine Staatslehre* (General Theory of the State), the most influential of which at the beginning of the century was that of Georg Jellinek. What is at issue, however, is not just the concept of the state per se, or the idea of a general theory of the state, disputed though they are, but the wider political connotations of the concept and the theory. It has been argued, and still is argued, that this tradition of state discourse is marred by its entrapment in monarchical and authoritarian conceptions that were dominant at the beginning of the century. In general, this concept of the state is characterised, we are told, by the presumption that there is such a thing as the state, which is susceptible to a general description or theory.

The second feature of this concept is the idea that the state existed and exists prior to any constitutional order and constraint. This priority is construed as being both historical and existential. It is historical in that the state existed before constitutions were drafted and granted or conceded by the state, that is, typically, by the monarchical head of state. It is existentially prior in that the state comes to the fore in the event of a paralysis of the constitutionally prescribed order. The third characteristic is that this concept of the state was expressed in distinctive legal forms, that is, as an association unified by a will and conceived of as a legal person. The fourth feature is that this juristic personality with its unified will is contrasted to society. The state is defined by its distance from society, to whose members, the citizens, it exists in a relationship of (state) command and (citizens') obedience. Society here is a non-political world primarily concerned with the satisfaction of the material and private needs of its members. The state has to maintain its distance from the pluralism of society, which it must consider as a threat to its integrity and unity. This state stands above society. The fifth feature is closely related to this. This concept of the state excludes political parties. Political parties which give expression to the diversity and pluralism of society cannot form part of the state. The state does not exclude political parties in the literal sense of prohibiting them but rather in the sense of relegating them to the sphere of society. Political parties as such cannot, then, form the political will of the state. The sixth feature is that this concept of the state has pronounced monarchical and authoritarian characteristics. It is the monarchical state or the author-itarian state even when those terms are not explicitly used. The general point is neatly summarised by Peter Häberle's reference at the end of the twentieth century to the title of Adolf Merkl's article of 1920: 'Die monarchische Befangenheit der deutschen Staatsrechtslehre' (The monarchical entrapment of German legal state theory).[14] The seventh feature is that this concept of the state was, usually self-consciously, German and is different from and was distinguished from western constitutional concepts.

As the title of Merkl's article indicates, at least some of the features of this concept of the state have long been disputed. More recently, it has been argued that the concept is so burdened by undesirable connotations that it should be abandoned altogether. In some quarters, there has indeed been a turn away from the discourse of the state. It is notable, for example, that a current introduction to disputed concepts in political theory does not include the state per se in its twenty-two topics.[15] On the other hand, there has been a renaissance of the discourse of the state over the last two decades. The contentious nature of this is evident in the complaint of one of the leading protagonists of this revival, Josef Isensee, of the use of terms like society, political system, government, governance and democracy as 'verbal surrogates for the unspeakable "state"'.[16]

The concept of politics itself is a second reference point. Here too is a concept of fluctuating prominence and disputed connotations, often linked to the fate of the concept of the state. According to Jellinek: '"Political" means "related to the state" [staatlich]: in the concept of the political one has already thought of the concept of the state'.[17] This has been taken to signify the predominance of the concept of the state to the point where, as indicated above, non-state actors, that is the citizens, are excluded from the political realm and consigned to an unpolitical realm concerned with the pursuit of private, material interests. In a related variation on the relation between the state and the concept of politics, advocates of a distinctive German vision of the state associated the state with the adoption of a standpoint above political parties. In that sense, the supposed unpolitical nature of Germans was transformed into a positive virtue. As such, it was first defended and then ridiculed by the novelist Thomas Mann. Quite how problematic the relationship between these concepts could become is evident in the assessment of the impact of National Socialism by Herbert Marcuse in 1934. As a Jewish-Marxist member of the exiled Frankfurt School, Marcuse had no sympathy for the new regime in Germany. Yet he conceded that in one respect the 'totalitarian view of the state represents progress' – that is, insofar as it finally did away with the unpolitical stance through its ruthless politicisation of the population.[18]

What we have here is on the one hand a concept of politics as an autonomous realm of activity, whether monopolised by the state or demarcated by other criteria that separate it out from economic and social concerns, and on the other hand the idea of an unpolitical stance being challenged by violent processes of political radicalisation. Both have ensured that the concept of politics has remained, if not exactly a theme of enduring reflection, at least a theme of recurrent dispute. It is part of that process that advocates of a focus on the nature of politics, which invariably means a specific conception of politics, have periodically bemoaned the faltering of interest in the concept. Thus, at the end of the nineteenth century, Otto Hintze complained that almost no-one regularly offered lectures in politics. A century later, Wilhelm Bleek, in a history of political science in Germany, added the following gloss to Hintze's complaint: 'At the turn of the nineteenth to the twentieth centuries the threads [of reflection on politics] had become so thin that they threatened to break'.[19] A not dissimilar lament came from Hennis in the 1960s.[20] What was at stake was in part the fate of political theory in academic curricula, but more important than that has been the connotations of specific conceptions of politics, especially the level of politicisation that is seen as desirable or inevitable and the question of whether politics is unavoidably conflictual in nature, issuing in Schmitt's characterisation of politics as the decision between friend and foe, or whether it is cooperative in nature.

A third reference point is provided by concepts of collective identity, especially those of the nation or *Volk*. The 'late' unification of Germany in 1871, which was in reality also a division of Germans between the newly created German *Reich* and the multi-ethnic Habsburg Empire, guaranteed that issues of national identity would be pervasive and problematic. In retrospect at least, the first half of the twentieth century seems to be marked by an increasingly virulent nationalism, linked to anti-semitism, that culminated in the hubris of National Socialism. Near-idolatry of the state and the nation seem to have gone hand in hand. Yet, from the outset, there was a tension between understanding collective identity as a pre-political phenomenon and understanding it as a product of the state. That tension was further complicated by disputes about whether distinctive national identity was tied to distinctive political institutions, including the German monarchies. These issues were given added intensity by the propaganda battle of the First World War, in which Allied propaganda sought to draw a distinction between German culture and German militarism. The response to what was seen as an attempt to divide the home front included an indiscriminate assertion of internal unity and distinctiveness that amounted to the proclamation of an ideological *Sonderweg* (special road).

The polemical use of concepts of collective identity reached its peak in the principled subordination of the concept of the state to that of the *Volk* in the Third Reich and in the Holocaust. For the exiles, the price of German collective identity was by definition the experience of statelessness, which in the case of Hannah Arendt became a central concept in her political thought.[21] It is, of course, precisely the trauma of the Third Reich that lies behind the passion of Habermas's comments on the appropriate form of collective identity. Habermas's preferred form of identity is *Verfassungspatriotismus* (constitutional patriotism), that is, a form of patriotism defined by identification with constitutional provisions rather than pre-political ethnic or linguistic criteria. That is no more universally accepted today than was the assertion of a propriety right over the concept of the nation by right-wing political theorists at the beginning of the twentieth century. Nor was the virulent assertion of the importance of collective identity any more free from anxiety about its fragility at the beginning of the century, in, for example, the fears of General von Bernhardi, than it was at the end of the century, in, for example, the fears of Arnulf Baring, although the implications of their fears were radically different.[22]

The concept of the *Rechtsstaat* is peculiar to German legal and political thought and forms the fourth point of reference. Although the term dates only from the early nineteenth century, it has been subject to considerable change.[23] By the end of the nineteenth century, it had largely shed its origins in natural law and was understood predominantly as a form of state in which administrative acts are performed on the basis of law and are subject to legal control. The law in question was understood as positive law, that is, as duly enacted statutory law. Other kinds of law, natural law or customary law, were specifically excluded. This was taken so far that Richard Thoma proclaimed before the First World War that even bad and outrageous law still counted as law.[24] This was the consequence of what he admitted was the paradoxical principle that 'Power subjects itself to the law which it has itself created and which in turn subjects itself to power as the instrument of power'.[25] Again, the prism of the end of Weimar and the Third Reich have affected the interpretation of this positivistic concept of the *Rechtsstaat*. Legal positivism, it has been argued, proved powerless in the face of the authoritarian form of government in the last years of Weimar and even more so in the Third Reich. Lacking any standards other than those decreed by power, it could provide no defence against a legal system in which outrageous law was the norm. Yet it is now increasingly recognised that there are problems with this account. First, statutory positivism was not undisputed. A group of figures known as the Free Law Movement criticised the positivist approach to law well before the First World War, primarily for underestimating the importance of judicial discretion in the interpretation and application of law. So influential were they that the young Gustav Radbruch wrote that 'In a few years free law has won all along the line so that . . . today one scarcely dares any more to confess opposition to it'.[26] That was an exaggeration, but then so too is the image of an unchallenged positivism. Second, the self-avowed positivists, Hans Kelsen, Richard Thoma and Gerhard Anschütz, were highly prominent defenders of the Weimar Republic.[27] The attack on Weimar came from the critics of legal positivism. Third, positivists like Thoma saw the threat to the *Rechtsstaat* in the discretion claimed for the administrative authorities.

The extent to which administrative or technocratic discretion forms a limit to the *Rechtsstaat* is one of the issues in which the disputes about this concept continue to the present day. Another abiding theme, linked to diverging approaches to the concept of the state, is whether state power can and should be conceived independently of constitutional principles that serve to restrain this pre-existing power. If anything, the issue of judicial interpretation has become more contentious given the prominent role of the Federal Constitutional Court in post-war Germany. These disputes, however, concern the form and justification of the *Rechtsstaat*, not the phenomenon or concept itself. While the concept of the state per se, and even the concept of collective identity, have been discredited in the eyes of some theorists, the same fate has not befallen the concept of the *Rechtsstaat*.[28]

One of the forms in which the old idea of the *Rechtsstaat* was maintained was in opposition to the emergent *Sozialstaat* (social state), which forms the fifth point of reference. Yet the challenge of the interventionist state was not a new one. It was already prominent at the beginning of the twentieth century.[29] Indeed, Isensee traces the concept of the *Sozialstaat* enshrined in the Basic Law of the Federal Republic back not only to Wilhelmine Germany but also to the 'older German tradition of the care of the territorial princes [for their subjects] as well as the "good police" [*guten Policey*]', that is to the paternalistic welfare policies of the territorial rulers prior to unification in 1871.[30] This, however, detracts from the experience of rapid change that accompanied the emergence of the interventionist state in the last quarter of the nineteenth century. Once again, the motives and responses which this brought forth defy any simple categorisation. Fear that this development posed a threat to some pristine essence of the state certainly existed, as did concerns that it amounted to state socialism; but so too did the hope that the enlarged scope of state activity would endow the state with a new sense of purpose and that the state would prove equal to the task of managing the conflicting interests of a modern industrialised society.

Hugo Preuss could still interpret some of these reactions as the revival of an old clash between urban and rural cultures in

Germany.[31] By the time of the Third Reich, however, despite the National Socialist invocation of blood and soil, it was clear to Ernst Forsthoff that the relative self-sufficiency of rural life was a thing of the past.[32] Forsthoff gave the idea of the *Sozialstaat* a distinctive form, explicitly separate from the conceptions of welfare associated with its early debates, compatible with the policies of the Third Reich. The rebirth of the idea of the *Sozialstaat* in the Basic Law of the Federal Republic did not end the disputes surrounding it. Indeed, Forsthoff took the lead in mobilising the concept of the *Rechtsstaat* against it.

In later responses, especially under the impact of globalisation at the end of the century, the problem was less of an excessively interventionist state and more of a state that could no longer manage the processes of globalisation and in which the old political mechanisms for ensuring the responsible management of society were no longer adequate.[33] This appears to resemble earlier debates, in the Weimar era, in which societal demands upon the state were seen as having led to its effective paralysis. Although there are some similarities, there are also significant differences insofar as some see a new range of possibilities, quite distinct from either the retreat to a powerful state, isolated from the demands of societal interests, or the mobilisation of state resources in the interests of social justice.

The sixth point of reference concerns the role of political parties, especially in parliamentary democracy, and organised forms of political dissent. As already indicated in the comments on the concept of the state above, political parties were regarded with reservation in many quarters at the beginning of the twentieth century. The idea of a German tradition of political thought inimical to parliamentary democracy is further strengthened by the predominant emphasis upon conservative or authoritarian attitudes in the Weimar Republic. In part, this bleak picture was painted by the post-war 'westernisers' of German political thought, for example by Ernst Fraenkel in his highly influential *Die repräsentative und die plebiszitäre Komponente im demokratischen Verfassungsstaat* (The Representative and Plebiscitarian Components in the Democratic Constitutional State) of 1958. According to Fraenkel, the inability to grasp the nature of representative parliamentary democracy lay in impact of the 'subordinate position assigned to parliament in the *Obrigkeitsstaat* [authoritarian state]', and crucially this incomprehension was said to be true of both the defenders and the critics of the *Obrigkeitsstaat*.[34] This is similar to the charge of entrapment in the conceptions of the monarchical state made much earlier by Merkl. Criticism of the deficiencies of the political parties of Wilhelmine Germany did not mean necessarily, however, that the critic was hostile to either political parties per se or parliamentary democracy. Anti-party rhetoric and the advocacy of a standpoint above parties were widespread in both Wilhelmine Germany and the Weimar Republic, sufficiently so for Gustav Radbruch to observe: 'That the government stood above the parties was precisely the legend, the life-giving lie of the *Obrigkeitsstaat*'.[35]

From both within the Third Reich and from the viewpoint of the exiles, the position of the National Socialist party within the new regime was far from clear. Schmitt adapted rapidly, capturing the ambiguity of the situation in 1933 under the heading *Staat, Bewegung, Volk* (State, Movement, People) which, he claimed, constituted the three components of the political unity in Germany.[36] On the eve of the Second World War, Ernst Rudolf Huber deployed the compound name 'movement-state' in another attempt to deal with the unresolved tensions in the Third Reich.[37] The reality of the party was, however, better grasped by the exiled Franz Neumann, who saw an ill-coordinated cartel of which the party was only one element.[38]

The re-establishment of political parties in the Federal Republic received doctrinal sanction in Gerhard Leibholz's theory of the *Parteienstaat*, which arguably ascribed political parties an even more prominent position than intended by the authors of the Basic Law.[39] The consolidation of parliamentary party democracy did not end disputes about the role of political parties, and the earlier disputes provided a ready stock of arguments and rhetoric. In the second half of the century, however, criticism of political parties or the practices of parliamentary democracy did not amount to the suggestion that they should be dispensed with.

The final reference point concerns Germany's position in the wider world. This is important because of the argument that Germany's international position had a direct and significant impact upon its domestic political organisation; that is, as Otto Hintze put it, a relatively authoritarian domestic order was made necessary by Germany's geographical position and the high level of potential pressure on its borders. It is also important because German political thought about the international order at the beginning of the twentieth century was quite diverse. Advocacy of the *Machtstaat* (power state) and disparagement of international law can be found quite easily, but so too can support for an emergent international community and support for international law. While the shock of war and almost universal resentment of the perceived injustice of the Versailles Treaty narrowed the agenda in some respects, the old disputes were revived and developed after the First World War.

The National Socialist vision of Germany as a *Reich* distinct in nature from other nations was accompanied by claims that there was a distinctive National Socialist theory of international law. That claim was no more successful than Carl Schmitt's attempt to define the legal status of Europe as a continental bloc under Nazi hegemony. As with the concepts deployed to explain the internal nature of the regime, so too in the case of its position and policies in the international order there was surprising scope for disagreement among the regime's more or less enthusiastic supporters.

The defeat of the Third Reich and the post-war division of Germany threw up a host of problems, including the question of whether it made sense to talk about the continuity of a German state and how the German nation was to be understood given the reality of the existence of two states on former German territory. They also largely displaced the discourse of power, at least as traditionally understood. Re-unification revived the discourse of power, as was evident in the protest against the 'power political resocialisation' of Germany.[40] Yet the connotations and context were different. The discourse of power could no longer be reconnected plausibly to the inherently expansive concept of the *Reich* understood as embodying a mission rather than the interests of one state among many.[41]

In this respect as in many others, German political thought was different at the end of the century, though German political theorists were quick to identify continuities. In fact, the entire century exhibited a complex blend of continuity and discontinuity. The following chapters seek to illustrate that fact.

Notes

1. Wilhelm Hennis, 'Legitimität' [1976], in Wilhelm Hennis, *Politikwissenschaft und politisches Denken* (Tübingen: Mohr Siebeck, 2000), p. 261.
2. Jürgen Habermas, 'Apologetic tendencies' [1986], in Jürgen Habermas, *The New Conservatism* (Cambridge: Polity, 1989), p. 227.
3. Duncan Kelly, *The State of the Political* (Oxford: Oxford University Press, 2003), p. 19.
4. See Detlef Lehnert, *Verfassungsdemokratie als Bürgergenossenschaft* (Baden-Baden: Nomos, 1998), and Detlef Lehnert and Christoph Müller (eds), *Vom Untertanenverband zur Bürgergenossenschaft*

(Baden-Baden: Nomos, 2003). In English, see Ernest Hamburger, 'Hugo Preuss: scholar and statesman', *Leo Baeck Institute Yearbook*, vol. 20 (London, 1975), pp. 179–206, and Peter Stirk, 'Hugo Preuss, German political thought and the Weimar Constitution', *History of Political Thought* 23 (2002), pp. 497–516.

5. Michael Stolleis, 'In the belly of the beast: constitutional legal theory (*Staatsrechtslehre*), under National Socialism', in Michael Stolleis, *The Law under the Swastika* (Chicago: University of Chicago Press, 1998), p. 98.

6. Helmuth Plessner, *Die verspätete Nation* [1959] (Frankfurt am Main: Suhrkamp, 1974). Max Horkheimer and Theodor W. Adorno, *Dialectic of Enlightenment* [1947] (London: Allen Lane, 1973).

7. Jürgen Habermas, 'Replik auf Beiträge zu einem Symposium der Cardozo Law School' [1996], in Jürgen Habermas, *Die Einbeziehung des Anderen* (Frankfurt am Main: Suhrkamp, 1997), p. 379.

8. See his comments in an interview in 1984, 'A philosophico-political profile', in Peter Dews (ed.), *Autonomy and Solidarity* (London: Verso, 1992), p. 151.

9. Kurt Sontheimer, *Antidemokratisches Denken in der Weimarer Republik* [1968] (Munich: DTV, 1994).

10. Christoph Gusy, 'Einleitung', in Christoph Gusy (ed.), *Demokratisches Denken in der Weimarer Republik* (Baden-Baden: Nomos, 2000), p. 12.

11. George Iggers, *Deutsche Geschichtswissenschaft* (Vienna: Böhlau, 1997) p. 249.

12. Kenneth H. F. Dyson, *The State Tradition in Western Europe* (Oxford: Martin Robertson, 1980), p. 19.

13. Christoph Möllers, *Staat als Argument* (Munich: Beck, 2000), p. 1.

14. Peter Häberle, *Verfassungslehre als Kulturwissenschaft* (Berlin: Duncker & Humblot, 1998), p. 620. Adolf Merkl, 'Die monarchische Befangenheit der deutschen Staatsrechtslehre' [1920], in Adolf Merkl, *Gesammelte Schriften*, vol. 1, part 2 (Berlin: Duncker & Humblot, 1995), pp. 4–12.

15. Gerhard Göhler, Matthias Iser and Ina Kerner (eds), *Politische Theorie. 22 umkämpfte Begriffe zur Einführung* (Wiesbaden: VS, 2004).

16. Josef Isensee, 'Staat und Verfassung', in Josef Isensee and Paul Kirchhof (eds), *Handbuch des Staatsrechts der Bundesrepublik Deutschland*, vol. 2 (Heidelberg: Müller, 2004), p. 8.

17. Georg Jellinek, *Allgemeine Staatslehre*, (Berlin: Julius Springer, 1929), p. 180.

18. Herbert Marcuse, 'The struggle against liberalism in the totalitarian view of the state' [1934], in Herbert Marcuse, *Negations* (Harmondsworth: Penguin, 1968), p. 39.

19. Wilhelm Bleek, *Geschichte der Politikwissenschaft in Deutschland* (Munich: Beck, 2001), p. 189.

20. Wilhelm Hennis, 'Politik und praktische Philosophie' [1963], in Wilhelm Hennis, *Politikwissenschaft und politisches Denken* (Tübingen: Mohr Siebeck, 2000), pp. 1–126.
21. See Margaret Canovan, *Hannah Arendt* (Cambridge: Cambridge University Press, 1992), pp. 33–4.
22. On Baring, see Lutz Niethammer, *Kollektive Identität* (Hamburg: Rowohlt, 2000), pp. 598–600.
23. See Ernst Wolfgang Böckenförde, 'Entstehung und Wandel des Rechtsstaatsbegriffs' [1969], in Ernst Wolfgang Böckenförde, *Recht, Staat, Freiheit* (Frankfurt am Main: Suhrkamp, 1991), pp. 143–69.
24. Richard Thoma, 'Rechtsstaatsidee und Verwaltungswissenschaft', *Jahrbuch des öffentlichen Recht der Gegenwart*, 4 (1910), pp. 201–2.
25. Ibid., p. 201.
26. Gustav Radbruch, *Gesamtausgabe*, vol. 17 (Heidelberg: Müller, 1991), p. 160.
27. Detlef Lehnert, 'Die Weimarer Staatsrechtsdebatte zwischen Legendenbildung und Neubesinnung', *Aus Politik und Zeitgeschichte* 51 (1996), pp. 3–14.
28. See Niethammer's observations on excising 'collective identity from our political vocabulary', *Kollektive Identität*, pp. 627–32.
29. Thus Michael Stolleis, 'Die Entstehung des Interventionsstaats und das öffentliche Recht', *Zeitschrift für neuere Rechtsgeschichte*, 11 (1989), pp. 129–47.
30. Isensee, 'Staat und Verfassung', p. 73.
31. See Lehnert, *Verfassungsdemokratie und Bürgergenossenschaft*, p. 251.
32. Ernst Forsthoff, *Die Verwaltung als Leistungsträger* (Stuttgart: Kohlhammer, 1938). See also Dieter Scheidemann, *Der Begriff Daseinsvorsorge* (Göttingen: Muster-Schmidt, 1991), pp. 6–7.
33. From different perspectives, see Niklas Luhmann, *Die Politik der Gesellschaft* (Frankfurt am Main: Suhrkamp, 2000), Ulrich Beck, *The Reinvention of Politics* [1993] (Cambridge: Polity, 1997) and Hermann Lübbe, *Aufklärung anlasshalber* (Gräfeling: Resche, 2001).
34. Ernst Fraenkel, *Die repräsentative und die plebiszitäre Komponente im demokratischen Verfassungsstaat* (Tübingen: Mohr, 1958), pp. 42–3.
35. Gustav Radbruch, 'Die politischen Parteien im System des deutschen Verfassungsrechts', in Gerhard Anschütz and Richard Thoma (eds), *Handbuch des deutschen Staatsrechts*, vol. 1 (Tübingen: Mohr, 1930), p. 289.
36. Carl Schmitt, *Staat, Bewegung, Volk* (Hamburg: Hanseatische Verlagsanstalt, 1933).
37. Ernst Rudolf Huber, *Verfassungsrecht des Grossdeutschen Reiches* (Hamburg: Hanseatische Verlagsanstalt, 1939), p. 288.
38. Franz Neumann, *Behemoth* (London: Gollancz, 1942), pp. 382–3.
39. See Wilhelm Hennis, 'Der "Parteienstaat" des Grundgesetzes' [1992], in

Wilhelm Hennis, *Auf dem Weg in den Parteienstaat* (Stuttgart: Reclam, 1998), pp. 107–35.

40. Thus Gunther Hellmann, 'Wider die machtpolitische Resozialisierung der deutschen Aussenpolitik', *WeltTrends* 12 (2004), pp. 79–88.

41. In this, I follow Heinrich August Winkler, *Die Zeit* (14 December 2000).

1

Political Thought in the Age of Monarchy

At the beginning of the twentieth century, the German-speaking lands were dominated by two states both of which presented, and still present, considerable difficulties for those attempting to understand them. In the north, the German *Reich* had been formed in 1871 in the wake of a successful war against France. Its formation was also the final stage in a prolonged struggle for power between the dynastic house of Prussia and the Habsburgs. The Franco-Prussian war was accompanied by the invocation of German unity. In speeches, newspapers and subsequently in memoirs, the war was presented as a justified defence of German honour, supposedly insulted by the French. Extensive analogies were drawn between 1870 and 1813, when Prussia had risen against Napoleon after a series of defeats and humiliations.[1]

Yet there were problems with this triumph of German unity, for the separate states, including Prussia, continued to exist within the new *Reich*. Indeed, the historian Friedrich Meinecke later recalled how he had become aware of a latent problem, namely the 'defensive struggle' of the 'Prussian state personality' against the rising tide of national unity.[2] The difficulty was compounded by the fact that formally the *Reich* was the creation of the German princes, and, in principle at least, considerable authority was held by the council, to which all member states sent delegates. Shortly after the creation of the *Reich*, Otto von Bismarck had declared to the parliament of the *Reich*: 'Sovereignty does not lie with the *Kaiser*; it lies with the totality of the united governments'.[3] To what extent such proclamations corresponded to reality was disputed throughout the life of the *Reich*. It is clear, however, that the manner of its creation and its formal constitutional basis presented theoretical problems about the nature of the state and sovereignty.

The Habsburg Empire to the south presented an even more confusing picture which is well captured by the author Robert Musil: 'On paper, it called itself the Austro-Hungarian Monarchy; in speaking, however, one referred to it as "Austria" that is to say, it was known by a name which it had, as a state, solemnly renounced by oath while preserving it in all matters of sentiment . . .'[4] This was but one of many ambiguities of this state, not the least of which was its attitude to German nationalism. The emperor, Franz Josef, was deeply suspicious of German nationalism, which was ultimately incompatible with the existence of his multi-ethnic empire in which Germans accounted for less than a quarter of the population. That was evident in his hesitation about celebrations intended to honour his sixty-year-long rule in 1908. When the celebrations took place, he responded to the praise lavished on him by Wilhelm II by describing the proceedings as a 'festive demonstration of the monarchic principle . . . to which Germany owes its power and greatness'.[5] Dynastic power took pride of place, and it was this *Hausmacht* or dynastic power that in his eyes held his lands together.

Although both regimes clearly paraded the legacy of the past, which was literally embodied in the figure of the aged Franz Josef, they were also grappling with the problems of modernisation. Both were confronted with increasing political mobilisation, an increasingly aggressive nationalism with anti-semitic strains, and recalcitrant, and in the case of Austria often dysfunctional, parliamentary bodies. For the Habsburg Empire, finding a solution to the problem of nationalities was simply a matter of life or death. The German *Reich* did not face that problem, but there was concern about the number of Poles living mainly in the east of the country. They were subject to considerable discrimination, as were other segments of the population. The Catholics and then the socialists had to endure prolonged periods of political persecution, though in both cases the outcome was, paradoxically, a strengthening of their respective political parties. Resort to dynastic or state power was a reality and, possibly equally importantly, a recurrent threat evident, for example, in the rhetoric of a coup d'état from above, that is, a dissolution of parliament followed by the imposition of a new constitution.

Economically, the German *Reich* was by far the most advanced. Urbanisation and industrialisation brought with them a host of problems to which the *Reich* responded with increased state intervention in society and the economy and a wave of legislation and legal codification, as reflected, for example, in the Civil Code of 1900. The growing importance of legislative activity was reflected from 1880 by the attempts of special interests to influence legislation upon which their prospects depended. All this brought with it a growth in the administrative apparatus of the state. It was indicative of this that one legal theorist proclaimed that 'The *Rechtsstaat* is the state of well-ordered administrative law'.[6]

The formation of the German *Reich* was perceived at the time as a significant change in the European balance of power even before accelerated industrialisation further enhanced German power. Popular associations, as well as the navy and special-interest groups, lobbied for an expanded fleet and the acquisition of colonies as Europe's system of alliances became more and more rigid and confrontational. Yet it is misleading to observe the political thought of the period before the First World War solely with the benefit of hindsight. Economically, integration in Europe had reached high levels, in terms of trade, capital mobility and labour mobility. A network of agreements regulating international trade and communications and even involving some international administrative activity made a great impression upon contemporaries. The Hague Conferences of 1899 and 1907 promised some mitigation of the horrors of war, even if their achievements seemed greater to popular consciousness than to more trained observers.

For German political theorists, then, the period before the First World War was one of rapid change, politically, economically and socially. It was a period in which the gap between constitutional and legal doctrine and the reality of state and social power expanded in some areas and contracted in others. It was a period in which political and social developments forced them to reconsider the nature of the state and law and to try to align those concepts with the activity, and shortcomings, of political parties and the expanding administrative activity of the state. It was, however, also a period which left many of them ill-prepared for the reality and increasingly ideological character of the First World War.

The state

In order to understand approaches to the state around the turn of the twentieth century, it is useful to go back to the work of Paul Laband. From the perspective of 1907, Philipp Zorn praised Laband's multi-volume *Staatsrecht des deutschen Reiches* (State Law of the German *Reich*), which appeared between 1876 and 1882, as the 'great masterwork of the entire German legal theory of the *Reich*'. Zorn picked out Laband's exclusion of politics and his principled fixation on the positive laws of the *Reich* as especially praiseworthy. Yet Laband had first made his name by his attempt to explain one of the most significant political and constitutional disputes of German nineteenth-century history. This was the so-called budget crisis of 1862–6, which had pitted Chancellor Otto von Bismarck against the liberals in the Prussian parliament in the 1860s. The crisis arose when the liberals refused to accept increases in military expenditure and the length of military service. Bismarck responded by proclaiming that there was a gap in the constitution, since there was no specified mechanism for resolving the dispute, and that in this event the state's more original right, derived from its historic primacy, provided the basis for government without an approved budget. Although the dispute was eventually set aside by the Indemnity Bill after Bismarck's triumph over Austria in 1866, the initial apparent assertion of state power over the constitution continued to trouble German jurists. Laband sought to draw the teeth of the controversy by introducing a conceptual distinction between different types of law, which effectively denied that Bismarck had violated the constitution by continuing to operate the machinery of state in the absence of a duly approved budget. By the same token, Laband believed that he had shown that there was no gap in the constitution. This was vital to his belief in his task of systematising law and his belief in the state as a *Rechtsstaat*. From this perspective, he found the notion of a gap in this fabric of law unbearable. Indeed, he asserted that there can no more be a gap in the legal system than there can be a gap in the law of nature. This, in turn, was linked to his definition of the state as an enduring personality. This admittedly 'fictitious' and abstract personality was, according to Laband, a necessary construct in order to grasp the unity and persistence of the state.

Despite Zorn's praise for Laband's work, he had some concerns about Laband's method. It was necessary, he argued, to see the *Reich* not just as a juristic construction dating back to 1866 but as an historical product of the aspiration to national unity. Politics had to be excluded, but history could be allowed back in.[7] In the same year and journal as Zorn's review of Laband's work, Laband himself responded to the complexities of the developing constitutional order of the *Reich* by invoking history and politics. He noted that frequent efforts to construe the *Kaiser* as a monarch were constitutionally untenable. *Kaiser* was simply the title bestowed upon the federal president [*das Präsidium des Bundes*], who was also the King of Prussia. However, he continued, for the 'naive conceptions of the people' the *Kaiser* was the 'perceptible symbol of national unity' around which the loyalty and self-sacrifice of the nation crystallised. In effect, Laband allowed the supposedly abstract personality of the state to take on all-too-human shape in the interests of political and historical expediency, despite his insistence in principle that the personality of the state could not be attached to any specific part of it, including the *Kaiser*.[8]

Although the conservative jurist Laband deviated from his principled position in order to support the existing form of government, his theoretical position was that the state had to be conceived as a legal order, as a personality, as composed of the twenty-five member states of the German *Reich* and not the ever-increasing millions of German citizens. The state thus appeared as something standing above those citizens. Laband faced criticism from different quarters, but the major fundamental challenge to his approach came from Georg Jellinek whose *Allgemeine Staatslehre* is one of the most influential works of twentieth-century German political thought. According to Jellinek, the focus almost exclusively on the legal aspect of the state had been misguided. The state has to be considered not just as a legal construct but as a social fact. Consistently with this two-sided conception of the state, Jellinek divided his general theory of the state into a social theory of the state and a legal theory of the state.[9]

From these two perspectives, Jellinek arrived at two closely related definitions of the state. From the viewpoint of his social theory, 'The state is a united association of sedentary men, equipped with an original power of domination'.[10] From the viewpoint of his legal theory, the state is 'the territorial corporation of a sedentary people, equipped with an original power of domination'.[11] It has been objected that the two definitions are so similar as to be indistinguishable; but it is not too difficult to bring out the significance of the different emphases. As a territorial body, the state claims a right to issue laws binding within that territory, not just for its own citizens but for residents who are not citizens or for those travelling through or conducting business within it. The territorial extent sets the limits of its remit. As a united association of men, the state brings together these men for some common purpose, the laws associated with this common purpose being compulsory for all of them.

A further concern about Jellinek's definitions of the state concerns his emphasis upon an 'original power of domination', suggesting something analogous to Bismarck's claim about a right of the state based upon its unconstrained and historically prior power. Yet Jellinek specifically rejected this interpretation. By 'original power', he meant simply that a state exercises this power in its own name, that this power is not derived from some higher political entity.[12] Although

Jellinek made the power of domination central to the state, he had no wish to transfigure the state into some quasi-natural entity standing above men or to venerate power for its own sake.

Jellinek's opposition to any hypostatisation of the state is evident in his comments on the idea of the personality of the state. He shared the idea that the state has to be construed as a personality but rejected the assumption that this entailed the embodiment of the state in a specific organ or institution within the state or in a physical person. This point was buttressed by methodological considerations drawn from the epistemology of Immanuel Kant. According to Jellinek, in conceiving of the unity of the state in terms of its individuality 'we use a conceptually necessary category for the synthesis of appearances, which is epistemologically justified so long as we do not ascribe transcendent reality to what is thought through it'.[13] It is consistent with this that he insisted that there is no substance distinct from individual men at the root of the state as a social formation and that this fact rules out all doctrines 'which conceive of the state as a permanent natural structure alongside or above men'.[14]

His opposition to any veneration of power is evident in his approach to the concept of sovereignty and in his theory of the auto-limitation of the state. Jellinek argued that the concept of sovereignty was too often treated as a claim to unconstrained power rooted in the idea of sovereignty as '*summum imperium, summa potestas*'.[15] Turning once again to Kant's theories for assistance, Jellinek argued that there is no more inconsistency in supposing that the state can restrict itself than there is in supposing that the individual can bind himself through ethical commitments. It was precisely this capacity for self-limitation that he turned into a definition of sovereignty: 'Sovereignty is not lack of limitation but rather the capacity of exclusive self-determination and therefore of self-limitation'. He added that if, as some wished, the state is seen as able to expand its competence at will, without any restraint, we will all be no more than 'state slaves' on licence.[16]

This does not mean that Jellinek needed to diminish his emphasis on domination as a central part of his definition of the state. For Jellinek, it is the distinctive characteristic of the state that it can enforce the rules that it creates and that there is no escape from this domination in the way that someone can escape from the rules of other associations, such as religious bodies, by the simple expedient of leaving them. Indeed, this state power (*Staatsgewalt*) forms part of Jellinek's highly influential doctrine of the three elements of the state, the other two being the state's territory (*Staatsgebiet*) and the population of the state

(*Staatsvolk*). For Jellinek, a state that lacks one of these elements is simply not a state at all.

It is now increasingly recognised that Jellinek exercised considerable influence over Max Weber.[17] Weber shared Jellinek's hostility to what he saw as the misuse of collective concepts, including that of the state. The concept of the state does not, he argued, refer to a substantive entity, but is rather a 'synthesis, which we propose for specific cognitive purposes'. More specifically, the ideal types which are formed of the state have specific political connotations, as was evident in the 'German "organicist" state metaphysics, for example, in contrast to the "societal" American conception'.[18] The disparaging reference to German state metaphysics is indicative of Weber's stance. He was, however, interested in and worried by the domination of men over men and the specific forms that it took in modern society. Central here is the concept of the state as an *Anstalt*. What was meant by this term was far from clear. Jellinek had complained that there was a general failure to define the term clearly, or even to attempt to do so.[19] Weber's definition brought some much-needed clarity to this issue. According to Weber, an *Anstalt* imposed rules that are valid for all those who exhibit specific criteria, for example birth or residence in a certain territory. Not all communities into which people are born qualify as an *Anstalt*. The linguistic community does not qualify, for it is also characteristic of an *Anstalt* that the rules that it imposes are rational and formally posited rules, typically laws. Finally, an *Anstalt* is typically an imposed order. Weber exhibited little sympathy for contractarian theories of the state. The state as an *Anstalt* is, according to Weber, an imposed order characterised by formally posited rational rules that are valid for all.[20]

While Weber dismissed contractarian theories of the state as fictions, that did not mean that he saw the state as nothing more than a relationship of coercion. In his account, coercion is the means specific to the state, but obedience of men to the laws of the state typically takes place for a variety of motives, as it does in Jellinek's theory. It is true, however, that Weber focused very heavily on the sociological approach to the state, taking one aspect of Jellinek's dualistic approach and pushing it to its limits. Others deployed legal theories but did so in overt disagreement with Laband. Thus, both Otto Gierke and Hugo Preuss argued that one of the cardinal errors of Laband's approach to the state was his reliance upon Roman private law as a model for interpreting and defining the state. According to Gierke, this led to a dubious analogy between the individual person as a legal subject in private law and the state as a legal subject in public law, the only difference being that in the case of the state 'instead of property rights, rights of domination are ascribed to the imagined subject'.[21] Behind this, so argued Preuss, lay the old theory of the patrimonial state that denigrated both the citizens and the state itself to the status of the property of the sovereign prince.

The vigour of Preuss's criticism of the old patrimonial theories applied more widely to his critique of the *Obrigkeitsstaat*, that is, the authoritarian state that Preuss presented as part of the German tradition of political thought. The problem lay in the distinctive impact of the modern centralising state that had appeared in all west European countries. Preuss argued that in France and England there was a 'natural substratum', that is, an incipient nation based on a more or less unified territory, underneath this ruthlessly centralising power. In Germany, by contrast, political fragmentation meant that there was 'no other starting point than the territories and the princes'. Germany, at this point, was not in fact a state at all and had to make do with a 'peculiar conglomerate of state surrogates'. The consequence of this was that 'this tragicomic caricature of the absolute monarchy often worked out grotesquely when some little dynast, in the purple of Byzantine majesty, strutted about as the successor of the caesars and later imitated the *l'état c'est moi* of the sun king with unbelievable seriousness'.[22] In Preuss's account, there was a distinctive and authoritarian German tradition. It was strong enough to suppress and stifle the urban self-government that Preuss favoured, but it was also fundamentally flawed and even ludicrous. The point of Preuss's polemic, of course, was to recommend that Germany abandon this flawed tradition in favour of more modern institutions and beliefs.

For Preuss, this meant learning from English practices and ideas, but he also drew on older and different Germanic traditions as explored by Gierke, that is, ideas of political community as a fellowship (*Genossenschaft*). Both Gierke and Preuss relied on the idea of mutual dependency and the legal binding of wills in order to claim that it makes sense to ascribe personality not just to individuals but to political associations in general, with the state being only one of these associations. They marshalled a host of arguments to make this seem plausible. Preuss, for example, took up the commonplace description of civil servants as organs of the state and the identification of the state with a ruler and asked: 'How, in all the world, can one imagine that a physical organ can be the organ of [another] physical individual distinct from him?'[23] The civil servant cannot be the organ of the ruler. Preuss argued, however, that the civil servant can be conceived as the organ of an association, that is, of a multiplicity of men which has a collective legal personality distinct from their individual legal personalities. That is inconsistent with Jellinek's methodological individualism; and Jellinek, not surprisingly, regarded Preuss's claims on this issue as sheer mysticism. Indeed, Preuss himself confessed that the concept of an organism was a 'puzzling overarching concept' for which there was no entirely satisfactory explanation.[24]

A more radical solution to the theory of the state was offered by Hans Kelsen. Whereas Weber had taken the sociological dimension of Jellinek's theory and pushed it further, Kelsen took up the legal dimension. With even greater emphasis upon the substantive existence of physical men, and nothing but them, he indicted both advocates of organicist theories like Preuss, and Jellinek himself who had no sympathy for organicist theories, for violating this principle. Against Jellinek's supposition of a state will, Kelsen protested that it 'must seriously be doubted that there is any kind of common purpose which all the men united within arbitrary state boundaries follow'.[25] In Kelsen's eyes, Jellinek's doctrine of auto-limitation fared no better. He attacked it at its weakest point, its reliance upon the analogy with the Kantian notion of duty. Jellinek's efforts 'founder on the fact that the state is no kind of man and can have no kind of duty which is possible only for a human will'.[26] Kelsen's own theory radicalised the long-standing proposition that the jurist had to strip away all contingent and non-juristic elements in conceptualising the state. At the end, this meant that Kelsen had reduced the state to a network of laws. It was a theory which ruthlessly exposed all traits of anthropomorphism in dealing with the state as a legal entity and which sought to cut off the exploitation of the personalisation of state power in order to justify the arbitrary use of power. But Kelsen paid a high price for the rigour of his assault upon the mystification of political power. By his own account, his theory could not deal with the reality of relations of domination and force. These fell outside the juristic purview.[27] Nor could Kelsen incorporate the act of legislation in his system of the state as a network of laws; for legislation, he argued, was itself neither a law nor a function of the state but a precondition of both. From the viewpoint of his own theory, the act of legislation had to remain, he conceded, 'the great mystery of the law and the state'.[28]

Although Kelsen put forward his critique in the name of the

objectivity of a science of jurisprudence, stripped of all political ideology, much of the force of his critique came from his ability to expose the political agenda that relied upon the veneration of state power and its supposed embodiment in particular organs of state, be it the monarch or the civil service. It is not difficult to recognise the political connotations of Kelsen's assault on the veneration of state power and his accusation that ascribing a will to the state is anthropomorphic projection.

The concept of politics

Approaches to the concept of politics were closely related to understandings of the state which provided a reference point for Jellinek in his assertion that '"Political" means "related to the state": in the concept of the political one has already thought of the concept of the state'.[29] Yet this apparently simple association was not undisputed. Thus, when Albert Schäffle sought to define the concept in an essay of 1897, he began by specifying what politics is not. It is not merely about the different forms which the state takes, it is not merely about Machiavellian shrewdness and cunning and it is not any and every activity of the state and the organs of state.[30] Seeking to steer between an overly restrictive use of the term and, more frequently, an inflationary use of the term, Schäffle eventually identified politics and the science of politics as concerned with the 'fluidity', the element of 'change', the 'yet to be created'.[31]

This contrast between the static and the dynamic was also evident in Laband's work. For Laband, politics conjured up images of caprice which he believed should be purged from constitutional law. In Laband's case, this was consistent with an affirmative view of the German *Reich* as established by Otto von Bismarck and with a positive approach to law which took state-enacted law as its sole reference point and eschewed any sympathy for natural-law doctrines which might provide an external criterion for the state and its activities. The historian and publicist Heinrich von Treitschke was no more sympathetic to natural law than Laband, and was equally committed to the Bismarckian form of the *Reich*. Treitschke, however, took a much more positive view of politics as the fluid and the dynamic, for here lay the scope for the 'riddle of personality' which set limits to history as a science despite Treitschke's own definition of politics as 'applied history'.[32] For Treitschke, the dynamics of history are driven forward by personalities, whether individual or the collective personality of the state. The historian Max Lenz was merely echoing Treitschke when he wrote:

> He [Bismarck] saw politics as what it really is: as a conflict of power against power, as leadership in war, in which the means of cunning is thoroughly allowed, but whose final form is always arms . . . Nothing was more hated by him than 'planless irresolution', nothing more contemptible than defensiveness, whether out of good nature or empty lack of awareness of the duties of power . . .[33]

It was precisely this kind of veneration of naked power transfigured into the essence of politics that Schäffle had sought to cut off in his essay on the nature of politics. Schäffle succumbed to neither facile assumptions about good nature nor neglect of considerations of power. His objection, rather, was that the unrestrained veneration of power is simply foolish. It is, at the end of the day, 'unpolitical'.[34] Many took pride in an unpolitical stance, associating this with the scientific objectivity of a jurisprudence purged of the caprice of politics and with the idea of the state as a stable order standing above the political fray. Others, like Schäffle, sought to recognise the clash of power they witnessed in their own society without succumbing to a veneration of power.

Drawing the line between an awareness of the constraints of power and a veneration of power which tips over into an ultimately self-destructive hubris was an important but difficult task, especially when political theorists were carried away by polemic and rhetoric. Both were prominent in Weber's 1895 inaugural lecture as Professor of Political Economy in Freiburg. The subject of Weber's address was the economic conditions in Prussia and especially the relationship between Germans and Poles in the region. Weber left no doubt that he was adopting a political stance and defining politics in the process: 'The science of political economy is a *political* science'.[35] Weber explained that this must be so, for although as 'an explanatory and analytic science, political economy is *international* . . . as soon as it makes *value judgements* it is tied to the particular strain of humankind (*Menschentum*) we find within our own nature'.[36] Weber spelled out that he was writing in the interests of German policy and culture, and his language is riddled with the rhetoric of Darwinian conflict: 'We do not have peace and human happiness to hand down to our descendants, but rather the *eternal struggle* to preserve and raise the quality of our national species'.[37] Yet there were several restraining factors in Weber's view of politics. For Weber, politics entailed the choice of values without any guarantee that there were any universally valid choices, but these were choices about, as he put it in the Freiburg address, 'what kind of people they [our descendants] will be'.[38] That in turn was linked to a personal and principled antipathy to irrationalism and emotionalism which he held to be deeply unpolitical. He associated the fashionable pursuit of 'experience' and 'publicity' for that experience with a loss of self-control and the requisite sense of 'distance' appropriate to private and public conduct. Furthermore, Weber did not glorify violence, even when he wrote with what he admitted was some brutality. Indeed, whereas Treitschke bundled together state, power, violence and personality in an all-encompassing view of the political, Weber sought to avoid the inflation of concepts.[39]

Much of what Weber put with rhetorical vehemence was expressed more reservedly by Jellinek. Jellinek also emphasised the dynamic and the element of choice in politics. Politics, as distinct from the theory of the state, equalled the 'theory of the attainment of specific state purposes, and therefore the consideration of state formations from specific teleological standpoints, which also supply critical standards for the judgement of state conditions and relationships'.[40] Yet Jellinek was far too sophisticated to hold rigidly to this distinction. Time and again throughout his *Allgemeine Staatslehre*, he emphasised that politics and the theory of the state could not be separated. There was, however, a significant difference between the norms of law and those of politics, for only the former were properly backed by power; the latter required 'free recognition'.[41]

While theorists like Jellinek, Schäffle and Weber sought to steer a course between the aestheticisation of politics and its disparagement as the realm of caprice, socialist theorists largely held to the view of politics as a matter of class conflict driven by economic forces. In reality, the orthodox view of politics as an epiphenomenon stood in crass contrast to socialist practice, though the bourgeois liberal jurist Preuss saw their attitude as indicative of a wider German, rather than specifically socialist, malaise: 'The dogmatic one-sidedness of the materialist conception of history with its underestimation of purely political motives marks out Marx and Engels more strongly as Germans than as social democrats'.[42] The socialist Eduard Bernstein could not directly confront the founding fathers in the same spirit. Nevertheless, implicitly at least, he operated with a fundamentally different conception of politics to that which prevailed in the majority of his own party. For Bernstein, that involved the claim that 'it would be better to talk of political rule [*Herrschaft*] rather than political power [*Macht*]'.[43]

The concept of the nation

Attitudes towards national identity were marked by memory of the recent political fragmentation of Germany and by the continuing existence of the multi-ethnic Habsburg Empire. This was evident in the north in a speech of 1896 by Laband in which he praised the 1871 constitution as 'the historical and legal landmark of redemption of the German people from fragmentation and powerlessness'.[44] The apparent fragility of national identity was indeed remarkably strong on the right. It was evident in August Julius Langbehn's *Rembrandt as Educator* of 1890. The appropriation of Rembrandt as a model of German identity was but one of the oddities of Langbehn's anti-modernist tract, which upheld the peasant and the artist as the basis of Germany's future. Uncertainty about the strength of national identity was present in much more aggressive characters than the despairing Langbehn. In another influential tract, *Germany and the Next War*, published in 1911, General Friedrich von Bernhardi worried that the development of German national identity had

> been hampered and hindered by the hereditary defects of its character – that is, by the particularism of the individual races and States, the theoretic dogmatism of the parties, the incapacity to sacrifice personal interests for great national objects for want of patriotism and of political common sense, often, also, by the pettiness of the prevailing ideas.[45]

Assertion of German identity and underlying fears about its solidity were often, but not invariably, linked with anti-semitism. The connection was aptly summarised by Preuss: anti-semitism 'is rather the national grimace of people without a true nation-state consciousness'.[46] As was indicated above, Weber was a fervent nationalist, but he was not anti-semitic. Even the antipathy to Poles evident in the 1895 Freiburg address faded. At the Second German Sociologists' Conference in 1912, Weber had undisguised contempt for 'opaque racial mysticism', and he dismissed the 'uncritical use of racial hypotheses' as a 'scientific crime'. A nation, he declared, 'is a community of feeling, whose appropriate expression would be its own state'. How a nation came into existence, he continued, is a complex process with diverse causes from case to case.[47] On the eve of the First

World War, the historian Friedrich Meinecke expressed a similar disdain for the crudities of some conceptions of national identity. He also noted the tendency for advocates of German as a *Herrenvolk* vis-à-vis other peoples to assume a similar posture towards fellow Germans.[48]

Contempt for the cruder notions of national identity did not mean that these men lacked a strong sense of national identity. Jellinek expressed his solidarity with Germans in Bohemia and Moravia as the Habsburg authorities planned to elevate Czech to the status of an official language alongside German in 1897. It was an intervention which was not welcomed by the Viennese press, which was close to the government.[49] One product of this intervention was Jellinek's *Recht der Minoritäten* (Right of Minorities), first published in 1898. Motivated by concern for the Germans as a minority within the Habsburg lands, Jellinek considered the various ways in which minorities could be defended against majorities. As the title suggests, his conclusion was simply 'recognition of the rights of minorities', though he was prepared to consider and countenance parliamentary obstruction as well.[50] It is notable, however, that Jellinek set limits to the politics of nationality. In his *Allgemeine Staatslehre*, he argued that neither religious nor national parties are genuine parties, for both necessarily lacked the comprehensive programmes appropriate to parliamentary activity.[51] Earlier he had sought to use the principles of majority rule to curtail the appeal of national parties. According to Jellinek, what made majority rule acceptable was the transient nature of the majority. The fortunes of political parties change, as do the party-political allegiances of individuals. But, he continued, this is not the case with national identity: 'The German of today cannot become the Slav of tomorrow, and if, exceptionally, he should, he would rightly meet with general contempt. Like religious parties, national parties are firmly circumscribed once and for all.'[52] Later, however, Jellinek placed more emphasis upon the voluntaristic idea of national identity associated with the French philosopher Ernest Renan, who described the existence of a nation as a daily plebiscite. Nations, he wrote, are social and historical constructs for which there are no fixed objective markers. Jellinek went a step further when he considered attempts to equate nation and state. He described these as being based on a readily discernible error, that is, that the unity of a people requires a political organisation to form the unity in the first place. Behind this point lay a general methodological principle which was central to Jellinek's political thought, namely that will and feeling could only be ascribed to physical individuals. Consequently, he stated: 'The national will [*Volkswille*] is not the physical will of a unity, but a juristic will formed out of physical acts of will [of individuals] on the basis of legal principles'.[53]

The presumption that the nation is a pre-political unity was incompatible with the methodological basis of Jellinek's thought. Yet Jellinek did not quite manage to adhere to this principle. Towards the end of his *Allgemeine Staatslehre,* he wrote that 'the federal state, like every other state, has a social, pre-juristic existence, to which the legal order can be attached, but which it cannot create'.[54] Behind this remark, however, lay disputes to which German political theorists devoted considerable energy which in retrospect easily seems disproportionate, namely disputes about the federal nature of the *Reich* and especially the formation of the *Reich*. Jellinek's remark occurred in the context of his criticism of theories which based the foundation of the *Reich* purely upon a treaty between the member states, or rather, the princes of those states. These theories were simply following Bismarck, who also argued that what the princes had once put together they could also take apart. Jellinek's own concern for national unity, as well as some scepticism about the princely houses, was evident when he attacked Otto Mayer. Mayer, wrote Jellinek, 'who declares that the *Reich* is a league of monarchs, finds the guarantee of the *Reich* in the federal loyalty [*Bundnistreue*] of the princes: a surety of the weakest kind . . .'[55]

Attitudes to the complex historical problem were compounded as they were mapped onto the internal conflict between left and right. The attempt of the right to appropriate the national idea met with indignation from Hugo Preuss. Nor was the irony, that the states which now made patriotism compulsory had previously persecuted advocates of national unity, lost on the sociologist Ferdinand Tönnies.[56] Both Preuss and Tönnies sought to reclaim the idea of national unity for the democratic tradition with which it had originally been associated. In Preuss's case, this also involved extensive comparison with England. Having referred to the ethnic diversity of England's, origins he wrote that '[o]ur belief in the spiritual advantage of a pure, unmixed population is a worthless superstition' and added: 'That the politically most able nation of the modern world emerged from such elements should give our recent nationalist fanatics cause for some reflection'.[57] Moreover, Preuss repeatedly claimed that it was English political institutions, above all the combination of local self-government and national representative government, which had formed a stable and common sense of citizenship.[58] In Germany, however, internal division went all too well with the 'brainless nationalist swindle'.[59] In making political institutions the cornerstone of stable national identity and demarcating this kind of 'patriotism' from chauvinism, Preuss came close to what would later be known as 'constitutional patriotism', that is, the foundation of collective identity upon pride in and identification with political institutions rather than pre-political forms of identity. An analogous approximation has been suggested for the socialist Eduard Bernstein, though German socialists in the *Reich* found it difficult to deal with the concept of national identity. Principled internationalism was combined with suspicion that the militarism endemic in the *Reich* would issue in a war of aggression. On the other hand, the socialists were keen to deflect the charge that they were *vaterlandslose Gesellen* who would abandon their country even in the event of a defensive war. Ground between these two pressures, they found it difficult to maintain a conception of national identity that was tied to distinct institutions, save for the remote future of a socialist society.[60]

The most distinctive response to the problem of national identity came from socialists in the Habsburg lands. As socialists, Karl Renner and Otto Bauer were confronted with this problem within their own party, which was one of the few pan-Austrian institutions, incorporating diverse nationalities, especially a substantial Czech section which fretted at the predominance of Austrian Germans in the leadership of the party. It was Bauer who produced the more sustained analysis of the national identity in his book of 1906, *The Question of Nationalities and Social Democracy*. The definition at which he ultimately arrived was: 'The nation is the totality of human beings bound together by a community of fate into a community of character'.[61] According to Bauer, the initial communities in which common descent and community had both played a role had long since disintegrated, giving way to a period in which the relationship between the dominant class, the effective bearer of national identity, and the masses was the decisive factor. As a Marxist, he naturally argued for the importance of capitalism in promoting the wider dissemination of this culture and in the 'awakening of the non-historical nations', including the Czechs. It was, however, only the future socialist state that would complete this process.[62]

Sophisticated though his analysis of the nations was, it was the solution to the contemporary problems of the multi-national state that was most innovative. Here, Bauer drew on the ideas of Karl Renner.

Renner was motivated by the difficulty of recognising nationality in a political and legal culture dominated solely by the concepts of the territorial state and citizen. As Bauer later summarised: in this 'centralist-atomistic' model, 'the legal order knows only, on the one hand, the state, and on the other, the individual, the individual citizen'.[63] Renner had noticed an anomaly here in which some protection was provided against the territorial principle. In international law, the foreign citizen, an Englishman, could find protection even in Prague, in the form of the diplomatic service of his own state. Renner paused to note that this was more than could be said for the Austrian German in Prague.[64] Spurred on by this, Renner drew a distinction between the territorial principle, defining people by place of residence, and the personality principle, defining people by national identity. According to the latter, those of the same nationality would constitute a legal entity regardless of place of residence. Renner went to suggest that the current functions of the government should be divided and regulated on the basis of either the territorial or the personality principle according to whether or not they were central to cultural identity. The distinction was facilitated by Renner's contrast of the defining qualities of state and nation. He followed the influential identification of the essence of the state as will, in order then to say that in the case of the nation 'the common feature does not concern the realm of willing, but rather of thinking and feeling . . . It touches a completely different human dimension. There, where the will in general is not in consideration, there can be no kind of dominating, sovereign will but only dominating intellectual and emotional tendencies . . .'[65]

The Rechtsstaat

One barrier against the contingency of politics and the irrationalism of national identity was the concept of the *Rechtsstaat*, even if this had lost its wider political connotations. Nevertheless, the idea of a state whose prime characteristic was the creation of an ever more dense and coherent system of law that determined the legitimate activity of the state as well as of the citizens was widely perceived as a major achievement. As indicated in the Introduction, this did not exclude awareness of the paradoxical character of deriving law from the power of the state while simultaneously defining the state as subject to law. It was, however, not necessarily the state as a legislative machine that was seen as a threat to the *Rechtsstaat*. Thus, when

Gerhard Anschütz reviewed the arguments for and against the existence of gaps in the legal order, he denied that there were any such gaps in administrative law. In elaboration, he considered the possibility that administrative bodies might act in the common interest, provided only that what they did was not expressly forbidden by law. He proceeded to reject this possibility unequivocally, for it is a characteristic of a 'police' state that the administration acts 'only according to considerations of utility; the conviction of the administrative organs in the utility of their action is the only limit to administrative power'.[66] Administrative power was the threat in the eyes of Anschütz, and the answer to it lay predominantly, but not exclusively, in legislation.

One supplement to this was provided by the judicial system. According to Thoma, who agreed that legislation was the primary guarantee against arbitrary administrative discretion, the exclusion of the courts from issues of public law had been alien to the German legal tradition but had gradually been asserted in the interests of executive and administrative discretion. A restricted role for the courts also followed from the orthodox positivist position that gave priority to the legislative machine and viewed judges as little more than mouth-pieces of statutory law. Yet, well before the turn of the century, Rudolf von Ihring and Oskar Bülow had attacked this model of statutory positivism. Bülow went much further than Ihering, but the latter had pointed the way by emphasising interests and considerations of utility in the development of law.[67] Bülow took up these ideas to argue for the fundamental indeterminacy of the legal order.[68] He dismissed the idea that it is possible in cases of doubt to discern the intent of the 'many-headed legislator', some of whose members may not have even understood the legal text they sanctioned. He added that the greatest transformation in the legal order, the introduction of Roman law, had been effected not by statute but by 'judicial lawmaking'.[69] On the eve of the First World War, Eugen Ehrlich was even more scathing. The whole idea of the legal order as an order without gaps 'never was anything but purely theoretical pedantry'.[70] Ehrlich brought out the wider political significance of what had become known as the Free Law Movement. The idea of the 'omnipotence of the state', and the presumption that 'the power to legislate is the highest power in modern society', glossed over the fact that law is predominantly a product of social forces and non-state associations.[71] The Free Law Movement was successful enough for Gustav Radbruch to proclaim with some exaggeration that few now dared to challenge it. One who had no reservations about attacking it for reversion to 'value-irrationalism' was Max Weber.[72] Weber suspected that the ideas of the Free Law Movement could only encourage judges to substitute their own arbitrary values for what was prescribed by the legislative machine.

The *Rechtsstaat* presented related problems for German Marxist theorists. Thus, Renner agreed that social forces could bring about a change in the meaning of law, including changes disadvantageous to the working class. More specifically, he argued that what was properly public right and power had been effectively conferred upon private individuals. Renner's argument was that fixed legal categories undergo a change of function unnoticed by the legal system. His conclusion was that

> The right of the capitalist is delegated public authority, conferred indiscriminately upon the person who will use it for his own benefit. The employment relationship is an indirect power relationship, a public obligation to service, like the serfdom of feudal times. It differs from serfdom only in this respect, that it is based upon contract, not upon inheritance.[73]

Law and the *Rechtsstaat* had no more provided stability and certainty than Bismarck's constitution.

Parties and parliament

It was widely recognised that political parties were one of the main agents for trying to channel and achieve social change. Their virtues, however, were intensely disputed. Often, German theorists at the beginning of the century have been regarded not only as unsympathetic to parliamentary government but also as unable to grasp its true nature, above all the role of the majority and opposition parties within parliament. That in turn is traced to a commitment to a so-called constitutional monarchism explicitly contrasted with parliamentary systems, where constitutional monarchism is defined by the supposed balance between governmental power and parliamentary power.[74] These views were indeed widely held. They were especially evident in comparisons with the English political system, though this was clearly used as a weapon in debates about Germany's future political system.[75] Opponents of parliamentary democracy and political parties argued that England was a crypto-republic, with the clear implication that moves towards greater parliamentary power would prove a threat to German monarchy. Supporters invoked the existence of monarchy alongside a powerful parliament in England as proof that greater parliamentary power need not be a threat to German monarchy. Ironically, this gave supporters of parliament an interest in exaggerating the power of the English monarchy.

The basic model of monarch on the one side and parliament, as the people's representative, on the other side was evident, for example, in Conrad Bornhak's review of constitutional change in 1910. Indeed, Bornhak argued that it was even truer than at the time of the foundation of the *Reich*. His reason was that while the constitution had envisaged a federal government, the *Kaiser* had effectively displaced the *Bundesrat*. He added that the contrast of *Kaiser* and parliament was also more consistent with popular perceptions.[76] Jellinek noted that the idea of a balance between monarch and parliament was one of three possible relationships between monarch and parliament. The others were either monarchic dominance or parliamentary dominance. Balance, he continued, was rare and could be nothing more than a temporary arrangement.[77] In Germany, political reality corresponded with the doctrine that ascribed power to the executive and allowed parliament only a restraining influence upon this power of domination (*Herrschermacht*).[78] Yet Jellinek left no doubt that in this respect Germany lagged behind the development of the modern state.

He also sought to cut the ground from under the feet of some of those who wanted to provide a principled justification of the subordination of parliament by denying that it was an organ of state. Parliament was said to be an expression of society, incapable of embodying a unified will. Behind this lay the charge that not the interests of the state but the interests of the parties were said to come to the fore in parliaments. Society and parties were presented as divisive and hence not political, as, by extension, was parliament. Jellinek replied that society did not and could not have a unified will but that a parliament had no choice but to have a unified will. What he meant by this was simply that any parliamentary body has only two options when presented with any proposal. It can affirm it or reject it. The argument against parliament as a political institution an organ of state was false in its understanding of society, parties and parliament.[79]

Equally important was the underlying reason for the actual weakness of the German parliament, which Jellinek located in the fragmentation of political forces. Hence, he concluded, the only way forward lay in a 'complete transformation of the parties and a fusion of the [parliamentary] fractions into large groups'.[80] Alfred Weber agreed. Indeed, he believed that the situation had deteriorated since 1890 as any prospect of a firm government coalition faded and all parties had retreated to a stance of pure opposition.[81] Jellinek added that the literature criticising the vices of the reality of parliamentary government was so extensive that it was difficult to grasp. Yet he ascribed this to the progress that the idea and reality of parliamentary government was making. As with all political institutions, it was only as parliamentary government moved from a desired ideal to a practical reality that its deficiencies, varying as they did from state to state, came to the fore.[82] The real issue was not whether the regime in the German *Reich* was in reality a dualistic one, but whether this was seen as desirable and appropriate to Germany, as it was by Bornhak, or was seen as ultimately incompatible with the modern state, as it was by Jellinek and by the brothers Alfred and Max Weber.

The interventionist state

The supposed contrast between the state as the embodiment of a unified will and society as the site of the conflicting clamour of special interests was complicated by the emergence of an increasingly interventionist state and by a wider debate over the future of the German polity. Given the rate of industrialisation especially in the German *Reich*, it is notable that it was still possible for a debate to take place about whether the German future would take the form of an agrarian or an industrial state. At the turn of the century, Adolf Wagner argued for the former. According to Wagner, the current phase of industrialisation was no more than a transient one that nevertheless threatened the harmony of rural society. Max Weber retorted that 'no rural idyll' could be retained, while Friedrich Naumann outbid Weber in their common opposition to Wagner and his allies: '*God wants technical progress. He wants the machine.*'[83] The strains imposed by rapid urbanisation and industrialisation and the reaction they induced were set in a wider context by Preuss shortly after these debates. According to Preuss, Germany was witnessing a 'new phase of the old struggle between country and city'.[84]

Both critics as well as the advocates of industrialisation and urbanisation claimed to represent the common man, including the industrial proletariat, against the vices of these processes of modernisation. What was also common to them was a sense of being overwhelmed by the process of modernisation in which advanced capitalism and a bureaucratic and interventionist state were related phenomena. Along with that sense of momentous change went a conceptual slippage which readily equated the interventionist state in general with some form of socialism. All this was gathered together in Max Scheler's proclamation on the eve of the First World War: 'The fact itself however, that the freedom-threatening medicaments of the increasing state socialism have become the only ones that are able to promote the maximum of national welfare, is itself the worst *consequence* of the *domination of the capitalist spirit*'.[85]

Not all felt as threatened by these developments as Scheler. As Michael Stolleis has argued, one response to the rise of the interventionist was the revival of the concept of the purpose of the state in the work of Ihering.[86] Even Jellinek, who was suspicious of expansive concepts of purpose and all too aware of how contingent purposes could be transfigured into either absolute values for the state per se or into the supposed distinctive purposes of various national polities, sanctioned the centralising interventionist state as an empirical reality.[87] According to Jellinek, one of the most important aspects of any discussion of the purposes of the state was what the state was not supposed to do. That was a sentiment which Weber also expressed, though on more tactical grounds, when faced with calls for greater state intervention. Weber was not a doctrinaire opponent of an active social policy; quite the contrary. He lamented the power of business interests as much for the supine attitude of state officials in the face of such power as anything else. Contrary to the supposition that state officials could adopt a standpoint above the clash of social interests, Weber asserted in 1909 that one could not expect anything from the replacement of the industrialist by the civil servant other than that 'the state power will be full of [concern] for the sensitivities of the employers'. Compared with the manufacturer, in economic matters the civil servants and white-collar workers 'are more papal than the Pope'.[88]

The international order

Weber could not resist setting his comments in the context of the international struggle for power, and countered the supposition of the supposed superior moral standing of German civil servants with the observation that 'Democratically governed countries with, in part, an undoubtedly corrupt civil service have attained very much more in the world than our highly moral bureaucracy . . .'[89] Weber's comment reflected a wider debate about the relationship between

Germany's domestic institutions and its international position. The idea, most clearly expressed by Otto Hintze, that its exposed international position in the centre of Europe required a hierarchically organised internal political order was one of many arguments for the distinctiveness of German institutions.

The need for the pursuit of power politics on the international stage had been a constant theme in Weber's work. Although Weber criticised the German government for its obsession with the trappings of power rather than the substance, he was not always that precise about what substantive goals Germany ought to be seeking. One common element among advocates of a great-power orientation was the transposition of the idea of a balance amongst the European powers onto the global stage. Common though this idea was, approaches to the international order cannot be reduced to a Darwinian power politics regulated at most by the idea of a balance of power. Thus, Heinrich Triepel argued for the existence of international law alongside domestic or municipal law. This dualistic approach to the legal order, embodied in the title of his book, *Völkerrecht und Landesrecht* (International and Municipal Law), was founded on the idea that the two forms of law regulated different subjects of law, coordinate states in the case of international law, citizens of states in the case of domestic law. Although he sought to hold these two forms of law apart, he did so in order to defend the existence of international law as a binding form of law against its detractors. This involved the claim that law rested not merely upon contracts or treaties but was the expression of an underlying international community. In Triepel's words: 'While the treaty [*Vertrag*] is supposed to serve the fulfilment of contrary interests, agreement [*Vereinbarung*] is intended to satisfy common or identical interests'.[90] Triepel's argument, so far as it rested on the conceptual distinction between contract and agreement, is flawed, as was pointed out at the time.[91] It is noteworthy, however, that Triepel slipped into using dubious analogies most blatantly not when seeking to make the two forms of law conceptually watertight, but when seeking to allow for the influence, albeit indirect, of international law upon domestic law.[92] In many respects, politically and intellectually, Triepel was relatively orthodox. Indeed, he was praised for defending international law from a strictly positivistic standpoint.

Yet others also responded to the same phenomena as Triepel. When discussing the general trend towards centralisation, Jellinek observed that although the final outcome was unclear there were already signs that the process would not halt at the boundaries of the individual state.[93] Indeed, Jellinek was more radical than Triepel. His definition of sovereignty enabled him to take a relatively relaxed view about the voluntary surrender of powers that were usually seen as essential to sovereignty. This could go so far, Jellinek concluded, that 'It is not only a theoretical consequence of the concept of sovereignty that it can exist as a *nudum jus* but also something demonstrable in the practical world'.[94] According to Jellinek, approaches to the international order were distorted not just by ill-defined concepts but also by a basic methodological error. The natural sciences and economics had made great strides by a radical isolation of the object of study. In the case of the international order, this had quite misleading consequences, for in 'reality never *the state* but always and only *states* are present' in the international order.[95] In other words, one had to start not with the autonomous, sovereign state but with the reality of a community of states. The Swiss jurist, Max Huber, also placed the community of states at the centre of his argument. Tracing the development of the nature of treaties across the centuries, he argued for a growing recognition of common interests, culminating in treaties that were in the interests of the 'totality of states' rather than the direct signatories.[96]

Although Huber had been drawn to international relations by Bertha von Suttner's pacifist novel, *Die Waffen nieder!*, Huber was no pacifist. He showed some sympathy for the supposition that war had a positive influence on human virtue and culture. Yet he thought he could see a growing reluctance of men to repeat what he described as the 'extraordinary' willingness to sacrifice themselves for the state in the nineteenth century.[97] Jellinek too anticipated a decline in inter-state wars, but he set two limits to the prospects of peace. First, civil wars were unavoidable. Not even the almost certain prospect of failure would deter parties convinced of their cause. Second, major ideological transformation would continue to be accompanied by violence: 'No great idea has achieved domination, whether in the religious, political or social fields, without having cost streams of blood'.[98]

The impact of the First World War

On the eve of the First World War, German political thought exhibited great diversity. Although some views, for example support of natural-law theories, were clearly marginalised, there was no 'orthodoxy' that had not been attacked. While some individuals appear easy to assign to an ideological camp, most camps had their renegades, and many individuals fitted into several or no camps. In retrospect, that is to be expected from societies as fragmented and, in some respects at least, as dynamic as the lands inhabited by Germans in this period. If anything is striking in retrospect, it is the extent of the diversity of political thought, the vehemence of the disputes and the willingness to push concept and argument to the limit. Those characteristics were aggravated by the apparent fragility of identity and frequently by a sense of being overwhelmed by the pace of change. A war, whose nature few had anticipated, could only accelerate these trends. Yet, at first, this was not how it seemed. The war brought with it proclamations of national unity which most intellectuals rushed to sign, or indeed initiated. Even in retrospect, Meinecke could still recall his enthusiasm for 3 August 1914. He was not unusual in this respect. Affirmation of national unity, in the shape of the proclamation by the *Kaiser* that he no longer recognised political parties but only Germans, were soon inflamed into claims that the war, and German victory, revealed the true meaning of history. So rampant were such views that Georg Simmel noted in one of his early panegyrics to national unity that 'In every respect it is to be rejected that Germany must be victorious, if history is to have a meaning'.[99] The rhetoric of inner value and expectation of victory, which amounted to little more than an indeterminate assertion of will, was deployed without restraint by Rudolf Eucken: 'If we only stand fast to ourselves, grasp the depths and inner force of our essence, then our genius will be with us and lead to victory, then even the gates of hell will not be able to overcome us'.[100] Even more ominous was the prophesy made by Paul Natorp: 'Were the German . . . not true to his vocation then will his name be eradicated from the earth'.[101]

These sentiments were accompanied by a set of contrasts, between the ideas of 1789 and the ideas of 1914 – between, in Werner Sombart's well-known contrast German 'heroes' and English 'traders'. In part, the contrasts and the exaggerated rhetoric were products of the clash between the propagandistic endeavours of the intellectuals of the warring powers. It was this which drove Germans to identify German culture and Prussian militarism in a way they would not have dreamed of doing before the war. Meinecke, for example, recalled that his 'Kultur, Machtpolitik und Militarismus' (Culture, power politics and militarism) of 1915 had been written to counter enemy attempts to draw a distinction between two Germanies, one peaceful and cultured, the other militaristic and wild.[102] This intellectual transfiguration of the war into an ideological conflict marked the transformation of the idea of a separate road of German political development into a widespread ideology.[103] It was also linked to a sense of embarking upon a new political venture with an indeterminate end goal, albeit one to which old concepts served as no guide. This was evident even in Alfred Weber, an advocate of democratic reform before the war, and after, who wrote that 'our old conceptual world, words like democracy and aristocracy, and similar ones, are absolutely unusable in the light of our contemporary reality . . .'[104]

Not all succumbed to this rhetoric. The Austrian Marxist Max Adler had little difficulty in mocking Max Scheler's variety of war philosophy: 'Such a theory brings us to the point where all the destructiveness of war is described as act of liberating love, as, for example, occurs especially strikingly in the destruction of the cathedral of Reim'.[105] Among the few who withstood the general inflammation, Adler emphasised Emil Lederer. Lederer sought to explain the complex, and paradoxical, development of the state as conditioned both by the socio-economic structure of countries and the evolving military structure. One of the paradoxes was that the absolutist state, which recognised no limits on its power in principle, had been in fact highly limited. It was unable to deploy the human resources of the modern state and was reliant upon paid armies: 'the state disposed of its citizens only by virtue of a contract'.[106] The modern state, however, could exploit the resources of a capitalist economy, including the manpower which could be diverted from non-essential occupations. By virtue of the principle of conscription, 'the limitless power of the state is realised; only now does it dispose over its population – far more than the absolute prince, for whom the land was his domain, for whom the citizens were his subjects'. But this side of the state was 'in its essence abstract, because [it is] beyond the social and economic differences that are given today'.[107] Whereas the prophets of a special German path thought that the mobilisation of 1914 was the expression of something distinctively German, Lederer saw the same abstract principle of conscription and military organisation at work in all the warring states. The state itself appeared with a Janus face. Internally, states were indeed distinguished by the peculiarities of their social, economic and hence political systems. Looked at from the outside, however, the state increasingly freed itself from its distinctive social and economic characteristics. As Meinecke had seen before the war, Lederer noted that modern nationalism in fact employed 'only a schematised and conventional national culture' that glossed over true national differences.[108] Moreover, the community formed by mobilisation was by definition a compulsory one that took no recognition of social peculiarities or positions. It was, in fact, not a genuine community at all but an 'abstract, organised multitude'.[109] It was characteristic of the power of the abstract state that in war one witnessed 'the complete abdication of the domestic organs of state, of the administration: in war the state of siege is proclaimed . . . The military is the state.'[110]

Lederer referred to the state of siege only in passing, but it inevitably stimulated more focused discussion. Werner Rosenberg responded to a judicial interpretation of the Prussian law of 4 June 1851, according to which the law established an independent right to issue unrestricted directives.[111] Rosenberg objected to this judgement, arguing that it was consistent neither with the intent of the legislators at the time nor the subsequent views of Prussian courts and jurists, or even the Prussian military authorities before the war. Rosenberg's vigorous defence of the rule of law was, as he acknowledged, disputed. Among those who took exception to Rosenberg's view was Carl Schmitt. Schmitt set the issue in a much wider context, of the literature on the concept of dictatorship and on the state of siege. Although Schmitt's conclusion was apparently equivocal, his real motive lay in the justification not only of the power of the military commanders but also in a certain conception of politics and the state. Schmitt conceded that in both cases it was still possible to maintain a conceptual difference between legislative and executive power – more so, in fact, in the state of siege. Schmitt added, however, that there was a 'concentration within the executive'.[112] The meaning of this became clear when Schmitt elaborated. He took up the idea of legislative and executive power, where the former, as the 'true expression of the sovereignty of the people', was accorded supremacy and the executive was interpreted simply as the 'arm' of the legislative brain; and he then wrote:

> But with such antitheses one does not do justice to the significance of the administration. Administration is more than the mere execution of positive legal definitions; the law is only the framework within which the creative activity of administration takes place. Also, the historical development did not occur in such a way that first the law . . . was declared and then its execution was taken in hand. In the beginning all state activity is administration; legislation and jurisdiction separated out later . . . The primeval condition, if it is permitted to use this word, remains administration . . .[113]

This was the 'concentration within the executive' which amounted to the invocation of a primeval conception of the political, reincarnated within the façade of the *Rechtsstaat*. Both Lederer and Schmitt had focused upon the enhanced power of the state during the war. Lederer saw this as the product of specifically modern conditions, leading to an intensification of the autonomy of the state from society in the same moment as this militarised state sucked up the substance of society, its very population, into an abstract machine indifferent to the real peculiarities of the warring nations. Schmitt presented this enhanced power as a return to an earlier condition, an explicit regression which did justice to the idea of 'administration'.

Political institutions, national unity and German distinctiveness were the themes of Preuss's *Das Deutsche Volk und die Politik* (The German People and Politics) of 1915. Although, to Preuss's surprise, it was favourably received in some quarters, especially in Austria, Gustav Schmoller responded with a bitter attack, including crude anti-semitic comments.[114] The underlying reason for the bitterness is not difficult to discern. Preuss asked why Germany had been so unsuccessful in the propaganda war with its enemies. He rejected the standard argument that resentment against Germany as a newcomer on the global stage was the problem. The real reason, he claimed, was the distinctiveness of German institutions and ideas and specifically the German tradition of the *Obrigkeitsstaat*. To press home the point, Preuss asked: had not foreign countries heard so much about German distinctiveness precisely from Germans?[115] It was, in fact, Preuss's book that turned the term *Obrigkeitsstaat* into a widely used polemical term. In Preuss's hands, the idea of an authoritarian political tradition became a weapon to explain German weakness, not strength, and to call for reform.

Preuss's biting and often sarcastic attack on what he identitifed as the *Obrigkeitsstaat* came through in his comments on German wartime unity: 'Such unanimity in external defence could, of course, be a surprise – hopefully a pleasant one – only for believers in the traditional politics of mistrust, that stamped every domestic opposition as an enemy of the *Reich*'.[116] Preuss effectively blamed the same suspicion for feeding the belief of Germany's wartime opponents that they could divide the German nation.[117] In this and much else, Preuss was concerned above all about the underlying understanding of politics. Hence he described the discriminatory Prussian electoral system, to which he was opposed, as a secondary matter. What really counted was the political 'energy' of the German people. What was lacking was parties capable of and willing to take on the role of government. That in turn was a product of a lack of 'political energy . . . oriented directly towards the practical activity of the state'.[118]

Schmoller sought to discredit Preuss with a mixture of anti-semitism and anti-urban resentment that unintentionally gave retrospective justification to Preuss's earlier reference to a 'new phase of the old struggle between country and city'. Schmoller claimed that Germany was not as undemocratic as Preuss suggested, but also sought to undermine aspirations for democratisation and parliamentarianism by comparing the reality of parliamentary regimes with idealised models: 'Even in the red republic the people as such has never and nowhere ruled'.[119] Underlying much of Schmoller's argument was the idea that parliamentary regimes relied upon demagoguery and the fickle, if not corrupted, mood of the masses, whereas German constitutionalism ensured a stable, honest and far-sighted administration.

That became more and more difficult to maintain as resort to demagoguery, especially by the more extreme annexationists, became all too evident. Indeed, it was not long before Max Weber was angrily proclaiming that 'In Germany we have *demagogy and the influence of the rabble without democracy*, or rather, *because we lack an orderly democracy*'.[120] There was little in the constitutional monarchy that Weber did not attack. The ideology of the 'communal wartime economy' and supposed spirit of integrity were both treated as mere sham. Yet Weber's proposals for reform in a series of articles in April–June 1917 fell short of a call for parliamentary government, as Robert Piloty pointed out. Weber had focused initially on problems of leadership selection and the clash between political leadership and rule by bureaucracy. What was missing was clear recognition of the core idea of a parliamentary system, namely that 'only a specific party tendency is allowed to lay its hands on the rudder at any given time'.[121] By the end of the year, however, Weber was giving explicit emphasis to the role of parties. Whereas Schmoller associated party and parliamentary government with fickleness, Weber argued that 'the *un*organised mass, the democracy of the street, is wholly irrational. It is at its most powerful in countries with a parliament that is either powerless or politically discredited, and that means above all where *rationally organised parties* are absent.'[122]

It was within organised political parties that responsibility was to be inculcated, and organised political parties were to provide the political platform for the caesaristic leader. But only the platform; for, in contrast to the leaders of parties of notables, the key to the political leader advocated by Weber was that 'he uses the means of *mass demagogy* to gain the confidence of the masses and their belief in his person, and thereby gains power'.[123] Weber expanded on the tension between parliamentary and plebiscitary selection of leaders, but even in the case of the latter he ascribed significant functions to parliament in educating prospective leaders, providing a platform for them, ensuring the existence of *'legal safeguards'* against them and a mechanism for *'eliminating'* leaders who had lost the trust of the masses. More broadly, he warned that any attempt to introduce democracy without a parliament would have dire consequences in Germany: 'Any merely *passive democratisation* of this kind would be the purest form of *uncontrolled bureaucratic rule*, with which we are very familiar here, and it would call itself a "monarchic regiment"'.[124]

Weber later lost sight of the importance of his warning, though that is not true of Robert Redslob, whose *Die parlamentarische Regierung in ihrer wahren und in ihrer unechten Form* (Parliamentary Government in its True and Unauthentic Form) of 1918 has been accused of contributing to the decision to opt for a directly elected head of state in the Weimar constitution. In fact, Redslob believed that French political experience had confirmed the suspicions of those who had resisted such an option in that country. What Redslob did admire in the 'true' English form of parliamentarianism was the existence of a mechanism for avoiding political paralysis through the dissolution of parliament. Redslob was also aware that even this mechanism could be subject to abuse. Reflecting on the actions of the French president Macmahon in 1877, he wrote that dissolution

> may not be used in order to break resistance and help a policy to victory . . . Dissolution is no kind of weapon of attack. It is a question, perhaps a plea, but it is no kind of coup de main . . . To appeal to a people, whose opposition one knows, means pursuing an act of repression, means not recognising a people as a judge and degrading it to the role of an instrument . . .'[125]

Weber, Preuss and Redslob were all looking for institutional mechanisms which would ensure political responsibility, as well as a commensurate political culture. Yet the strains of war suggested different priorities, even to those supportive of democratisation. For Friedrich Naumann, what mattered most was the myth which would unite the nation. He still found this in the monarch, 'equipped with a remarkable mystique', who could integrate the working masses as citizens of the state.[126] Weber identified a quite different source of unity:

The modern state is the first to have the concept of the '*citizen of the state*' (*Staatsbürger*). Equal voting rights means in the first instance simply this: at this point of social life the individual, for once, is *not*, as he is everywhere else, considered in terms of the particular professional and family position he occupies, nor in relation to differences of material and social situation, but purely and simply *as a citizen*. This expresses the political unity of the nation (*Staatsvolk*).[127]

It is clear that German political thought before 1914 was part of a contested political culture. Even the idea of a German political tradition was part of an often highly polemical debate about how the German empires would have to respond to the challenges of modernisation. Certain ideas were highly prominent, most obviously the concept of the state, or highly distinctive, most obviously the *Rechtsstaat*, but the precise connotations of those concepts were also disputed. It is also clear that the war of 1914–18 was disorientating, divisive, and tied up with a radicalisation of the idea of a distinctive German political tradition, both by advocates and critics of that tradition.

Notes

1. F. Becker, *Bilder von Krieg und Nation. Die Einigungskriege in der bürgerlichen Öffentlichkeit Deutschlands 1864–1913* (Munich: Oldenbourg, 2001), pp. 292–376.
2. Friedrich Meinecke, *Strassburg/Freiburg/Berlin 1901–1919. Erinnerungen* (Stuttgart: Koehler, 1947), p. 41.
3. Quoted in Richard Thoma, 'Grundzüge des Staatsrechts des deutschen Kaiserreichs und seiner Einzelstaaten', in Gerhard Anschütz and Richard Thoma (eds), *Handbuch des Deutschen Staatsrechts*, vol. 1 (Tübingen: Mohr, 1930), p. 72.
4. Quoted in Allan Janik and Stephen Toulmin, *Wittgenstein's Vienna* (New York: Simon and Schuster, 1973), p. 36.
5. Quoted in Brigitte Hamann, *Hitler's Vienna* (Oxford: Oxford University Press, 1999), p. 96.
6. Otto Mayer, quoted in Michael Stolleis, 'Die Entstehung des Interventionsstaats und das öffentliche Recht', *Zeitschrift für neuere Rechtsgeschichte* 11 (1989), p. 141.
7. Philipp Zorn, 'Die Entwicklung der Staatsrechts-Wissenschaft seit 1866', *Jahrbuch des öffentlichen Rechts der Gegenwart*. 1 (1907), pp. 64–6.
8. Paul Laband, 'Die geschichtliche Entwicklung der Reichsverfassung seit der Reichsgründung', *Jahrbuch des öffentlichen Rechts der Gegenwart* 1 (1907), p. 14.

9. Georg Jellinek, *Allgemeine Staatslehre* [1913] (Berlin: Julius Springer, 1929), pp. 10–12.
10. Ibid., p. 181.
11. Ibid., p. 183.
12. Ibid., p. 181.
13. Ibid., p. 161.
14. Ibid., p. 175.
15. Georg Jellinek, *Die Lehre von den Staatenverbindungen* [1882] (Goldbach: Keip, 1996), p. 26.
16. Jellinek, *Allgemeine Staatslehre*, pp. 481–2.
17. See especially Max Anter, *Max Webers Theorie des modernen Staates* (Berlin: Duncker & Humblot, 1995).
18. Max Weber, 'Die "Objectivität" sozialwissenschaftlicher and sozialpolitischer Erkenntnis' [1904], in *Gesammelte Aufsätze zur Wissenschaftslehre*, 2nd edn (Tübingen: Mohr, 1951), pp. 200–1.
19. Jellinek, *Allgemeine Staatslehre*, pp. 165–6.
20. See Max Weber, 'Über einige Kategorien der verstehenden Soziologie' [1913], in Weber, *Gesammelte Aufsätze zur Wissenschaftslehre*, pp. 466–74; Max Weber, *Wirtschaft und Gesellschaft* [1921] (Tübingen: Mohr, 1972), pp. 27–30; Anter, *Max Webers Theorie*, pp. 47–51.
21. Otto Gierke, 'Labands Staatsrecht und die deutsche Rechtswissenschaft', *Schmollers Jahrbuch* 7 (1883), p. 1126.
22. Hugo Preuss, *Die Entwicklung des deutschen Städtewesens* (Leipzig: Teubner, 1906), pp. 125–6.
23. Hugo Preuss, 'Über Organpersönlichkeit', *Jahrbuch für Gesetzgebung, Verwaltung und Volkswirtschaft im Deutschen Reich* 26 (1902), p. 560. The argument relies on the notion that an organ is a part of a larger whole and not a mere instrument of someone or something else. See Hans Kelsen, *Hauptprobleme der Staatsrechtslehre* [1923] (Aalen: Scientia, 1981), pp. 697–8. The main part of the text was first published in 1911.
24. Preuss, 'Über Organpersönlichkeit', p. 575.
25. Kelsen, *Hauptprobleme der Staatsrechtslehre*, p.173.
26. Ibid., p. 399. See also pp. 431–2.
27. Ibid., pp. 702–3.
28. Ibid., p. 411.
29. Jellinek, *Allgemeine Staatslehre*, p. 180.
30. A. Schäffle, 'Über den wissenschaftlichen Begriff der Politik', *Zeitschrift für die gesamte Staatswissenschaft*, 5 (1897), pp. 580–1.
31. Ibid., p. 593.
32. Heinrich von Treitschke, *Politics*, vol. 1 [1898] (London: Constable, 1916), pp. xxxvii, xxxiii. On the following comment on Treitschke, see Ulrich Langer, *Heinrich von Treitschke* (Düsseldorf: Droste, 1998), p. 343.

33. Max Lenz, 'Bismarck als Diplomat' [1915], in Max Lenz, *Wille, Macht, Schicksal* (Munich: Oldenbourg, 1922), p. 152.
34. Schäffle, 'Über den wissenschaftlichen Begriff der Politik', p. 598.
35. Max Weber, 'Nation state and economic policy' [1895], in Max Weber, *Political Writings* (Cambridge: Cambridge University Press, 1994), p. 16.
36. Ibid., p. 15.
37. Ibid., p. 16. The claim by Wilhelm Hennis that here Weber must be 'read in a "political-anthropological" manner, and not nationalistically', 'A science of man', in Wolfgang J. Mommsen (ed.), *Max Weber and his Contemporaries* (London: Allen and Unwin, 1987), p. 37, is unpersuasive. See Anter, *Max Webers Theorie des modernen Staates*, p. 137. Hennis would have been on sounder ground if he had dropped the 'not'.
38. Weber, 'Nation State and Economic Policy', p. 15.
39. On antipathy to emotionalism, see Lawrence A. Scaff, *Fleeing the Iron Cage* (Berkeley, CA: University of California Press, 1989), pp. 170, 184. On the 'pathos of distance', see Stephen E. Asheim, *The Nietzsche Legacy in Germany 1890–1990* (Berkeley, CA: University of California Press, 1994), p. 42. Both Anter, *Max Webers Theorie*, p. 25 and Wolfgang J. Mommsen, *Max Weber and German Politics 1890–1920* (Chicago: Chicago University Press, 1984), pp. 33, 42–3, 45, agree that Weber did not fetishise or aestheticise violence.
40. Jellinek, *Allgemeine Staatslehre*, p. 13.
41. Ibid., p. 21.
42. Hugo Preuss, 'Weltkrieg, Demokratie und Deutschlands Erneuerung', *Archiv für Sozialwissenschaft und Sozialpolitik*, 44 (1917): pp. 256–7. See also his comment: 'Strange that one believes it necessary to continually warn the most unpolitical of all cultural nations of the enchantress, politics . . .', 'Verwaltungsreform und Politik', *Zeitschrift für Politik* 1 (1907), p. 96.
43. 'The conquest of political power' [1898], in H. Tudor and J. M. Tudor (eds), *Marxism and Social Democracy: The Revisionist Debate 1896–1898* (Cambridge: Cambridge University Press, 1988), p. 305.
44. Quoted in Peter C. Caldwell, *Popular Sovereignty and the Crisis of German Constitutional Law* (Durham, NC: Duke University Press, 1997), p. 37.
45. F. von Bernhardi, *Germany and the Next War* [1911] (London: Edward Arnold, 1914), pp. 112–13.
46. Quoted in Detlef Lehnert, *Verfassungsdemokratie als Bürgergenossenschaft* (Baden-Baden: Nomos, 1998), p. 169.
47. Max Weber, *Gesammelte Aufsätze zur Soziologie und Sozialpolitik* (Tübingen: Mohr, 1924), pp. 490, 492, 487.
48. Friedrich Meinecke, 'Nationalismus und nationale Idee' [July 1914],

in Friedrich Meinecke, *Politische Schriften und Reden* (Darmstadt: Toeche-Mittler, 1979), pp. 86–7.

49. Klaus Kempter, *Die Jellineks 1820–1955* (Düsseldorf: Droste, 1998), pp. 328–30.

50. Georg Jellinek, *Das Recht der Minoritäten* [1898] (Schutterwald: Klaus Fischer, 1996), p. 89. Later on, he showed more concern about the paralysing effects of such practices: 'Parliamentary Obstruction', *Political Science Quarterly* 19 (1904), pp. 579–88.

51. Jellinek, *Allgemeine Staatslehre*, p. 116.

52. Jellinek, *Das Recht der Minoritäten*, p. 65.

53. Jellinek, *Allgemeine Staatslehre*, p. 145.

54. Ibid., p. 775.

55. Ibid., p. 779.

56. Ferdinand Tönnies, 'Nationalgefühl' [July 1914], in Ferdinand Tönnies, *Gesamtausgabe*, vol. 9 (Berlin: de Gruyter, 2000), p. 407.

57. Hugo Preuss, 'Eine Bibliographie des Englischen Parlaments' [1886], in Hugo Preuss, *Staat, Recht, Freiheit* (Tübingen: Mohr, 1926), p. 513.

58. See *Die Entwicklung des deutschen Städtewesens*, p. 235.

59. Hugo Preuss, *Deutschland und sein Reichskanzler* (Berlin: Habel, 1885), pp. 25–7.

60. Thus Dieter Groh and Peter Brandt, *'Vaterlandslose Gesellen'. Sozialdemokratie und Nation 1860–1990* (Munich: Beck, 1992), especially pp. 112–20. For Bernstein, see Manfred B. Steger, *The Quest for Evolutionary Socialism* (Cambridge: Cambridge University Press, 1997), pp. 197–204.

61. Otto Bauer, *The Question of Nationalities and Social Democracy* [1907] (Minneapolis: University of Minnesota Press, 2000), p. 117.

62. Ibid., pp. 176–93 and 107.

63. Ibid., p. 222.

64. Karl Renner, 'Staat und Nation' [1899], in Karl Renner, *Schriften* (Salzburg: Residenz, 1994), p. 30.

65. Ibid., p. 24.

66. Gerhard Anschütz, 'Lücken in den Verfassungs- und Verwaltungsgesetzen', *Verwaltungsarchiv* 14 (1906), p. 325.

67. Rudolf von Ihering, *Law as a Means to an End* (South Hackensack, NJ: Rothman, 1968). This is a translation of the fourth edition of the first volume of *Der Zweck im Recht* (1903). The first was published in 1877.

68. James E. Herget defines this as involving the following: '(1) The formal legal authorities . . . do not bind the courts in their decisions, and the judicial power may even be exercised to contradict those authorities. (2) The authoritative sources themselves contain ambiguous and contradictory principles. (3) Law is consequently not fixed and objective, but indeterminate and subjective . . . (4) to explain the judicial process

it is necessary to go outside the authoritative sources to other social phenomena.' 'Unearthing the origins of a radical idea: the case of legal indeterminacy', *The American Journal of Legal History* 39 (1995), p. 60.

69. Oskar Bülow, 'Statutory law and judicial function' [1885], *The American Journal of Legal History* 39 (1995), pp. 89 and 85.

70. Eugen Ehrlich, *Fundamental Principles of the Sociology of Law* [1913] (New York: Russell and Russell, 1962), p. 430.

71. Ibid., pp. 389–90.

72. Max Weber, *Wirtschaft und Gesellschaft* [1922] (Tübingen: Mohr, 1972), pp. 504–13. This was probably written in 1913–14.

73. Karl Renner, *The Institutions of Private Law and Their Social Function*, 2nd edn [1929] (London: Routledge & Paul, 1949), p. 115. Renner's method was 'to examine only the economic and social effect of the valid norm, so long as the norm does not change' (ibid., p. 55). For Ihering's attack on the 'sacredness of property' and his 'social theory of property', see Ihering, *Law as a Means to an End*, pp. 389–97.

74. See for example Christoph Schönberger, *Das Parlament im Anstaltsstaat* (Frankfurt am Main: Klostermann, 1997).

75. Richard J. Lammer, *Der englische Parlamentarismus in der deutschen politischen Theorie im Zeitalter Bismarcks (1857–1890)* (Lübeck: Matthiesen, 1963).

76. Conrad Bornhak, 'Wandlungen der Reichsverfasssung', *Archiv des öffentliche Rechts* 26 (1910), pp. 381 and 391. Earlier, Bornhak had even advocated a revived monarchism as a solution to England's ills: 'Die Entwicklung der konstitutionellen Theorie', *Zeitschrift für die gesamte Staatswissenschaft* 51 (1895), p. 617.

77. Jellinek, *Allgemeine Staatslehre*, p. 705.

78. Georg Jellinek, *Verfassungsänderung und Verfassungswandlung* [1906] (Goldbach: Keip, 1996), p. 58.

79. Jellinek, *Allgemeine Staatslehre*, pp. 578–9.

80. Jellinek, *Verfassungsänderung und Verfassungswandlung*, p. 59.

81. Alfred Weber, 'Konstitutionelle oder parlamentarische Regierung in Deutschland' [1907], in Eberhard Demm (ed.), *Politische Theorie und Tagespolitik* (Marburg: Metropolis, 1999), p. 37.

82. Jellinek, *Verfassungsänderung und Verfassungswandlung*, pp. 68–70.

83. Both quoted in Kenneth D. Barkin, 'Conflict and concord in Wilhelmian social thought', *Central European History* 5 (1972), p. 66.

84. Quoted in Lehnert, *Verfassungsdemokratie als Bürgergenossenschaft*, p. 251.

85. Max Scheler, 'Die Zukunft des Kapitalismus' [1914], in *Die Zukunft des Kapitalismus und andere Aufsätze* (Munich: Francke, 1979), p. 77.

86. Stolleis, 'Die Entstehung des Interventionsstaats', p. 140.

87. Jellinek, *Allgemeine Staatslehre*, pp. 230–65.

88. Max Weber, 'Debattereden auf der Tagung des Vereins für Sozialpolitik

in Wien 1909', in *Gesammelte Aufsätze zur Soziologie und Sozial-politik*, pp. 416–17.

89. Ibid., p. 418.

90. Carl Heinrich Triepel, *Völkerrecht und Landesrecht* (Leipzig: Hirsch-feld, 1899), p. 53.

91. Contracts could involve identical interests, as when two parties con-tracted to endow some public institution or charity. See L. von Bar, 'Grundlage und Kodification des Völkerrechts', *Archiv für Rechts-philosophie* (1916), p. 146.

92. See Triepel, *Völkerrecht und Landesrecht*, pp. 258 and 271.

93. Jellinek, *Allgemeine Staatslehre*, pp. 261–3.

94. Jellinek, *Die Lehre von den Staatenverbindungen*, p. 54. His favoured example at the time was Bosnia and Herzegovina, whose sovereign remained the Porte despite being administered by the Habsburg Empire.

95. Ibid., p. 93.

96. Max Huber, 'Beiträge zur Kenntnis der soziologischen Grundlagen des Völkerrechts und der Staatengemeinschaft', *Jahrbuch des öffentlichen Rechts der Gegenwart* 4 (1910), p. 91.

97. Ibid., pp. 114, 116, 120.

98. Georg Jellinek, 'Die Zukunft des Krieges' [1890], in Georg Jellinek, *Ausgewählte Schriften und Reden*, vol. 2 (Aalen: Scientia, 1970), p. 539.

99. Georg Simmel, 'Deutschlands innere Wandlung' [1914], in Georg Simmel, *Gesamtausgabe*, vol. 16 (Frankfurt am Main: Suhrkamp, 1999), p. 23.

100. Quoted in Hermann Lübbe, *Politische Philosophie in Deutschland* (Munich: DTV, 1974), p. 183.

101. Ibid., p. 192.

102. Friedrich Meinecke, *Strassburg/Freiburg/Berlin 1901–1919*, p. 199.

103. Thus Rudolf Vierhaus, 'Die Ideologie eines deutschen Weges', in Rudolf von Thadden (ed.), *Die Krise des Liberalismus zwischen den Weltkriegen* (Göttingen: Vandenhoeck & Ruprecht, 1978), p. 99.

104. Quoted in Marcus Llanque, *Demokratisches Denken im Krieg* (Berlin: Akademie, 2000), p. 66.

105. Max Adler, 'Zwei Jahre . . . ! Weltkriegsbetrachtungen eines Sozialisten' [1916], in Max Adler, *Ausgewählte Schriften* (Vienna: Österreichischer Bundesverlag, 1981), p. 117.

106. Emil Lederer, 'Zur Soziologie des Weltkrieges', *Archiv für Sozialwis-senschaft und Sozialpolitik* 39 (1916), p. 366.

107. Ibid., p. 361.

108. Ibid., p. 376.

109. Ibid., p. 382.

110. Ibid., p. 365. As Christian Jansen notes, it is interesting that it was possible to publish such views: *Professoren und Politik* (Göttingen: Vandenhoeck & Ruprecht, 1992), p. 133.

111. Werner Rosenberg, 'Die rechtlichen Schranken der Militärdiktatur', *Zeitschrift für die gesamte Strafrechtswissenschaft* 37 (1916), p. 808.
112. Carl Schmitt, 'Diktatur und Belagerungszustand', *Zeitschrift für die gesamte Strafrechtswissenschaft* 38 (1917), pp. 156–7.
113. Ibid., p. 157.
114. Hugo Preuss, *Das deutsche Volk und die Politik* (Jena: Eugen Diederichs, 1915). For his surprise, see *Obrigkeitsstaat und grossdeutsche Gedanke* (Jena: Diederichs, 1916), p. 5. For Schmoller's attack, see his 'Obrigkeitsstaat und Volksstaat: ein missverständlicher Gegensatz', *Schmollers Jahrbuch* 40 (1916), pp. 423–34.
115. Preuss, *Das deutsche Volk und die Politik*, p. 59.
116. Ibid., pp. 46–7.
117. Ibid., pp. 67–8. See also p. 161.
118. Ibid., p. 185.
119. Schmoller, 'Obrigkeitsstaat und Volksstaat: ein missverständlicher Gegensatz', p. 2034.
120. Max Weber, 'Parliament and government in Germany under a new political order' [1918], in Weber, *Political Writings*, p. 220.
121. Robert Piloty, 'Das parlamentarische System', *Archiv für Rechtsphilosophie* 11 (1917–18), p. 127.
122. Max Weber, 'Parliament and government in Germany', p. 231.
123. Ibid., p. 220.
124. Ibid., p. 222.
125. Robert Redslob, *Die parlamentarische Regierung in ihrer wahren und in ihrer unechten Form* (Tübingen: Mohr, 1918), p. 132. For the debate about Redslob, see Peter Stirk, 'Hugo Preuss, German political thought and the Weimar Constitution', *History of Political Thought* 23 (2002), pp. 497–516.
126. Llanque, *Demokratisches Denken im Krieg*, p. 235.
127. Max Weber, 'Suffrage and democracy in Germany' [1917], in Weber, *Political Writings*, p. 103.

2

Contested Democracies

The end of the First World War brought with it the collapse of the two German regimes and the disintegration of the Habsburg Empire. The monarchic principle that Franz Josef had proclaimed as the source of German greatness evaporated with remarkable speed. The point was not lost on Hugo Preuss: 'The suddenness with which the change took place, which set aside with a single blow 22 dynasties in a Germany considered as especially monarchist, is, however, so astonishing that one can understand the suspicious doubt about the permanence and fundamental character of the rapid transformation'.[1] Preuss went on to explain that the collapse of the dynastic order was less surprising than it seemed, for the grip of this order on Germany had already been hollowed out. Especially in retrospect, his comments readily seem to have a different, prophetic meaning; for, although the monarchy was finished as a form of government, both the Weimar Republic and the Austrian Republic were of short-lived duration, and this has often been traced to the incompleteness of the break with the past which took place in 1918. Even during the short life of these republics, the extent of the break with the past was one of the issues that divided German political theorists.

The new republics, especially the Weimar Republic, were contested democracies facing critics from the right and the left. Both constitutions were compromises. Both were the product of political conflict that threw the role of professional politicians and the concept of politics into sharp relief. That does not mean that the old pretence of adopting a standpoint above parties had disappeared. It was still necessary for Gustav Radbruch to complain of the hypocrisy even of those involved in party politics, for whom politics 'belongs to the things one does but does not willingly talk about'.[2] Attitudes to party political conflict and the republics were also still bound up with conceptions of the state. Across the political spectrum, critics denounced the Weimar Republic as a 'sham state', while on the right the concept of the state was invoked as an alternative to the Republic and, more specifically, as a distinctively German alternative to what was seen as an all-too-western Republic.[3]

That rebuke was rooted in the impact of the war and the Versailles Treaty, whose provisions induced resentment across the political spectrum. One of the provisions of the peace treaties that were seen as especially unjust was the prohibition of a union between Germany and an Austria now largely separated from the other nationalities of the old empire. The continued existence of two German states was but one of the challenges to the concept of national identity. Within those states, the growth of National Socialism with its virulent anti-semitism posed a threat to national unity. The legacy of persecution and Marxist antipathy to the state as an instrument of class domination also served as a barrier to political integration, despite the fact that the socialist parties had been a major force behind the creation of the democratic republics. Indeed, in the case of the Weimar Republic, the socialist Ernst Fraenkel could plausibly describe the SPD as the 'guardian of the constitution'.[4]

The history of the Weimar Republic has inevitably been coloured by its collapse and by the National Socialist era that followed. The failure to meet the challenge of National Socialism has been explained less as a case of the murder of the democratic republic than of its suicide. This judgement seems all too reasonable in the light of the less-than-enthusiastic confession by the historian Friedrich Meinecke that he was a monarchist by heart but a republican by reason.[5] Others have emphasised not so much the flaws within the republic and its sup- porters as the strength of the attack from outside, that is, from those implacably imposed to a republican and democratic parliamentary order. However one judges the ultimate failure to prevent the succes- sion of the Third Reich, to read the political thought of the period solely through the filter of what succeeded it is to deploy a perspective that was not available to political theorists of the time – not even to most of the critics of Weimar. Towards the end of the Republic, as parliamentary government gave way to rule by presidential decree, the prospects of the Republic were clearly bleak, though that fact and the uncertainty about the future were both evident in the title of an article by the socialist lawyer Otto Kirchheimer: 'Weimar . . . and what then?'[6]

The Weimar Republic and to a lesser extent its Austrian counterpart experienced a process of accelerated modernisation and increased state intervention. The aspirations of the socialists were partly res- ponsible for this, but deeper industrial, social and generational changes contributed to it. Periodic economic dislocation, including hyper-inflation in Germany in 1923, and then the world economic crisis at the beginning of the 1930s that hit both Germany and Austria especially hard, aggravated political discontent. Economic crisis was perceived as part of a wider crisis affecting all aspects of social and political life, as academic disciplines and intellectual traditions. 'Die säkulare Bedeutung der Weltkrise' ('The secular significance of the world crisis'), to use the title of an article by the economist Wilhelm Röpke, seemed almost limitless in its ramifications. Only astronomers, he suggested, could reflect upon a stable order.[7] Even the advantages of hindsight and distance from the tumult of events have not lessened this impression. As the historian Detlev Peukert has put it, 'Nowhere else in Europe had both traditional values and political and social reforming ideas been so called into question as they had been in post-war Germany, and nowhere else had public life been so politicised and polarised'.[8]

As already indicated, the position of the two states in the international order was a contributing factor to the sense of discontent. The Versailles Treaty with its ascription of responsibility for the First World War to Germany and its allies was almost universally bitterly resented. Anglo-Saxon hegemony, increasingly American rather than British, jostled alongside what as seen as French lust for revenge. Yet, despite the parlous international position of the two republics, there were attempts to promote international law, and even the most virulent critics of this agenda occasionally feared that it might prove attractive.

The concept of politics

The contested republics encouraged an emphasis upon the conflictual character of politics while the clash of values suggested a relativist approach, though this could take a prosaic form orientated towards democratic institutions or degenerate into the cultivation of myth. In Munich in 1919, amid the violence associated with the proclamation of a Soviet Republic of Bavaria, Max Weber addressed the theme of 'The profession and vocation of politics'. Politics, according to Weber, is 'striving for a share of power or for influence on the distribution of power . . .'[9] The inherent limits on this aspiration are evident in Weber's reference to a 'share of power'. The aspiration to a share of power is also limited by the existence of powerful bureaucracies, characteristic of modern political and economic life. It was precisely these constraints that led Weber to look to charismatic plebiscitary leaders, even though their character and status at the head of party machines 'means a "loss of soul" (*Entseelung*) for the followers, what one might call their spiritual proletarianisation'.[10]

Weber's main concern, however, was the character of the politician. He did not share the principled contempt for professional politicians expressed in Oswald Spengler's 'Preussentum und Sozialismus', also of 1919, whose recommendations for reform included 'no organised parties, no professional politicians, no periodic elections'.[11] Weber did set very high hurdles for those who pursue politics as a vocation. These hurdles were primarily internal. That is consistent with his interest in the 'inner justification' of power, its meaning for those who were in a position of power. The politician, according to Weber, is confronted with a series of ethical conflicts and with 'his responsibility for what may become of *himself* under pressure from them'.[12] This means balancing an ethic of conviction, embodied in the politician's commitment to a cause he has chosen, and an ethic of responsibility, which obliges the politician to attend to the consequences of his actions, in full knowledge that some of those consequences at least will be unknown to him at the time he acts.

Weber knew that most political leaders fail to fulfil the vocation of politics thus understood. The combination of 'passion, a sense of responsibility, judgement' that Weber required were too often absent. In their place, the 'mere "power politician"' parades his strength; but this, Weber assured his audience, is pretence: 'The sudden inner collapse of typical representatives of this outlook (*Gesinnung*) has shown us just how much inner weakness and ineffectuality are concealed behind this grandiose but empty pose'.[13] It is not difficult here to recognise the representatives of the monarchic principle and the German military leaders who sought to hide their responsibility for defeat behind the assertion that the German army was stabbed in the back by the collapse of the home front as these 'typical representatives'.

There is a considerable difference between Weber's emphasis upon the contingency of politics and the ethical paradoxes that threaten to destroy the integrity of the politician on the one hand, and the panegyric to the cult of leadership in the historian Hermann Oncken's 'Politik als Kunst' ('Politics as Art') on the other. Oncken emphasised the irrationality of the masses, only to endow the true political leader with an 'instinctual certainty' that allows him to manipulate them for his purposes. The gap between Oncken and Weber appears even greater, as Oncken proclaimed that the 'professional political machine', that is the machinery of party politics, damages the 'divine gift' which the politician supposedly enjoys.[14]

The irrationality of political life also fascinated and initially worried Carl Schmitt. He recognised what he saw as the power of political myths: 'In the power to [create] myth lies the criterion for whether a people or another social group has a historical mission and whether its historical moment has come'.[15] Schmitt identified the crucial component of myth in brief comments on the myth of the bourgeoisie. The bourgeois character had originally been a figure of fun, a caricature, developed by French authors. Even then, what mattered to Schmitt was the emotion that he found in 'the hate of socially déclassé geniuses, like Baudelaire . . .' It was this hated caricature of the bourgeois that Marx and Engels then enshrined in a 'world historical' framework: 'They gave it the significance of the final representative of a humanity divided into classes, of the final enemy of mankind in general, of the final *odium generis humani*'.[16] For Schmitt, the power of the myth of the nation is more powerful than the socialist myth of class. He also criticised the rhetoric of an enemy of humanity, which was too close to the anti-German Anglo-Saxon propaganda of the First World War. The enmity in his account of political myth, however, became the key to his definition of politics.

He opened his 'Der Begriff des Politischen' (The Concept of the Political) with the assertion that 'The concept of the state presupposes the concept of the political' and the claim that no definition of the state was required in order to understand the meaning of the political.[17] This is a direct inversion of the definition given earlier by Jellinek that gives priority to the concept of the state.[18] Schmitt's own definition of the political relied upon a simple distinction: 'The specific distinction to which political action and motives can be reduced is that between friend and enemy'.[19] He added that this is the 'most intense and extreme antagonism' and left no doubt that he was not deploying 'metaphors or symbols'. The enemy cannot, according to Schmitt, be interpreted as an economic 'competitor' or as a 'debating adversary'. The enemy is a 'public' enemy not a 'private' one.[20] This is politics defined from the perspective of international conflict, from the perspective of war, though the possibility of its extension to the domestic realm in the unstable conditions in Germany was not difficult to discern.

Schmitt incorporated this bellicist understanding of politics as a form of human activity into the grammar of politics. For Schmitt all political concepts, images and words have a *polemical* meaning. They are focused on a specific conflict and are bound to a concrete situation; the result (which manifests itself in war or revolution) is a friend–enemy grouping, and they turn into empty and ghostlike abstractions when this situation disappears.[21]

Schmitt emphasised that this applies to literally all concepts, from concepts like state and sovereignty through to the concept of reparations in the Versailles Treaty. All of these concepts, images and words can lose their meaning as the specific antagonisms that gave birth to them disappear. All that remains is the possibility of extreme antagonism that manifests itself in violence.

The socialist Hermann Heller agreed that the possibility of a resort to violence could not be excluded. For Heller, the conflict of interests is an abiding feature of politics. Not all such conflicts will lead to a resort to force. Men, he wrote, are unlikely to take up arms over a dispute about which side of the road to drive on, but they will do so over disputes about monarchical or republican government and about a socialist or capitalist order.[22] He contemptuously dismissed socialist longing for a future society free of conflict as the 'expression of an unheroic character' that is unable to face up to reality and takes flight in expectations of 'this worldly redemption'.[23] Yet conflict is neither the goal nor the meaning of politics. Schmitt's distinction, Heller argued, is not specifically political at all but quite indeterminate. Indeed, the existence and persistence of political communities, that is, of political order, has to appear as something 'highly unpolitical' if one accepts Schmitt's definition. Schmitt's argument, he continued, relies on deriving the word politics from 'polemos', whereas its true origin lies in the word 'polis'.[24] Politics cannot be separated from the normative meaning of communal life any more than it can be separated from the reality of the conflict of interests.[25]

Weber, Oncken, Schmitt and Heller all addressed the conflictual nature of politics, albeit from radically different perspectives, and accepted that politics in this sense is inescapable. The unpolitical stance or the longing for a world free of politics in this sense is sheer illusion. The rhetoric of the unpolitical stance was, however, still widespread. Conservatives like Spengler and Arthur Moeller van den Bruck were caught between the recognition of the disappearance of the old imperial order, with its supposed ability to embody a common good above the political fray, and contempt for the contingency and conflict of interests inherent in politics. The ambivalence was expressed in the desire that politics 'ought to become superfluous' but that the road to this goal was littered with 'political problems'.[26] Among legal theorists, according to Rudolf Laun, the old claim that they were engaged in an objective 'science' divorced from the contingency of the struggle for power was still professed as something self-evident. Laun himself did not share it. The theory of the state can least of all, he asserted, ignore the reality of power, and theorists of the state should have no fear of expressing their own political and subjective standpoints, so long as they do so openly and acknowledge the existence of opposing political standpoints.[27]

The relativism behind Laun's suggestion was given more sustained and forceful expression by Hans Kelsen. In his *Allgemeine Staatslehre*, Kelsen distinguished between a general theory of the state as a discipline from politics as a discipline. The former enquires about the nature and possible forms of the state. The latter enquires about whether the state should exist at all and, if it should, what the best form of state is. Politics as a science also deals with the appropriate means to bring about the desired form of state. Of these two aspects of politics, the ethical and the technical, it was the ethical dimension that was more important to Kelsen, for here value judgements come into play whose validity cannot be demonstrated.[28] This value relativism was a uniform assumption among the self-avowed positivists among whom Kelsen counted himself.[29] Yet Kelsen's basic assumption of value relativism is not as neutral as it might sound, as becomes clear at the end of his book. There, Kelsen aligned the relativist position with a specifically democratic form of politics. Only the relativist, who can accept the possibility that his judgement might err, can accept that his preference can be overridden by a majority vote. The alternative, he argued, is the belief in absolute truth that forms the basis of 'a metaphysical and specifically religious–mystical world view'.[30] Belief in absolute truth is also incompatible with the 'politics of compromise' that Kelsen held to be essential.[31] In the increasingly politicised and polarised Weimar Republic and the Austrian Republic whose constitution Kelsen had drafted, compromise was increasingly difficult to achieve, though a relativist stance is arguably the only one that offered any prospect for such deeply divided societies.[32] It was a stance that the opponents of the contested republics did not share, as Kelsen knew.

National and collective identity

Visions of national unity drove the opposition to the democratic order of the new republics, to the extent that any positive vision of the state was a secondary issue.[33] Obsession with national unity was compatible with quite diverse judgements about the recent past. According to one embittered critic of Weimar and Versailles: 'Today we are not a nation. We lost the war, we had to lose the war, because we were not a nation.'[34] Echoing the rhetoric of the war years, according to which only victory would demonstrate national unity and national identity, he drew the conclusion of disunity from the fact of military defeat. Others, no less hostile to the democratic order, took a strikingly different view. Ernst Jünger saw a 'new nationalism' freed from the shackles of the past, ironically by the experience of defeat and internal revolution:

> Please do not misunderstand me when I say that the modern nationalism owes this favourable configuration of its opportunities for action in a high degree to the collapse of 1918. This effect was, however, not in the least intended by the revolutionaries, in whose destructive work liberalism celebrated its filthiest, and hopefully its last, triumph ... A further advantage of the November revolution for nationalism is that the revolution cleared away obstacles that it could have set aside on its own only with the greatest difficulty. Think of the youth of 1813 whose greater German will shattered in the face of the dynasties.[35]

For Jünger, it was not the ideological ballast of the *Obrigkeitsstaat* that pointed the way forward.

Proponents of racist theories also exhibited a mixture of assertiveness and uncertainty. Alfred Rosenberg, who mistakenly believed that his *Der Mythus des 20. Jahrhunderts* (The Myth of the Twentieth Century) would be approved as the authorised ideology of the Third Reich, proclaimed:

> For us today the state is no longer an idol before which we have to lie in the dust; the state is not even a purpose, but is rather only a means of preserving the *Volk*. One means among others, such as the church, law, guild, science should also be. Forms of state change, and the laws of the state pass away; the *Volk* endures.[36]

Yet Rosenberg's 'myth' – myth in the sense of a belief in the power of race equal to the Christian conviction in the power of God – was haunted by visions of chaos. These images of racial miscegenation, of Bolshevik and Mongol threats, were so strong that Rosenberg called for a united Nordic front that would cut across the division between the victors and the defeated of the First World War.[37]

The prophet of the Nordic idea, Hans F. K. Günther, was averse to the prospects of war, if only because he believed that this Nordic race, being inherently courageous, would suffer disproportionate losses in the event of war.[38] Anti-semitism played a relatively minor role in Günther's racial theory, but he exercised considerable influence on the broader racial theory of Hitler. The overriding feature of Hitler's racism was his anti-semitism, and he was more confident of finding a solution to the threat he perceived in the very existence of Jews, namely their physical exclusion or extinction. His racial theory had other implications for his perception of German unity as well. He accepted Günther's distinction between the *Volk* and race (*Rasse*) and the idea that the German *Volk* was composed of different racial elements of varying value. Indeed, in his *Mein Kampf* he claimed that Germans exhibited less unity than other nations. Whereas others drew together in times of crisis following a herd instinct, Germans did not. Yet he drew a perverse comfort from this lack of instinctive unity. For, he continued, this lack of unity was derived from a lack of fusion of the different racial elements that meant that the valuable racial elements had been preserved in a more pristine state than in other nations. The implication is clear. German unity could be reconstructed around the best racial elements.[39]

Ideas of nationality were tied up with concerns about the legitimacy of the Weimar Republic, the supposed need for a certain level of social homogeneity for a viable democracy and the role of politics and the state as mechanisms of integration. In the work of Schmitt, the 'nationally homogeneous state' was presented as the basis of democracy and 'elimination or eradication of heterogeneity' as the policy which democracies adopt in its absence. That Schmitt had in mind national, rather the social, heterogeneity is clear from the two examples he presented in illustration of his claim: 'contemporary Turkey, with its radical expulsion of the Greeks and its reckless Turkish nationalization of the country, and the Australian commonwealth, which restricts unwanted entrants through its immigration laws . . .'[40]

The divisiveness of the racist doctrines was quite evident to Heller, according to whom the 'effect of this materialist nonsense . . . is suited in the highest degree to tear apart the unity of the German nation'.[41] Heller's concern for national unity set him in opposition to the theoretical stance of many fellow socialists. He, along with some of the young socialists who gathered at Hofgeismar, believed that the principled opposition to the concept of nationalism was a tactical mistake rooted in antipathy to the state and the right-wing monopolisation of the discourse of nationalism at the end of the nineteenth century.[42] Heller also raised wider theoretical objections to the opposition to nationalism. It is true, he argued, that the workers of all nations are subject to the same basic economic fate. They do not, however, 'experience it as a community, but differently, according to their national character'.[43] Marx and Engels had erred in constructing their concepts of man, society and even the goal of socialism in abstraction from the division of mankind into separate communities, that is, in the modern-era nations. Their concept of man was, he continued, taken from eighteenth-century natural law; it was in fact the '*homo oeconomicus* of liberalism'.[44] They postulated first an artificial concept of an economic society in abstraction from the plurality of human and then projected a political abstraction, in which the state has died away, of an undifferentiated humanity.[45] The bitterness that Heller's views induced was evident at the conference of young socialists in 1925, leaving Heller protesting: 'Because I have expressed myself positively about the question of the nation, I am supposed to be pretty much a traitor!'[46]

While Heller sought to reclaim the concept of the nation both for the left and for Weimar, Kelsen, with his roots in the multi-ethnic Habsburg Empire, took a radically different position. He noted that the unity of a people (*Volk*) is often taken as a basic precondition of a democratic order but that this unity was in reality highly problematic: 'Divided by national, religious and economic contradictions, it appears . . . rather as a bundle of groups than a coherent mass . . .'[47] Assertions of a community of feeling, of solidarity, are little more than political postulates in the service of national or state ideologies. Helmut Plessner went even further in *Grenzen der Gemeinschaft* (The Limits of Community), arguing that the 'sentimental sacrifice of a right to distance between men' was incompatible with human nature and ultimately futile.[48] Although arguing from different starting points, Plesssner from anthropology, Kelsen from legal theory, both converged in setting limits to the claim of the community and nation over the individual. For Kelsen, the unity of the *Volk* is no more than the unity brought about by the law. Kelsen pushed this basic point further – for the law, he wrote, regulates specific human actions. The unity of the *Volk*, therefore, is the unity only of that specific set of actions, not a unity of people. In Kelsen's words: 'Man as a whole, that is in all his functions, according to all the directions of his spiritual and corporeal life, never belongs to the social community, not even to that which grasps him most firmly, to the state'.[49] Again, Kelsen's recommendation was that men should live without myths, even the myth that Schmitt held to be the most powerful of all.

The concept of the state

The fact that Preuss welcomed the fall of the dynastic houses did not mean that he saw the threat from the tradition of the *Obrigkeitsstaat* as something that had definitively passed. The dynastic houses had played a prominent role in his account of this authoritarian state, but his concept of the *Obrigkeitsstaat* was not dependent upon them. Thus, he warned the new socialist government against installing an 'inverted *Obrigkeitsstaat*', that is, against substituting the authority of the proletariat for the authority of the princes.[50] He defined the *Obrigkeitstaat* more generally as the form of state where the legitimate monopoly of violence possessed by the state is in the hands of 'a dynasty, a class, a caste, an authority [*Obrigkeit*]'.[51] Similarly, Richard Thoma agreed that a hereditary monarchy is in no way necessary. The Catholic Church, with its elected head who in turn appoints the cardinals, provides another example, as do 'republican directorates' that co-opt members to fill vacancies.[52] Both effectively agreed that the essence of the *Obrigkeitsstaat* is the presence of self-recruiting elites. Gustav Radbruch had a different emphasis, though this can also be found in the work of Preuss and Thoma. According to Radbruch: 'That the government stood above parties was precisely the legend, the life-giving lie of the *Obrigkeitsstaat*'.[53] It was a lie because the supposed standpoint above parties was no more than 'crypto-party government' which hid its real nature from public gaze and sought to disparage other partisan viewpoints, from which it was itself no different.

Preuss was also confronted with the argument that the form of state enshrined in the Weimar constitution was alien to the German political tradition. The notion that it was western in provenance and bound up with the hated Versailles treaty to the point of signifying a capitulation before the victor's conception of the state was commonplace. Even at the time of the debate on the constitution, Preuss's draft constitution was under attack for being little more than a compilation of what was to found in other constitutions, to which he replied: 'The constitution is understandable only to him who understands the German nation in its distinctiveness'.[54] Alongside Preuss's assertion of the German provenance of the constitution, he defended the constitution by attacking its critics for being obsessed with the authoritarian traits of Bismarck's Germany. This was, he wrote, under the title 'Die "undeutsche" Reichsverfassung': 'the root of the delusion that wants to recognise only this military and authoritarian form of state as appropriate to the German and wants to reject as "un-Germanic" all those other streams whose living spirit is interwoven in German history'.[55]

Oswald Spengler's *Preussentum und Sozialismus* is a prime example of such a conception of the state. For Spengler, Prussia was the embodiment of the true form of state which operated like a machine overseen by civil servants who understood themselves as servants of the community as a whole.[56] He presented this in stark contrast to English conceptions: 'In England the island replaced the organised state . . . This animosity to the state found expression in the word *society* which repressed the *state* in its ideal sense.'[57] The problem, according to Spengler, was not that these English conceptions were inappropriate per se. It was that they were inappropriate for Germans. The 'private man', the prominence of commercial interests, parliamentary government and the role of political parties were all elements of English society. Germans, however, could only be caricatures of these Englishmen, though he held that some Germans had become precisely that. He designated those Germans who opposed his own conception of the state as 'the internal England' that had brought about the 'parliamentary revolution' in Germany 'which guaranteed the final victory of the external England of the entente powers through the collapse of the state'.[58] Yet, for all Spengler's invocation of the distinctiveness of the Prussian state, the contours of his own conception of the state are strikingly vague. This was typical in one sense of the anti-democratic rhetoric of the state; for its proponents, as Kurt Sontheimer has pointed out, were concerned less with the constitutional detail of the state than with the idea that it was the appropriate form of the state for Germans.[59] Indeed, in the case of Spengler, the distinctiveness of the state itself, despite its contrast with the concept of society, evaporates in a looser authoritarian atmosphere of 'command and obedience in a strictly organised community, whether it is called state, party, working class, officer corps or civil service . . .', which is then equated with the state.[60]

Kelsen noted the expansiveness and elusiveness of Spengler's approach at the beginning of his *Allgemeine Staatslehre*. For Kelsen, the concept of the state is a matter of the legal definition of the state. It is not to be identified with specific organs or agencies. The state is nothing more than an objectively valid complex of norms, that is, a complex of norms independent of the wishes or wills of those subject to that complex of norms. The state, in brief, is identical with the legal order specified in positive law. The supposition that 'the state as a power stands "behind" the law . . . "bears" it, "produces" it, "guarantees" it and so on' is nothing more than a needless duplication of law as a coercive order.[61] The state is not a natural entity, nor is it reducible to psychological or sociological processes. The widespread supposition, which Kelsen located in the sociology of his day, that the state is a form of especially intense interaction, cannot explain the mystery that intense interaction forms men into distinct and antagonistic classes, nations and religions while intense interaction is simultaneously supposed to bind men into a state in a way that transcends those antagonisms.[62]

At every opportunity, Kelsen sought to strip away the veils, anthropomorphic projections and theological residues that he discerned in contemporary and past theories of the state. Once this was done, all that remains is the complex of legal norms that regulates specified forms of human behaviour. The supposed irresistible power of the state, for example, is evidently false, for the thief is only punished if he is caught. Although he argued that the principle of the irresistible power of the state was theoretically meaningless, Kelsen recognised that it did serve a practical political purpose, namely the veneration of the power of the state, in the same way, he argued, that priests are more interested in venerating the power of God than understanding what God is.[63] Similarly, the supposition that the state has an emergency right in the interests of its self-preservation Kelsen dismissed on the grounds that 'Behind the candid assurance that the state must "live" usually lies only the ruthless will that the state must live in such a way as those who avail themselves of a "state emergency right" hold to be correct'.[64] Kelsen's criticism did not stop at the fictions of the democratic state, despite his commitment to democracy. He noted, for example, that, in part, the significance of the personification of the state was that it served to veil the fact of the rule of men over other men that is an affront to the democratic ideal of equality: 'I want to be ruled by the state and not by something of my kind, as if the state were not merely the mask for something of my kind'.[65]

Kelsen's identification of the state and the legal order met with considerable resistance both from those who wished to sweep away the contested republics and from those willing to defend them. Although Heller shared Kelsen's commitment to the democratic order, he vigorously disputed Kelsen's theory of the state. Against Kelsen's focus on the legal order and his definition of sovereignty as a complex of norms that recognised no higher norm above it, Heller insisted that the state had to be understood as a sociological reality and that the concept of sovereignty had to be ascribed to a specific subject. The state, according to Heller, is a territorially based decision-making unity. Sovereign acts require a real, individual decision. Sovereignty, however, is not to be ascribed to any organ of the state or to the imagined, personified state. Like Preuss, he traced the difficulties he discerned in German state theory back to the nineteenth century. It was the *'tergiversatio'* before the choice between the sovereignty of the monarch or the people that lay behind the 'inability of German state theory to identify an appropriate subject of sovereignty and the bloodlessness of its concept of the state . . .'[66]

In this respect, Heller argued, German theory of the state lagged behind American theory, for the latter had been able to locate the *'Sovereignty of the State'* in the nation and the people. By separating 'state' and 'government', American theorists had avoided slipping into the equation of the two concepts and had avoided, consequently, the error of locating sovereignty in the government.[67] Heller was well aware of the objection that the vast numbers of citizens in the modern state cannot be the source of sovereignty because their diversity is incompatible with the unity of will associated with the idea of sovereignty. Heller's response to this objection is quite simple: 'Unity of will through the majority principle and representation are the technical means through which the people as a unity dominates the people as a multitude, through which the people can become the sovereign subject'.[68] He added, however, that the idea of a general will is the precondition of both the majority principle and the concept of representation.

Carl Schmitt took even greater exception to Kelsen. Whereas Kelsen identified the state with law, Schmitt identified sovereignty with the decision about when the law does not apply. In the opening sentence of his *Political Theology*, he proclaimed: 'Sovereign is he who decides on the exception'.[69] Schmitt insisted that this decision extends to the suspension of the constitution in 'its entirety'. He glossed over the fact that in the Weimar constitution, under article 48, the president's emergency powers did not extend to the suspension of the constitution in its entirety, but he did note that these powers were subject to parliamentary control. For Schmitt, however, this amounted to an attempt 'to repress the question of sovereignty by a division and mutual control of competencies'.[70] Schmitt argued by setting up rigid antitheses and insisting on the need for a decision. He agreed with Heller that pre-Weimar Germany had been marked by an unresolved tension between monarchical and popular sovereignty. For Schmitt, this was a 'dilatory compromise', as were all compromises. He conceded that the eventual triumph of one of these principles could occur gradually, as it had in England, but this experience was, he insisted, irrelevant to continental Europe.[71]

In one sense, Schmitt conceded that a decision had been taken on the basis of the Weimar constitution: 'The German people has given itself this constitution'.[72] Yet he kept rediscovering dilatory compromises and the need for a radical decision about the state of the exception. Whereas Schmitt sought to locate sovereignty in a specific organ of state, Heller replied that any decision about a state of emergency ultimately belonged to the same subject that decided upon and maintained the normal constitutional order, that is, the multitude unified through representation and the majority principle.[73]

As the political position in the Weimar Republic deteriorated into rule by presidential decree, reluctantly tolerated by parliament, Schmitt set out a series of 'state forms' all of which existed in unresolved tension within the Republic. The 'legislative state', that is the 'parliamentary legislative state', rules through general and enduring norms. It is the rule of law in which command and domination have supposedly disappeared. In the 'jurisdictional state', judges decide, typically in concrete cases. In the 'governmental state', the *'sovereign personal will'* and *'authoritarian command'* of a head of state are predominant. In the 'administrative state', decrees orientated to the objective and practical resolution of problems 'according to the nature of the case' are decisive.[74] Schmitt effectively dissolved the state into a series of competing state forms, but with the persistent intent of discrediting the parliamentary legislative state. Although Schmitt typically claimed that the decision between these competing state forms had yet to be made, he suggested that an administrative state, as manifest in the practice of rule by decree, was more appropriate to the dictator, by which he meant the president issuing the decrees, than a 'parliament separated from the executive'.[75] Schmitt had effectively returned to the fusion of power that he had discerned in administrative rule during the First World War.[76]

Even before the turn to rule by presidential decree, Rudolf Smend had complained about the limits of parliamentary government and the principles of contracts, voting and majority rule in integrating citizens into the state. These forms of functional integration, as Smend called them do contribute to this task but are not sufficient in themselves. The dissolution of the state into a series of formal relationships that he discerned in Weber and Kelsen led, he claimed, to alternating alienation from the state and 'unpolitical worship of power'.[77] If the state is to fulfil its task of integrating citizens into the political community, a common system of values has to be espoused and made manifest in the symbols and ceremonies of the state. For Smend, this task, the distinctively political task of the state, took priority over the constitution itself, though the basic rights enshrined in constitutional law were also the expression of the common values that were to hold the state together.[78] Smend's plea for integration seemed, however, increasingly implausible in a polarised and politicised Germany.

The bourgeois Rechtsstaat *and the social* Rechtsstaat

One possibility was that the *Rechtsstaat*, law and the judiciary might help to promote integration where other concepts and institutions faltered. Yet, as Gustav Radbruch argued, positive statutory law in modern Germany lacked the pathos of unity. The very language of law had sloughed off the discursive and persuasive style of earlier law. Whoever looks for poetry in German law will, he continued, have to go far back into the past. Similarly, modern law lacks the 'style of conviction', that is, it no longer seeks to bring out the purpose of the law and the reasoning behind it. Nor does it have an 'educative style'. It seeks to influence behaviour by the power of command rather than by educating the citizen. Its style is 'rigorously ascetic'.[79] Precision not persuasion is its goal.

This emphasis upon cold, ascetic positive law does not mean that Radbruch was insensitive to the wider cultural and political significance of law. To the contrary, he placed great emphasis upon it. He stated that freedom from the state defines the *Rechtsstaat* in contrast to the *Polizeistaat* that intervenes in the affairs of citizens at its discretion. The freedom involved in participation in the state defines the *Volksstaat* in contrast to the *Obrigkeisstaat*.[80] This restriction of the *Rechtsstaat* to the preservation of negative liberty was questioned by Radbruch when he surveyed German legal culture more broadly. He argued that, even where freedom from the state was relatively secure, so long as the *Obrigkeitsstaat* lived on, that is, so long as participation in the state was curtailed, the *Polizeistaat* and the associated spirit of submissiveness also lived on. It was not that he saw his contemporaries as averse to a resort to law. It was, rather, that their sense of justice was exhausted in civil legal proceedings, often accompanied by an exaggerated emphasis upon the honour of the litigants. What was missing was the sense of being a member of a law-governed community, of being part of an association rather than simply being an individual confronted with a set of comprehensive laws.[81]

Radbruch here called into question the widespread distinction between the passive freedom of the private man, of the bourgeois, as protected by the *Rechtsstaat*, and the active freedom of the citizen, as expressed in the people's state or the democratic state. So too did Ferdinand Tönnies. He drew the same distinction as Radbruch but then noted that there is a 'quasi-political' activity that they seem to share, namely the freedom of association, the freedom to assemble and form associations for whatever purpose. Here, 'bourgeois' freedom passes over into political freedom.[82] Smend took up the same distinction to make a wider point. According to Smend, the whole idea of the 'bourgeois *Rechtsstaat*' in which the unpolitical bourgeois rested content with his freedom from the state was inconsistent with the reality of constitutional development. This concept is, he wrote, 'a polemical concept intended to serve as a foil for an opposed conceptual world, whether this be democracy, authoritarian or dictatorial forms of state, or finally the much-invoked "total" state'.[83] In reality, even the security of private property had also been a 'piece of political emancipation'.[84]

In his *Verfassungslehre* (Constitutional Theory) of 1928, Schmitt also construed the *Rechtsstaat* as a polemical concept. The first polemical contrast, wrote Schmitt, lies in the idea that 'the freedom of the individual is *in principle unlimited* while the power of the state to intervene in this sphere is *limited in principle*'.[85] More specifically, such intervention by the state as does take place is valid 'only *on the basis of a law* . . .' The entire activity of the state is determined by a network of carefully circumscribed competencies. The independence of the judiciary is an 'organisational' characteristic of this state. Finally, the full ideal of this form of state presumes that all activity of the state, including disputes between any of its organs, is subject to adjudication.[86] Schmitt's antipathy to this ideal is evident in his conclusion that 'The state is not only a judicial organisation; it is also something different from a mere neutral arbitrator or mediator. It essence lies in the fact that it takes *political decisions*.'[87]

Four years later, Schmitt declined to use the word *Rechtsstaat*, claiming that it was susceptible to so many different interpretations that it meant little at all. Propagandists of all kinds deployed it in order to 'defame [their] opponent as the enemy of the *Rechtsstaat*'.[88] Although Schmitt professed to avoid the word, the characteristics he had associated with it still very much concerned him, and his criticism of those characteristics, typically as reliant upon no longer tenable distinctions, amount to an attack on the concept even in the absence of the word. One focus of his criticism was the concept of statute law. Schmitt had long been concerned with the indeterminacy of law, which he had exploited to emphasise the inescapable element of decision in legal judgements, though this was accepted by positivists like Kelsen and Radbruch without great anxiety. Radbruch even invoked the English common-law system as an example of how such indeterminacy could be moderated, along with broader references to how the collegial nature of adjudication and systems of appeal can generate greater consistency.[89] Amid the resort to rule by presidential decree, Schmitt argued that his contemporaries had lost the ability to distinguish effectively between statute law, supposedly characterised by its generality and enduring nature, and decrees, supposedly char- acterised by their temporary nature and focus on specific situations. In effect, he claimed that the *Rechtsstaat* evaporated with the dis- tinctiveness of the law that defined it.[90]

In 'Die Wendung zum totalen Staat' ('The turn to the total state'), Schmitt began with what he again identified as a polemical concept, namely society, which had been developed in opposition to the monarchical, military and bureaucratic state of the nineteenth century. This state, he said, echoing his argument in his *Verfassungslehre*, had left society to its own devices in wide fields, including economic activity and freedom of conscience. It practised neutrality and non- intervention. But this was no longer the case: 'now the state is becoming the "self-organisation of society"'.[91] By this, he meant that the state had extended its remit in response to social pressure, especially the demands of the socialists for welfare provisions, and in response to interest groups of diverse kinds. The outcome, in Schmitt's eyes, was the emergence of an 'economic state', a 'welfare state' and a 'culture state'. There was no longer any sphere of society in which neutrality and non-intervention by the state was regarded as a matter of principle.[92] For Schmitt, this amounted to a transition to the 'total state'. He noted that critics of this trend had turned to the courts in order to find a counterweight to the legislative activity that had expanded the state's remit, but this was a mistake, for the courts could invoke only statute law or 'indeterminate and disputed principles' against the legislator. More assistance might be expected, he suggested, from the government.[93]

The resort to the courts to which Schmitt referred was bound up with a methodological dispute about the status of positive statutory law. Although the positivist approach to law and the state had been under attack well before the war, the methodological dispute took on sharper form in the more highly politicised and polarised post-war world. The dispute had several dimensions, but the key issues were whether or not law was constitutional and statute law alone or whether it also included a higher law, and whether or not political and sociological factors played a legitimate part in the deliberations of theorists and judges. Summarising one of the debates in 1926, Günther Holstein set out the position of the critics of positivism with respect to Article 109 of the Weimar Constitution, which specified the equality of Germans before the law. The critics claimed that this principle of equality is 'a *legal principle of supra-positive significance*' and that it 'is valid precisely *for the legislator*, who should create written law and, as the creator of statutes, may not infringe this legal principle . . .'[94] Supra-positive law gave judges a criterion on the basis of which they could claim to restrict the legislative activity of parliament. For the relatively conservative judicial establishment, this meant, in practice, defending the traditional social and economic order in the name of this higher law.[95]

There was, however, no strict correspondence between positions in the methodological dispute about statute law and natural law and attitudes to the democratic republics in general or to their legislative activity. Nor did the self-professed positivists necessarily accept the beliefs that their critics ascribed to them. Thus Thoma, who emphasised the supremacy of parliament, distinguished his understanding of positivism from the 'one-sided logicism' of Laband that failed to incorporate 'the sociological interest in the dynamics of constitutional law and the political interest in the evolution of constitutional law'.[96] On the other hand, the socialist Heller attacked what he saw as the dominant positivism, including the presumption that law had to take a purely general form, in order to promote the transformation of the 'pure *Rechtsstaat* into the democratic-social welfare state'.[97]

As Weimar approached its end, both democracy and welfare state were under attack. So too was the *Rechtsstaat*. From the perspective of 1931, Ernst Fraenkel identified a crisis of the *Rechtsstaat*. The increasing resort to rule by decree seemed to have benefited the judiciary insofar as the decline in parliamentary legislative activity reduced the tension between law and judicial interpretation with its disputed resort to natural law. Fraenkel, however, identified a crisis of justice alongside the crisis of the legislature. The crisis for the judiciary arose, he claimed, from the fact that 'The independence of the judiciary from the commands of the administrative authorities has its correlate in dependence on the law'.[98] Like Schmitt, Fraenkel pointed to the increasing difficulty in distinguishing between what was law and what was decree as part of the problem. It was aggravated by the tendency in the judiciary to agree with Schmitt's invocation of the principle of Thomas Hobbes that authority, not truth, determines the law. In the light of the threat to the dependence of the judiciary on law, and hence to its independence from the administration, Fraenkel urged the importance of a second correlate of judicial independence, namely freedom of the press and the maintenance of a public sphere. The corruption of the public spirit and public sphere would be, as Heller warned in 1929, the inevitable consequence of any dictatorship in western Europe.[99] The choice, said Heller, lay between fascist dictatorship and the social *Rechtsstaat*.[100] The contrast would be recalled when Germany began to reconstruct a democratic order.

Parliamentary democracy

The role of political parties and the viability of parliamentary democracy were the most contested issues in the new republics. The possibility of a socialist dictatorship, of rule through the workers'councils that had sprung up amid the collapse of the old regime, conjured up Preuss's fear of an 'inverted *Obrigkeitsstaat*'. By the time the Marxist Georg Lukács wrote about 'The question of parliamentarianism' in 1920, the Weimar Republic was established on the basis of parliamentary rule, not rule by the workers' councils. For Lukács, parliamentarianism was in principle a threat to the revolutionary cause. It is, he argued, at best a defensive weapon for the proletariat, though the very possibility of criticism within parliament confuses the proletariat insofar as such criticism tends to become a substitute for action, that is, the seizure of power. The risk is especially great, he continued, when an immature proletariat achieves an electoral great victory. Nor were his objections purely tactical. One of the problems of parliamentarianism is, he said, the 'inordinate degree of independence, even licence' of parliamentary deputies.[101] From this, he concluded that the best hope lay in the workers' councils, for 'the council is compelled to act – otherwise it ceases to exist'.[102]

This principled incompatibility between the proletarian cause and parliamentary democracy was denied by the socialist Carl Landauer.

According to Landauer, the framework for parliamentary democracy is provided on the one hand by the existence of common interests stretching across classes. On the other hand, it is provided by the fact that conflicts of interest, if only between demands for absolute equality and demands for preferential treatment of skilled workers, would persist even in a socialist society.[103] To these general conditions, he added that political parties are characterised by the fact that they profess ideas which they claim to be appropriate for all sections of society. He extended this into his view of class conflict when he argued that a party animated by the sentiment of class conflict 'means only that one expects the implementation of the social ideal of liberation not from the altruism of the oppressor but rather from the egoism of the oppressed'.[104]

In emphasising that parties should espouse social ideals that they hold to be valid for all members of society, Landauer was responding to the idea that parliaments composed of political parties based on the free recruitment of their members and elected on a territorially defined basis should be replaced by corporatist bodies representing economically defined estates. Towards the end of the Weimar Republic, Ferdinand A. Hermens complained of a veritable army of prophets of the corporatist state.[105] Among the leaders of this army were the Austrian Othmar Spann and Edgar J. Jung. Although Spann dismissed democracy in favour of the corporatist state, and Jung proclaimed a 'genuine democracy', the substance of their ideas was very similar, namely the rejection of parliamentary party democracy and its replacement by a combination of 'organically' formed bodies emerging from below combined with some higher spiritual and political leadership from above that was supposed to guide and unify the political process. With explicit reference to fascist Italy as a model, Jung proclaimed that there, ' "parliament" arises indeed not only in a mosaic fashion from below to the top, but also through the influence from above'.[106]

Hans Kelsen's response to such ideas was to point out the inherent implausibility of any organisation of the population of a modern state on occupational grounds. The complexity and dynamics of modern societies would require hundreds, if not thousands, of ever-shifting occupational groups. The corporatist model cannot, he argued, deal with the fact that economic interests are not the only issues that divide people. The fact that one person is a farmer and another is a lawyer provides no guarantee of their views on the regulation of marriage law or the relationship between the church and the state. The outcome, he continued, could only be authoritarian imposition from above.[107] Hermens made the same point in the light of the reality of the corporatist state in Italy.[108]

As late as 1931, Hermens mistakenly believed that because 'all the positive preconditions of democracy exist in Germany a fascist dictatorship could have at most a today, but no tomorrow'.[109] Hermens was not unaware of the difficulties facing the democratic order in the Weimar Republic, among which he counted the proportional electoral system. The following year, Thoma expressed a similar confidence: 'After overcoming the [present] dangers, the parliamentary system will again function tolerably well, and better than tolerably has a form of state never functioned in the entire history of the world'.[110] Thoma's confidence came from the conviction that party competition and rule by the leaders of political parties were simply inescapable in a modern democracy. Parties, however, he continued, invoking Max Weber's definition, have to be understood as voluntary groups, formed on the basis of individual initiative for the purposes of political competition. They are not, as they had been in part in the *Obrigkeitsstaat*, communities of sentiment or confession.[111] Gustav Radbruch entered similar concerns about the nature of German political parties. He claimed that these were characterised by a combination of rigid organisational structures and binding programmes more akin to the beliefs of religious confessions. Parliamentary politics, he added, cannot be conducted as if parties are engaged in a religious war.[112] Thoma and Radbruch did not hesitate to point out the vices of the German party system, but they did so in the hope that they could contribute to the better functioning of the parliamentary party system.

That cannot be said of Schmitt. His identification of the vices of German parliamentary democracy was intended as an identification of the vices of parliamentary democracy in principle. Schmitt claimed that the intellectual principle that had justified parliamentary democracy was the belief that parliamentary discussion led to a consensus about the truth. He insisted that this belief was central to the liberal world-view, in which he rooted parliamentarianism. Whether in politics, economics or law, it is exactly the same: 'That the truth can be found through an unrestrained clash of opinion and that competition will produce harmony'.[113] Schmitt could then appeal to what he knew to be commonplace assumptions about the futility of parliamentary debate and the power of committees hidden from the public gaze in order to conclude 'that parliamentarianism thus abandons its intellectual foundation . . .'[114]

While seeking to discredit the principle of parliamentarianism, Schmitt claimed to defend true democracy. He defined the latter by reference to Rousseau's assumption of a general will with which the law and dissenting individuals are supposed to conform. Schmitt proclaimed that this democracy rests on a 'series of identities', including the 'identity of governed and governing'.[115] That in turn was said to be dependent upon the homogeneity of the people. Given such homogeneity, the democratic identity of governed and governing can be confirmed, he claimed, by an act of acclamation.[116]

Schmitt's argument relies upon the plausibility of its assumptions; and, while these appealed to many political theorists, critics had little difficulty identifying their questionable nature. Tönnies, though accepting Schmitt's distinction between liberalism and democracy, argued that neither liberal theorists nor statesmen would want to make the constitutional validity of a law dependent on the idea that it expressed the 'truth'.[117] Kelsen attacked Schmitt's more basic assumption that democracy entails the unity of governed and governing in which the governing represent the general will of the people. For Kelsen, Schmitt's identities are based in a series of fictions. The idea that parliament is supposed to represent the will of the people, that thereby the sovereignty of the people is manifest, that there is such a thing as the will of the community are all fictions which served to advance the cause of democracy in the struggle against monarchic and aristocratic power but which can also be turned against parliamentary democracy. Where Schmitt invoked the pathos of sovereignty, unity and the general will, Kelsen insisted upon the prosaic reality of the diversity of individual human will, the majority principle that assured that the least possible number of such wills is overridden and the division of labour embodied in a representative parliament.[118]

Versailles and international law

Attitudes towards international law and the international order were strongly coloured by the war and ensuing peace treaties, especially the Treaty of Versailles. Supporters of the new republics and their critics, fervent nationalists and critics of the ideology of community, joined in condemnation of the victors' view and conduct of the war and the peace they imposed. Helmuth Plessner, the critic of the ideology of community, for example, condemned the admission in 1914 by the German Chancellor that the invasion of Belgium was a violation of international law as a sin against Germany, as indulging in the 'luxury of the harmony of conscience of a rentier . . .'[119] The nationalist historian Max Lenz showed even less restraint, declaring that whoever joined the League of Nations committed themselves to the 'pitiless' subjection of Germans 'in the name of humanity, of world peace and cosmopolitan justice'.[120]

Plessner's assumption that statesmen are obliged to subordinate their personal convictions and interests to the higher interest of the state is also the theme of Friedrich Meinecke's *The Doctrine of Raison d'État and its Place in Modern History*. This *raison d'état* is peculiar to each state, and each state has an ethical value. The ethical quality of the state facilitates the statesman's subordination of his own conscience and interests to the dictates of *raison d'état*. Yet Meinecke also argued that this power politics had acquired a new and dangerous quality with the greater resources available to modern states. Moreover, Meinecke had come to question what he described as 'the false deification of the State, which has continued in German thought since the time of Hegel . . .'[121] Meinecke was unable to resolve the tension he saw between the dictates of power and the dictates of ethics, and the idea that both could be fused in the higher dictates of the state had been badly shaken. Yet, whereas Lenz saw ideas of international law as a mere sham behind which lay the interests of rapacious victorious states, Meinecke accepted that interests lie behind law and the rhetoric of peace but also these ideas have a certain autonomy or life of their own.[122]

Meinecke's observations, like those of many others, are clearly marked by the vicissitudes of war and the subsequent peace – though, as his reference to what he saw as a misguided German tradition shows, broader considerations were also at work. That is also true of attempts to revive pre-war assumptions that trade, international administrative cooperation and the network of often technical agreements provide the basis for an expansion of international law. Fritz Stier-Somlo incorporated this into a general assumption about the sociological basis of law. Arguing from the experience of German history, he claimed that law and political institutions eventually had to adapt to underlying trends. He invoked the failure of legal persecution of German Catholics and socialists as evidence of the power of social trends to which the law has to adapt. In principle, the same applies to the international order, but Stier-Somlo was cautious about the pace of such developments not only because of the exigencies of the postwar world but also because of his general claim that this sociological basis of law is more difficult to form at the international level.[123]

There was also continuity in the shape of the insistence upon the state as the sole source and subject of international law and the insistence on the idea of a right of self-preservation, by virtue of which the state could revoke any agreements it had entered into. This did not amount to a denial of international law per se, but it did make the validity of international law relative to the interests of the state. That was clearly the intent of the conservative Erich Kaufmann, but the strength of the supposition that the creator of international law could also revoke that law was also evident in Thoma's mobilisation of it against Jellinek's doctrine of auto-limitation of the state. Thoma also showed some interest in the ideas of Kelsen and Alfred Verdross, who represented a minority view that radically challenged pre-war conceptions.[124] Kelsen's approach combined the same emphasis upon the legal nature of the state and criticism of all anthropomorphic projection and naturalistic analogies that he deployed in his interpretation of the state at the domestic level. For Kelsen, the existence of a multiplicity of states regulated by international law cannot ultimately be explained without the presumption that international law has some objective validity independent of the will of the various states. The basic principle of the equality of states presumes the existence of a norm that prescribes this equality. Furthermore, these states are themselves legal orders, not natural entities as persons. Kelsen dismissed the presumption of an international right to self-preservation as a residue of natural law which was just as implausible as the supposition that the law of the individual state intended 'under all circumstances to preserve the life of all the men subject to it'. Indeed, it is even more implausible, for international law recognises the right of states to defend their interests by resort to war.[125]

The radical insistence that the only real substance at the root of law is individual people, or rather the behaviours of individual people, led Alfred Verdross to consider the suggestion that the very concept of the state can be dispensed with. Verdross agreed that all the 'mystique' and 'heroic pathos' associated with the concept of the state has to be swept away, but the concept of the state does identify a stark reality of international law which he illustrated through the case of state liability. The liability of the state means 'that in the case of the non-fulfilment of obligations the reaction is applied not immediately against specific individuals but against the totality of the men dwelling on a specific territory, namely the state territory, and their possessions . . . The "state" functions in international law as a unity of liability.'[126]

The commitment of Kelsen and Verdross to international law and their sustained attack on any attempt to endow the state with any kind of naturalistic substance does not entail pacifism or blindness to the harshness of the international order. It was intended to sweep away the principled objections to international law as such and to promote the development of international law. For Schmitt, international law as he saw it developing in the post-war world posed a major threat. Like Lenz, he railed against the subjection of his country to treaties in the name of humanity and world peace, behind which he saw the imperialist ambitions of the Anglo-Saxon powers, especially America. Schmitt's antipathy to the language of humanity and world peace was rooted in his definition of politics:

> For as long as a people exists in the political sphere, this people must . . . determine for itself the distinction of friend and enemy . . . When it no longer possesses the capacity or will to make this distinction, it ceases to exist politically.[127]

Schmitt worried that Germany would lose this capacity if Germans accepted American ambitions to distinguish between just and unjust wars and, more broadly, to shape international law according to their interests. He claimed that this is 'perhaps even more dangerous than military repression and economic exploitation. A people is first defeated when it subjects itself to a foreign vocabulary, to a foreign conception of what law, and especially international, is.'[128] At that point, however, Schmitt did not identify a distinctive German conception of international law.

The political thought of the contested republics reflected their politicised and polarised character. The polemical construction of traditions of political thought, whether western or German, had become more bitter. Precisely the intensity of the disputes reflected the fact that the outcome was uncertain. Yet few were really prepared for the reality of the answer to Kirchheimer's question: 'Weimar – and what then?'

Notes

1. Hugo Preuss, 'Republik oder Monarchie? Deutschland oder Preussen?' [1922], in Hugo Preuss, *Staat, Recht Freiheit* (Tübingen: Mohr, 1926), p. 448.
2. Quoted in Christian Jansen, *Professoren und Politik* (Göttingen: Vandenhoeck and Ruprecht, 1992), p. 219.
3. Ibid., pp. 221, 226.

4. Ernst Fraenkel, 'Die Krise des Rechtsstaates und die Justiz' [1931], in Ernst Fraenkel, *Gesammelte Schriften*, vol. 1 (Baden-Baden: Nomos, 1999), p. 454.
5. Friedrich Meinecke, 'Verfassung und Verwaltung der deutschen Republik' [1919], in Friedrich Meinecke, *Politische Schriften und Reden* (Darmstadt: Toeche-Mittler, 1979), p. 281.
6. Otto Kirchheimer, 'Weimar – and what then?' [1930], in Otto Kirchheimer, *Politics, Law and Social Change* (New York: Columbia University Press, 1969), pp. 33–74.
7. Wilhelm Röpke, 'Die säkulare Bedeutung der Weltkrise', *Weltwirtschaftliches Archiv* 37 (1933), p. 1.
8. Detlev Peukert, *The Weimar Republic: The Crisis of Classical Modernity* (Harmondsworth: Penguin, 1993), pp. 266–7.
9. Max Weber, 'The profession and vocation of politics' [1919], in Max Weber, *Political Writings* (Cambridge: Cambridge University Press, 1994), p. 311.
10. Ibid., pp. 350–1 (translation modified).
11. Oswald Spengler, 'Preussentum und Sozialismus' [1919], in Oswald Spengler, *Politische Schriften* (Munich: Beck, 1933), p. 64.
12. Weber, 'The profession and vocation of politics', p. 365.
13. Ibid., p. 354.
14. Hermann Oncken, 'Politik als Kunst', in Gerhard Anschütz et al. (eds), *Handbuch der Politik*, vol. 1 (Berlin: Walther Rothschild, 1920) pp. 8–14.
15. Carl Schmitt, 'Die politische Theorie des Mythus' [1923], in Carl Schmitt, *Positionen und Begriffe im Kampf mit Weimar–Genf–Versailles 1923–1939* (Hamburg: Hanseatische Verlagsanstalt, 1940), p. 11.
16. Ibid., p. 16.
17. Carl Schmitt, 'Der Begriff des Politischen', *Archiv für Sozialwissenschaft und Sozialpolitik* 58 (1927), p. 1. See also Carl Schmitt, *The Concept of the Political* [1932] (Chicago: University of Chicago Press, 1996), p. 19.
18. As pointed out by Christoph Möllers, *Staat als Argument* (Munich: Beck, 2000), p. 61.
19. Schmitt, *The Concept of the Political*, p. 26.
20. Ibid., pp. 27–9.
21. Ibid., p. 30.
22. Hermann Heller, 'Der Sinn der Politik' [1924], in Hermann Heller, *Gesammelte Schriften*, vol. 1 (Tübingen: Mohr, 1992), pp. 433–4.
23. Hermann Heller, 'Sozialismus und Nation' [1931], in Heller, *Gesammelte Schriften*, vol. 1, p. 496.
24. Hermann Heller, 'Demokratie und soziale Homogenität' [1928], in Heller, *Gesammelte Schriften*, vol. 2 (Tübingen: Mohr, 1992), p. 425.
25. See also Marcus Lanque, 'Politik und republikanisches Denken: Hermann Heller', in Hans J. Lietzmann (ed.), *Moderne Politik* (Opladen: Leske & Budrich, 2001), pp. 37–61.

26. Thus Hermann Graf Keyserling quoted in Raimund von dem Bussche, *Konservatismus in der Weimarer Republik* (Heidelberg: Winter, 1998), p. 39.
27. Rudolf Laun, 'Der Staatsrechtslehrer und die Politik', *Archiv des öffentlichen Rechts* 43 (1922), pp. 148–75. See also Robert Piloty, 'Politik als Wissenschaft', in Anschütz et al. (eds), *Handbuch der Politik*, vol. 1, p. 5.
28. Hans Kelsen, *Allgemeine Staatslehre* (Berlin: Springer, 1925), p. 27.
29. See, for example, Gustav Radbruch, 'Einführung in die Rechtswissenschaft' [1929], in Gustav Radbruch, *Gesamtausgabe*, vol. 1 (Heidelberg: Müller, 1987), p. 229.
30. Kelsen, *Allgemeine Staatslehre*, p. 369. See also Kelsen, *Vom Wesen und Wert der Demokratie* [1929] (Aalen: Scientia, 1981), p. 100.
31. Kelsen, *Allgemeine Staatslehre*, p. 370.
32. This point is made by Werner Heun, 'Der staatsrechtliche Positivismus in der Weimarer Republik', *Der Staat* 28 (1989), pp. 399–400.
33. Kurt Sontheimer, *Antidemokratisches Denken in der Weimarer Republik* (Munich: DTV, 1994), p. 30.
34. Quoted in ibid., p. 253.
35. Ernst Jünger, 'Der neue Nationalismus' [1927], in Ernst Jünger, *Politische Publizistik* (Stuttgart: Klett-Cotta, 2001), pp. 285–9.
36. Alfred Rosenberg, *Der Mythus des 20. Jahrhunderts* [1930] (Munich: Hohenheichen, 1934), p. 526.
37. Ibid., pp. 113–14.
38. Hans-Jürgen Lutzhöft, *Der nordische Gedanke in Deutschland 1920–1940* (Stuttgart: Klett-Cotta, 1971), p. 261.
39. Adolf Hitler, *Mein Kampf* [1925–6] (London: Radius, 1969), pp. 360–1.
40. Carl Schmitt, *The Crisis of Parliamentary Democracy* [1926] (Cambridge, MA: MIT, 1988), p. 9.
41. Heller, 'Sozialismus und Nation', p. 454.
42. See Heller's comments in 1925 as recorded in Franz Osterroth, 'Der Hofgeismarkreis der Jungsozialisten', *Archiv für Sozialgeschichte* 4 (1964), p. 550.
43. Heller, 'Sozialismus und Nation', p. 472.
44. Ibid., p. 480.
45. Ibid., pp. 491–2.
46. Heller, 'Staat, Nation und Sozialdemokratie' [1925], in Heller, *Gesammelte Schriften*, vol. 1, p. 561.
47. Kelsen, *Vom Wesen und Wert der Demokratie*, p. 15.
48. Helmuth Plessner, *Grenzen der Gemeinschaft* [1924] (Frankfurt am Main: Suhrkamp, 2002), pp. 28–9.
49. Kelsen, *Vom Wesen und Wert der Demokratie*, pp. 15–16.
50. Hugo Preuss, 'Volksstaat oder verkehrter Obrigkeitsstaat?' [1918], in Preuss, *Staat, Recht, Freiheit*, pp. 365–8.

51. Hugo Preuss, 'Die Bedeutung der demokratischen Republik für den sozialen Gedanken' [1925], in Preuss, *Staat, Recht, Freiheit*, p. 489.

52. Richard Thoma, 'Staat', in L. Elster et al. (eds), *Handwörterbuch der Staatswissenschaften*, vol. 7 (Jena: Fischer, 1926), p. 732.

53. Gustav Radbruch, 'Die politischen Parteien im System des deutschen Verfassungsrechts', in Gerhard Anschütz and Richard Thoma (eds), *Handbuch des deutschen Staatsrechts*, vol. 1 (Tübingen: Mohr, 1930), p. 289.

54. Quoted in Josef Isensee, 'Staat und Verfassung', in Josef Isensee and Paul Kirchhof (eds), *Handbuch des Staatsrechts der Bundesrepublik Deutschland*, vol. 2 (Heidelberg: Müller, 2004), p. 73.

55. Hugo Preuss, 'Die "undeutsche" Reichsverfassung' [1924], in Preuss, *Staat, Recht, Freiheit*, p. 479.

56. Spengler, 'Preussentum und Sozialismus', p. 63.

57. Ibid., p. 33.

58. Ibid., p. 69.

59. Sontheimer, *Antidemokratisches Denken*, pp. 168, 197.

60. Spengler, 'Preussentum und Sozialismus', pp. 47–8.

61. Kelsen, *Allgemeine Staatslehre*, p. 17.

62. Hans Kelsen, 'Der Begriff des Staates und die Sozialpsychologie', *Imago* 8 (1922), pp. 97–102.

63. Kelsen, *Allgemeine Staatslehre*, pp. 100–1.

64. Ibid., p. 157.

65. Ibid., p. 67.

66. Hermann Heller, 'Souveränität' [1927], in Heller, *Gesammelte Schriften*, vol. 2, p. 92.

67. Ibid., pp. 94–5.

68. Ibid., p. 97. For an example of the objection, see above, Chapter 1.

69. Carl Schmitt, *Political Theology* [1922] (Cambridge, MA: MIT, 1985), p. 5.

70. Ibid., p. 11.

71. Carl Schmitt, *Verfassungslehre* [1928] (Berlin: Duncker & Humblot, 1993), p. 54.

72. Ibid., p. 60.

73. Heller, 'Souveränität', pp. 127–8.

74. Carl Schmitt, *Legalität und Legitimität* [1932] (Berlin: Duncker & Humblot, 1998), pp. 7–9.

75. Ibid., pp. 80–1.

76. See above, Chapter 1.

77. Rudolf Smend, 'Verfassung und Verfassungsrecht' [1928], in Rudolf Smend, *Staatsrechtliche Abhandlungen* (Berlin: Duncker & Humblot, 1994), p. 123.

78. Ibid., p. 264.

79. Radbruch, 'Einführung in die Rechtswissenschaft', pp. 239–41.

80. Ibid., p. 251.
81. Gustav Radbruch, 'Das Güterverfahren und das deutsche Rechtsgefühl' [1918], in Radbruch, *Gesamtausgabe*, vol. 1, pp. 432–4.
82. Ferdinand Tönnies, 'Bürgerliche und politische Freiheit', in Anschütz et al. (eds), *Handbuch der Politik*, vol. 1, p. 174.
83. Rudolf Smend, 'Bürger und Bourgeois im deutschen Staatsrecht' [1933], in Smend, *Staatsrechtliche Abhandlungen*, pp. 314–15.
84. Ibid., p. 317.
85. Schmitt, *Verfassungslehre*, p. 126.
86. Ibid., pp. 130–4.
87. Ibid., p. 134.
88. Schmitt, *Legalität und Legitimität*, p. 18.
89. Radbruch, 'Einführung in die Rechtswissenschaft', p. 329.
90. Schmitt, *Legalität und Legitimität*, pp. 78–81.
91. Carl Schmitt, 'Die Wendung zum totalen Staat' [1931], in Schmitt, *Positionen und Begriffe*, p. 151.
92. Ibid., pp. 151–2.
93. Ibid., pp. 154–5.
94. Günther Holstein, 'Von Aufgaben und Zielen heutiger Staatsrechts- wissenschaft', *Archiv des öffentlichen Rechts* 11 (1926), p. 3.
95. See Peter C. Caldwell, *Popular Sovereignty and the Crisis of German Constitutional Law* (Durham, NC: Duke University Press, 1997), especially pp. 145–70.
96. Richard Thoma, 'Einleitung', in Anschütz and Thoma (eds), *Handbuch des deutschen Staatsrechts*, vol. 1, p. 5.
97. Hermann Heller, 'Grundrechte und Grundpflichten' [1924], in Heller, *Gesammelte Schriften*, vol. 2, p. 291.
98. Fraenkel, 'Die Krise des Rechtsstaates und die Justiz', p. 430.
99. Hermann Heller, 'Rechtsstaat oder Diktatur' [1929], in Heller, *Gesam- melte Schriften*, vol. 2, p. 455.
100. Ibid., p. 462.
101. Georgy Lukács, 'The question of parliamentarianism' [1920], in Rodney Livingstone (ed.), *Georg Lukacs: Political Writings 1919–1929* (London: NLB, 1972), p. 61.
102. Ibid., p. 63.
103. Carl Landauer, 'Sozialismus und parlamentarisches System', *Archiv für Sozialwissenschaft und Sozialpolitik* 48 (1922), pp. 749, 752–3.
104. Ibid., p. 758.
105. Ferdinand A. Hermens, 'Parlamentarismus oder was sonst?' [1932], in Ferdinand A. Hermens, *Zwischen Politik und Vernunft* (Berlin: Duncker & Humblot, 1969), p. 58.
106. Edgar Julius Jung, *The Rule of the Inferior* [1927], vol. 2 (Lewiston: Mellen, 1995), p. 145.
107. Kelsen, *Vom Wesen und Wert der Demokratie*, pp. 47–52.

108. Hermens, 'Parlamentarismus oder was sonst?', p. 59.
109. Ferdinand A. Hermens, 'Die verhinderte Demokratie in Deutschland' [1931], in Hermens, *Zwischen Politik und Vernunft*, p. 76.
110. Quoted in Sontheimer, *Antidemokratisches Denken*, p. 152.
111. Richard Thoma, 'Der Begriff der modernen Demokratie in seinem Verhältnis zum Staatsbegriff', in Melchior Playi (ed.), *Hauptprobleme der Soziologie* (Munich: Duncker & Humblot, 1923), pp. 61–3.
112. Radbruch, 'Die politischen Parteien im System des deutschen Verfassungsrechts', p. 289.
113. Schmitt, *The Crisis of Parliamentary Democracy*, p. 33.
114. Ibid., p. 49.
115. Ibid., p. 26.
116. Schmitt, *Verfassungslehre*, p. 247.
117. Ferdinand Tönnies, 'Demokratie und Parlamentarismus', *Schmollers Jahrbuch* 51 (1927), p. 10.
118. Kelsen, *Vom Wesen und Wert der Demokratie*, pp. 26–37.
119. Plessner, *Grenzen der Gemeinschaft*, p. 121.
120. Max Lenz, 'Knechtschaft', in Max Lenz, *Wille, Macht, Schicksal* (Munich: Oldenbourg, 1922), p. 181.
121. Friedrich Meinecke, *Machiavellism: The Doctrine of Raison d'État and its Place in Modern History* [1924] (New Brunswick, NJ: Transaction, 1998), p. 429.
122. Friedrich Meinecke, 'Der Geist von Locarno' [1925], in Meinecke, *Politische Schriften und Reden*, pp. 400–1.
123. Fritz Stier Somlo. 'Zur Soziologie des internationalen Rechts', *Jahrbuch für Soziologie* 3 (1927), pp. 125–39.
124. For Kaufmann, see Martti Koskenniemi, *The Gentle Civilizer of Nations* (Cambridge: Cambridge University Press, 2002), pp. 249–61. For Thoma's comments, see 'Staat', pp. 750–1.
125. Hans Kelsen, 'Unrecht und Unrechtsfolge im Völkerrecht' [1932], in Hans Kelsen, *Drei Kleine Schriften* (Aalen: Scientia, 1994), p. 567.
126. Alfred Verdross, *Die völkerrechtswidrige Kriegshandlung und der Strafanspruch der Staaten* (Berlin: Engelmann, 1920), pp. 36–7.
127. Schmitt, *The Concept of the Political*, p. 49.
128. Carl Schmitt, 'Völkerrechtliche Formen des modernen Imperialismus' [1932], in Schmitt, *Positionen und Begriffe*, p. 179.

3

The Third Reich

The twelve years of the National Socialist Third Reich have received more scholarly attention than any other period of similar duration for the obvious reasons of the brutality of the regime, its novelty, its instigation of the Second World War and above all the Holocaust. Those same features have made the interpretation of the regime especially problematic and contentious. The facts that an explicit constitution was never written and that an authorised ideology was never sanctioned have hampered the efforts of later commentators, as they did the efforts of theorists supportive of the regime at the time, to make sense of what the regime actually was. This lack of explicit central direction was recognised by a National Socialist official, who noted that often people waited in vain for instructions on how to act:

> Unfortunately, the same will be true in the future; but in fact it is the duty of everybody to try to work towards the Führer along the lines he would wish. Anyone who makes mistakes will notice it soon enough. But anyone who really works towards the Führer along his lines and towards his goal will certainly both now and in the future one day have the finest reward in the form of the sudden legal confirmation of his work.[1]

In terms of the broader issues of political theory, the nature of the state, law, administration and the international order, this prescription captured the uncertainty which theorists were faced with but erred in suggesting that they would ever find final confirmation of their views.

While some older theorists who were hostile or unsympathetic to the regime, such as Smend, Anschütz and Thoma, wrote little or avoided the central political issues, younger ambitious men rushed to fill the gap, often taking the posts of those who had been driven into exile or retirement. They vied to demonstrate their commitment to the regime, and many engaged in personal conspiracies in order to discredit their competitors. This was accompanied by an inflationary use of what was taken to be appropriate vocabulary that induced the National Socialist jurist Gottfried Neesze to complain of 'speechifying and enthusiasm about blood and earth, race, honour, community, *Volk*' behind which lay the old concepts of constitutional theory.[2] Neesze's point, of course, was that this new vocabulary had to be taken more seriously and the break with the past had to be captured in the concepts of constitutional theory. In Neesze's mind, failure to do so could amount to 'sabotage', a charge he did not hesitate to level at Otto Koellreutter despite the fact that Koellreutter was one of the few established jurists to commit himself openly to the National Socialist party before the seizure of power.[3]

The sense of a break with the past and of a renewal of German spirit and energy was widespread. The break with the past meant in the first place a break with Weimar. For historians especially, that could mean the supposed reassertion of a link with the Prussian and imperial tradition that had been severed in 1918. Younger historians, however, were more inclined to see the *kleindeutsch* solution of Bismarck as insufficiently ambitious.[4] For many historians and legal theorists, the revolutionary transition represented by the advent of the Third Reich signified a break with the entire liberal era. From this perspective, the German Reich that collapsed in 1918, together with the theories it spawned, was recast as liberal in spirit and principle, or at best as a beleaguered 'soldiers' state' that was crippled by its concessions to the civilians.[5] The idea of national renewal and the end of a liberal era came together in the supposition that Germany was embarking on a new, distinctively German political path. Here, the old liberal models were no guide. Even the once-favoured *Allgemeine Staatslehre* was consigned to the past. Carl Schmitt dismissed this 'category' as a 'typical concern of the liberal nineteenth century'.[6] The very word *allgemein* (general) suggested a form of state of universal validity. That was incompatible with the idea that the National Socialist state was distinctive and distinctively German. There was not even any attempt to formulate a comparative theory or model of fascist states.[7]

The reality of the Third Reich was itself a paradox of the perceived omnipresence of the state and what the historian Michael Geyer has described as an 'extreme dilution of domination into an endless series of partial statelike organisations'.[8] It was, according to Geyer,

> a state consisting of public actors – some of them were legally 'private' like industries, some belonged to the executive like the military, and some were altogether hybrid mixtures like the German Labour Front – which gained their autonomy from their ability to coerce and to gain independent access to resources.[9]

Here, it was not the convergence of these competing actors that allowed the system to function but the distance between them. It was this reality that also allowed political theorists to pick up different aspects of the system even if they were sometimes frustrated by the ambiguity of the 'hybrid mixtures' within the Third Reich.

It was rare for the confusion to be identified as bluntly as it was by the State Secretary of the Interior, Wilhelm Stuckart: 'inflation of administrative authorities, war between administrative authorities, duplication of work and idleness of administrative authorities . . . reduction of legal security through the increased possibility of mutually conflicting administrative decisions', all of which threatened the most valuable asset 'that a state possesses, namely the trust of the people'.[10] Nevertheless, Stuckart effectively acknowledged that the disintegration of any coherent order was far from confined to the National Socialist movement, that is, to the realm of the Party and its numerous affiliated organisations.

The pace of change, economic recovery and rearmament, anti-semitic persecution, the hollowing-out of the legal system by the security apparatus, increased if erratic state intervention in the economy, and above all expansion and war all forced theorists to attempt to grasp the nature of the regime in the light of the most recent developments. The union with Austria in 1938, in whose authoritarian constitution of 1934 some had seen the only alternative to National Socialism, the occupation of the Czech lands in 1939, and the occupation of most of Europe in the Second World War opened up new problems and perspectives that further challenged the viability of traditional concepts. Moreover, responsiveness to the dynamics and the complexity of the Third Reich had to be combined with assertions of the unity of the Third Reich – for it was unity that supposedly, if erroneously, distinguished it from the despised liberal order of the past.

The state

Otto Koellreutter made an early attempt to define the new state under the heading 'Der nationale Rechtsstaat' (The national *Rechtsstaat*). He specified that the realisation of this form of state did not entail a 'change of the form of the state', but what he meant by that was simply that a restoration of the monarchy was not possible. The new national *Rechtsstaat* is, he argued, different by virtue of the political idea that animates it. The elemental power of this new 'political substance' is evident in the ease with which it has swept aside the autonomy of the states within the *Reich*. Despite this emphasis upon radical change, Koellreutter clearly wanted to retain some characteristics of traditional approach insofar as he wanted to retain the autonomy of the civil service. He wrote that there has to be a 'clear separation of the political leadership as the representative of political value and the professional civil service as the representative of the legal value . . .'[11]

It was Koellreutter's desire to retain the concept of the *Rechtsstaat* at all that induced Neesse's suspicions, though the number of those who wished to retain the concept in one guise or another was quite substantial.[12] Gustav Adolf Walz accepted that the concept was relevant to what he saw as the regime's commitment to justice and because general binding norms enunciated in legislation would still be required; but that did not warrant using the term *Rechtsstaat* as a general characterisation of the regime, for that would amount to confusing the means that the regime might employ with its essence.[13] Walz also considered the term 'authoritarian state'. That was favoured by Schmitt's pupil Herbert Krüger as well. For Krüger, 'the authoritarian state principle is the constitution of the National Socialist state'.[14] Walz, however, was not convinced. He argued that the concept of the authoritarian state had specific, recent political connotations, namely reliance on presidential power as enshrined in the Weimar constitution and a reformulation of the basic rights enshrined in the second part of the Weimar constitution.[15] The underlying political point was that the concept of the authoritarian state conjured up the viewpoint of those who had sought to establish an authoritarian alternative to both the democratic order of Weimar and to the National Socialists. Walz was little more sympathetic to the idea that the new regime should be characterised as a corporatist state. That was favoured by many who had long looked on the idea of a corporatist state, often as represented by fascist Italy, as an alternative to the Weimar Republic. Yet even Werner Sombart, who also favoured this idea, had to concede that it was at best only partially applicable to the new Germany. Of the various functions originally performed by the estates, the cultivation of a specific mentality among their members, the confirmation of non-egalitarian principles through the conferment of privileges, and educational, economic and political state functions, only fragments of the functional tasks of the estates could be revived, and even these only for segments of the population.[16]

Walz's preferred designation was the '*völkischer Führerstaat*', which he claimed captured the distinctive national identity and sense of unity in the new state as well as the concentration of executive and legislative power in the leader, who was the leader of the *Reich*, the *Volk* and the party.[17] Ernst Forsthoff, another protégé of Schmitt, showed some reservations about relying so heavily on the idea of leadership. Leadership, he argued, is bound up with the personal qualities of the leader and the leader's ties to his followers. But such qualities and ties are transient in that they do not endure beyond the life of the leader. It is acceptable, he continued, that a movement held together by leadership can dissolve with the death of the leader; but this is not acceptable for the state, which is 'the form of the political existence of a people'.[18] Walz also complained that there was something 'unmetaphysical' in the personal qualities of the leader. The desired metaphysical principle remained somewhat elusive, though it is clear that what Walz meant by this was some ideology of a quasi-religious nature that provided an unquestionable sanction for the authority of the 'total state', that is, the state that swept away the liberal *Rechtsstaat* with its reliance on law and the distinction between state and society. In seeking to explain what he meant by 'total state', Forsthoff had to combine the general antipathy to formal bureaucracies – though he insisted that some element of bureaucratically guaranteed calculability is necessary – and the idea of a form of authority that entailed personal responsibility and personal power of command. He found this in the figure of the *Reichsstatthalter*, that is, the position of Reich Governor created by the new regime to co-ordinate the states of the Reich. Several years later, Arnold Köttgen argued that these political commissars had been a transitional phenomenon whose role and whose distinctiveness from the civil service had subsequently faded.[19] Köttgen was arguably right about the Reich Governors, though Forsthoff had picked up Hitler's inclination to use special authorities or commissars to circumvent the crises to which the regime was prone as well as to promote his racist and anti-semitic visions. The fact that Köttgen and Forsthoff were each partially right is bound up with the difficulty that each had in responding to an ever-changing reality whose ultimate destination could not be defined.

Schmitt made one of the most enduring attempts to capture this dynamic under the title *Staat, Bewegung, Volk* (State, Movement, People).[20] He claimed that each term could be used to express the 'political unity' of the new order but also to capture a specific side of it: 'the state in the narrower sense as the political-static part, the movement as the political-dynamic element and the *Volk* as the unpolitical side, thriving under the protection and shadow of the political decisions . . .'[21] Having set up a tripartite framework, Schmitt then argued that unity is established insofar as the movement 'presses through and leads' the state and the *Volk*.[22] While clearly legitimating the leading role claimed by the Nazi movement as a whole, Schmitt also claimed that the interaction of these elements under the guiding role of the movement provides an alternative to the dualistic conceptions typical of the liberal democratic order which counterposes state and *Volk*, government and *Volk*, citizen and civil servant, or state and party.[23] Schmitt still thought it necessary to warn against allowing these political decisions in the new order to become subject to the courts, for the equality of the contending parties inherent in due legal process might allow the 'open or concealed enemy of the new state' to put itself on the same level as the state or the movement.[24]

Reinhard Höhn had been encouraged by Schmitt but soon became a bitter rival. He constantly harried those whom he suspected, rightly or wrongly, of less-than-wholehearted commitment to the new order. Yet he agreed with Schmitt on the dangers of subjecting the state and movement to due legal process and turned this into a broader attack upon the 'juristic state personality, the "foundation and corner stone" of previous constitutional law. . . .'[25] In a survey of the development of German constitutional thought, Georg Jellinek emerged as Höhn's main target. Jellinek, Höhn complained, had dissolved all human relations into relations between individual personalities. While other theorists had hesitated to reduce the state to the same level and had tended to deny the state's subjects 'subjective–public' rights against the state, Jellinek had construed the state as an 'abstract state personality' precisely in order to make such rights possible: 'In order to be able to give the individual subjective public rights, he had to place the state, as much as is possible, on the same level with the personality of the individual'.[26] For Höhn, breaking the hold of this concept of the state was the major challenge and achievement of the political thought of the new order: 'The foundation and corner stone of constitutional law is no longer the legal person of the state; rather the national community is the new starting point . . . The state as a legal person and the concept of the community are mutually exclusive'.[27]

Höhn's attack on the idea of the personality of the state was widely applauded. Neesze described it as Höhn's 'undisputable service'.[28] Yet the wider implications of Höhn's assault on the concept of the state were contested. Ernst Rudolf Huber, for example, described the replacement of the concept of the personality by that of the community as the replacement of one abstract concept by another. Huber regarded the concept of community as important but argued that its indiscriminate use would merely undermine its true value.[29] In his *Verfassungsrecht des Grossdeutschen Reiches* (Constitutional Law of the Greater German *Reich*) of 1939, the most substantial work of its kind in the Third Reich, Huber mounted a cautious defence of the concept of the state. He had to defer to Hitler's repeated insistence that the state is an instrument and not a purpose in its own right, but he claimed that this did not require dispensing with the concept of the state or degrading it to the name of a 'dead apparatus'. Huber found an answer to his difficulty in distinguishing between the state in a narrower sense, as an administrative and military organisation, and the state in a wider sense as the totality of the national order, as a 'living organism'. He then suggested that the former might be designated as 'state organisation' and the latter as the *Reich*.[30]

While Huber deployed the concept of the *Reich* in order to salvage the concept of the state, two years later Schmitt produced a brief article with the title 'Staat als ein konkreter, an eine geschichtliche Epoche gebundener Begriff' (The state as a concrete concept, bound to an historical epoch). He discussed the origins of the concepts of state and sovereignty in the sixteenth century but made clear that the era in which the state was the general organisational political form was coming to an end. Equally significant was his claim: 'The German *Volk* also had to go through the narrow pass of state sovereignty before it was possible for a new German *Reich* to win back for Germany leadership in Europe'.[31]

The initial attempts to grasp the nature of the new regime were followed by mounting attacks on old concepts mixed with defensive attempts to cling on to at least some of the old connotations of the state while adapting to the regime. The more ambitious, both personally and intellectually, staked everything on National Socialist victory.

The concept of politics: leadership contra administration

Long-standing concern with political leadership combined with National Socialist veneration of the *Führer* to give it a central place in the attitude to the concept of politics in the Third Reich. In the case of Schmitt, this continued to be related to his understanding of the relationship of the political to the state. The assumption that the political is bound up with the state presumes, he argued, that the state is the sole or normal form of political unity. This, however, he rejected as being no longer the case on the grounds that the *Volk* is now the normal form of political unity.[32] Yet Schmitt also continued to claim that the state has to be defined from the perspective of the political.[33] Attempts to determine an objective sphere of politics, distinct from economics, technology and religion or to separate out a non-political social sphere, had all failed. Even apparently trivial matters such as the music played during a military march could become highly political issues. Schmitt concluded that this 'proves how much today a *unified political leadership capable of taking decisions* is necessary for every people, in order to preserve the primacy of the political decisions (the primacy of politics) . . .'[34]

Schmitt sought to tie down this concept of political leadership by distinguishing it from other activities to which he thought it might be wrongly assimilated. Thus, political leadership has nothing to do with legally constrained activity. It is to be distinguished from any kind of 'supervision' and above all from ideas of 'trusteeship' and 'education'. He warned his readers that they must guard against the possibility 'that a specifically German and National Socialist concept [of political leadership] is muddied and watered down by assimilation to alien categories'.[35] Schmitt then stated what this specifically German and National Socialist concept was: 'the unconditional racial identity [*Artgleichheit*] between the leader and the followers [*Gefolgschaft*] . . .'[36] Schmitt left no doubt that he meant racial identity in the strict sense of the term. Referring to recent speeches in which the idea of race [*Rasse*] had been central, he added that this central role was 'no kind of theoretically conceived postulate'.[37]

Huber referred to Schmitt approvingly in his treatment of the nature of politics; but, despite having a similar focus upon leadership, the emphasis is significantly different. Thus Huber invoked Schmitt's well-known distinction between friend and enemy but asserted that this was only one criterion and that politics was of no value in itself without reference to a 'vital form, whose will, decision and act appear in the political'.[38] This is both close to Schmitt, insofar as it refers to a 'political unity', and somewhat distant from him, insofar as Huber sought to sidestep the centrality of Schmitt's distinction between friend and enemy. The real difference emerged, however, when Huber claimed that the historical continuity of political will required a 'bearer' of this will that endured through contingency and transformations of history and that this 'bearer of politics is the state . . .'[39] Huber's attempt to make the concept of the state central did not diminish his enthusiasm for the 'leadership state' (*Führerstaat*). Indeed, Huber took the concept of sovereignty from the repertoire of attributes of the state in order to hand it over to the leader in its most unconstrained form, including 'originality, exclusivity and universality, irresistibility . . .'[40]

It was not only constitutional theorists who defended the primacy of politics and centrality of leadership. Helmut Schelsky and Arnold Gehlen did so from the perspectives of the history of political thought and philosophical anthropology. Schelsky sought to reclaim the seventeenth-century English philosopher Thomas Hobbes from what he saw was an individualistic and rationalistic misinterpretation. The error, he argued, lies in confusing Hobbes's approach to the explanation of the physical world, including the human body, with his approach to the distinctive qualities of human nature, that is, speech. Speech facilitates a certain distance from the environment by means of a more proficient calculation, of which animals are not capable, and it enables men to advise each other. It is, however, a third quality of speech that Schelsky emphasised. It means that 'we can command and understand commands'.[41] Here lies the source of society, peace and discipline. Speech not instinct is decisive. From this, Schelsky concluded: 'The primacy of politics can scarcely be more clearly developed already in the picture of man'.[42] The total state is rooted in human nature. Gehlen also appealed to the distinctiveness of human nature. For Gehlen, human nature is distinctive by virtue of human deficiencies when compared with other species. Lacking the certainty of instinct and the physiological adaptation to specific situations and forms of behaviour, man is exposed to risks and suffers from a lack of orientation in a way that other species are not. Yet this deficiency also provides an opportunity, for man has the capacity to form himself. Man is an object of discipline for himself. From this need for discipline, Gehlen developed an abstract justification for leadership which he then recoupled to the regime's racial agenda.[43]

While Schelsky and Gehlen deployed arguments about human nature in order to assert the primacy of politics construed in terms of leadership and discipline, Hans Peter Ipsen sought to identify the nature of politics by a comparative analysis of acts of state which, as such, were held to be beyond the remit of the judiciary, and hence political. Ipsen's goal was to strip away any limitation on the acts of those bodies that 'qualified', as he put it, as sovereign. Each such body, whether the state or the party, can determine for itself the specific cases in which it acts that count as sovereign and hence as completely beyond judicial review. This does justice, he claimed, to the irrationality of the political.[44] An enumeration of such acts is neither possible nor desirable, for it violates the very concept of sovereign acts. He rejected even the legislative sanction of police powers beyond the realm of the judiciary in the Third Reich as insufficient recognition of the autonomy of the police.[45] Ipsen was aware that this proliferation of sovereign authorities was potentially problematic, hence his assurance that 'The "separation of leadership and administration" make the "dynamic element of leadership free" from the administrative element, without thereby setting up contradictory competencies'.[46] Despite this bland assurance, Ipsen conceded that some process of accommodation (*Ausgleich*) would be necessary, though that in turn was subordinated to political imperatives.[47] Ipsen came close, in fact, to giving expression to that 'extreme dilution of domination into an endless series of partial state-like organisations' which characterised the Third Reich, though he had to draw back from this conclusion in the interests of the façade of unity.

The distinction between leadership, or literally the leadership of men (*Menschenführung*), and administration (*Verwaltung*) was one of the central themes and dilemmas of political thought in the Third Reich. The assertion of the primacy of politics, understood as leadership in contrast to administration, was one of the main themes of political thought in the Third Reich. Again, Höhn adopted a consciously radical position on the distinction between the two. He specified that Hitler was leader (*Führer*) of the movement and the *Volk* and leader (*Leiter*) of the state, where the state is defined as an apparatus of authorities and civil servants. Within the state, there is no leadership but only command and obedience.[48] This distinction between leadership and administration was bound up with the idea that leadership is characterised by the voluntary submission of the followers of the leader and that the leader either represents or forms the *Volk*. The linkage with the movement was summarised in the frequent assertion that 'leadership is the sole task of the movement'.[49]

Although no-one denied the importance of the principle of leadership, Höhn's strict interpretation was not followed by all. Huber sought to mitigate it by protesting about the inflationary use of the term 'leader'. It is, he argued, particularly inappropriate in the economic context.[50] Johannes Heckel, however, took exception to Huber's extension of political leadership to the soldier, which, he claimed, 'burdens the army with tasks and responsibilities which do not correspond to its military profession . . .'[51] Huber's extension of the leadership principle to the army, despite his protest against its inflationary use elsewhere, followed from his opposition to the effective downgrading of the army and state implied by Höhn's restriction of the leadership principle to the National Socialist movement. Huber argued that all organisations, including the movement, require structures of command and obedience. At the same time, the army and administration are, he claimed, 'leadership orders which rest on voluntary sacrifice, responsibility and faithfulness'.[52]

Despite and because of the high level of politicisation and the sensitivity of discussion of the general concept of the state, there was what has been described as a 'turn towards administration' in the political thought of the Third Reich.[53] In part, this was a continuation of the response to the reduction in the role played by the legislative state that had already taken place in Weimar. It also seemed to offer some minimal refuge from the pressures from the National Socialist movement and the more radical political theorists. That meant showing that administration was not the mere administration of things but had some higher political dignity. This was what Forsthoff sought to achieve under the slogan 'provision for existence' (*Daseinsvorsorge*). He made clear that this is not to be equated with 'welfare' (*Fürsorge*).[54] He argued, rather, that modern, urbanised mankind is dependent for its very existence upon the provision of services, like the water and electricity supply, that can no longer be guaranteed at the level of the individual or family. What is at stake here is not how men live, but whether they will live at all. It is, he continued, these administrative tasks that define the prime activity of the modern state. Forsthoff duly acknowledged Höhn's distinction between leadership and administration but then promptly insisted that the administration he had in mind is no mere mechanistic process. It is, rather, 'a sovereign function of great political dynamism'.[55] Forsthoff also sought to connect his vision of administration as 'provision for existence' with the importance ascribed to the national community. He claimed that the enhanced dependence on this form of state administration is complemented by a vital 'unreflective trust', for without this 'feeling of being secure' there was a danger that the national community would 'dissolve in panic-ridden visions'.[56]

Forsthoff's attempt to balance the claims of political leadership and administration, in this case by enhancing the political profile of administration, was but one of numerous attempts to discern and legitimate some form of order amid the conflicting visions of the Third Reich. It was no more successful than any of the others in ending the tension between the competing claims of leadership and administration. That tension became more problematic as National Socialist rule extended over German Austrians and then over non-German peoples. German administration over these peoples had an extent and quality that did not seem to fit the narrow scope generally ascribed to mere administration. Werner Best, who was to have extensive practical experience of occupation in the service of the SS, finally cut the Gordian knot by claiming that the word 'administration' (*Verwaltung*) has its origins in a more comprehensive concept of ruling (*Walten*). This concept of comprehensive rule had been broken up and administration reduced to a subordinate activity controlled by legislation and administrative courts. In the light of Germany's hegemonic position, however, all that had to be abandoned. Administration, according to Best, had to be understood once again as comprehensive ruling, and the distinction between ' "political" rule' and ' "executive" administration' had to be discarded.[57]

Volk, *movement and law*

The primacy of the *Volk* was often presented as the unshakeable foundation of German political unity compared to the transience of the state. The endurance of the *Volk*, the more or less explicitly quasi-religious veneration of the *Volk*, the comparative transience of the state and the sense of threat to the unity of the *Volk*, were commonplace elements of one stream of thought in the Third Reich. Although the *Volk* was supposedly the enduring foundation of unity, it was also argued that the *Volk* had only been assigned its rightful place in the wake of the National Socialist revolution. Thus Höhn quoted Laband's assertion that the German *Reich* established in 1871 could not be understood as the creation of ever-increasing millions of German citizens as evidence of the earlier inability to grasp the true nature of the *Volk*.[58] Similarly, he complained that when Jellinek turned his gaze away from the juristically conceived state, all he saw was 'simple chaos'.[59] In contrast to these liberal conceptions, the *Volk* was presented as primary in the sense of directly incorporating the individual members of the community. Indeed, the individual, that is, the member of a society conceived as distinct from the state, equipped with basic rights, was to be replaced by the concept of the 'national comrade' (*Volksgenosse*) who had no need of such rights.[60] Whereas the liberal individual understood himself in contrast to the national community, the national comrade was supposed to be incorporated within the community.

The attempt to present the *Volk* as natural, substantive and inclusive proved difficult to reconcile with other elements of the Third Reich and with the account of pre-National Socialist Germany as a record of fragmentation culminating in defeat and the Weimar Republic. Unity, that is, the supposed reality of the national community, had to be construed as both the product of Hitler and the National Socialist movement, on the one hand, and as something pre-existing on the other hand. This effectively left considerable scope for significantly different emphases and mutual recrimination. Amid the enthusiasm of the early days of the regime, Wilhelm Sauer could proclaim that the Nordic racial type is no virtue per se, that race in general is not a value in itself but only a precondition and that the *Volk* is a mere natural organism.[61] The need for some form of political supplement to this natural substratum was summarised in Sauer's slogan: 'the race [*Volk*] is nature; the state is form; the nation [*Nation*] is content, value, culture . . .'[62] As Germany instigated the Second World War, Huber also insisted that although race (*Rasse*) was the natural foundation of the *Volk*, an 'historical idea' or 'historical mission' was required in order to form the 'political *Volk*'. In doing so, he felt obliged to rebut Höhn's accusation that in distinguishing between the natural and the political *Volk* he was tearing apart race and history.[63] For Krüger, Hitler was the source and creator of the community. Köttgen agreed: 'The historical fact of a living national community [*Volksgemeinschaft*] rests on the life and work of this *Führer* . . .' Yet he promptly added that this leadership had risen up from the life of the *Volk* and the movement.[64] The circularity of the argument is plain, but it provided some defence against the charge of either underestimating Hitler's role or underestimating his roots in the *Volk* and the movement.

There was also some ambivalence about the role of the movement, especially the National Socialist Party, though Schmitt's characterisation of the regime as a 'movement state' (*Bewegungsstaat*) was widely adopted. The central difficulty concerned the relationship of the party to the state. On the one hand, the unity of party and state was invoked, both as a general principle and as a practice exemplified in Hitler's position as head of state and leader and in the union of party and state offices at a lower level. On the other hand, the distinction between political leadership and administration, as well as a desire to emphasis the difference between Germany and Italy, where the state was ascribed a more dominant role, pointed to an emphasis upon the parallel existence of party and state. Thus, Ulrich Scheuner wrote of a 'characteristic duplication' of sovereign structures.[65] Approaching the relationship from the side of the party, Walter Sommer picked out the fact that it had its own assets, administration, law and courts as indicative of its autonomy. The Party, he proclaimed, has no need to intervene in the state, for such intervention would only distract it from its own tasks. Yet Sommer also noted that Hitler had warned that if the state administration failed to fulfil key tasks, they would be transferred to the Party.[66] Sommer was responding to what in reality was a fluid demarcation line that agencies of the Party could break through, especially if prompted by even vague suggestions from Hitler.

A similar ambivalence ran through attitudes towards the law. On the one hand, there was a desire to discard what was seen as the abstract, normative conception of law that was equated with the liberal order in favour of a more substantive conception rooted in the feelings of the unified community or the racial identity of the German *Volk*. In the racial legal theory of Helmut Nicolai, race defines the nature of law, the ability to judge particular cases and the fact of the commission of a crime. Having discarded the idea of free will in favour of a racial determinism, Nicolai saw the purpose of law as deterrence in cases of minor infringement and as the 'elimination' of 'unhealthy' racial elements in more serious cases.[67] Despite the anti-semitic rhetoric that recurs through his works in this period, anti-semitism did not play a structural role in Schmitt's attempt to redefine the nature of law. Schmitt asserted that there were only three approaches to law, the first two of which he discarded, namely normative and decisionistic approaches. Having earlier espoused decisionism against normativism himself, he now chose to emphasise the connection between the two. He picked out reliance upon general abstract rules, the characteristic of normativist approaches, that were nevertheless posited by men rather than existing independently of human will, as the characteristic of the individualistic positivism of the nineteenth century.[68] That what is offered as objective and generally valid is rooted in what is contingent and subjective, he now claimed, reveals the inability of the positivist conception to provide any reliable guidance. In place of these discredited options, Schmitt suggested that the alternative lies in terms of thinking in terms of 'concrete orders'. What Schmitt understood by this term is evident from his reference to institutions such as 'marriage, family, estate, state', and to the idea that the terms employer, white-collar worker and blue-collar worker were being replaced by the terms 'leaders and followers within a factory', that is, that the liberal idea of a set of relationships, governed by abstract general norms, into which individuals entered at their discretion was to be replaced by the role they occupied within the National Socialist community and the law peculiar to that role.[69]

On the other hand, this supposedly more 'concrete' order dissolved into a fluid pattern as Schmitt pointed to the emergence of 'so-called general clauses', that is, to general concepts of 'good ethics, faith and belief', that could be attached to any law or judicial interpretation.[70] This, coupled with his explicit rejection of the *Rechtsstaat* understood as a form of constitutional restraint, pointed towards Best's vision, although Schmitt would personally clash with Best on several occasions since Best was not convinced that Schmitt had sufficiently accepted the importance of race in the new order.[71] According to Best,

> preventive police tasks of the political police have not found a legal regulation. They cannot find them, for the preventive police tasks of the political police . . . cannot be written down and given normative form for all time. The tasks of the political police . . . are not freely selected but prescribed by the enemy.[72]

A National Socialist theory of international law

Throughout the course of the Third Reich, attitudes towards the international order were prescribed by the international enemy, in the sense that German theorists held that Germany had been subordinated to an alien and imperialist model of international law. In part, they hoped that the principles of this enemy, which were embodied in the Versailles Treaty and the Geneva-based League of Nations, could be turned against this enemy. Just as they praised the ability of the National Socialist movement to exploit what they saw as the weaknesses of the Weimar Republic's liberal democracy in order to overthrow it, so too they hoped to exploit the principled equality of states in international law in order to enhance Germany's position, and occasionally openly blurted this out.[73] The close connection between internal enmity, the hostility towards Weimar, and external enmity, towards Versailles and the League of Nations, was evident in the title of a collection of essays by Schmitt, published in 1940: *Positionen und Begriffe im Kampf mit Weimar–Genf–Versailles 1923–1939* (Positions and Concepts in the Struggle with

Weimar–Geneva–Versailles). Schmitt's illustration of the connections evident in this struggle was, according to Hermann Jahrreiss, 'a great gain which we must not lose sight of again'.[74] At the same time, other supporters of the regime sought to exploit what they saw as the strengths of the political ideas of the Third Reich in order to formulate a new, distinctively National Socialist approach to the international order. In part, this was a logical consequence of Schmitt's warning at the end of the Weimar Republic that a people is first defeated when it subordinates itself to a foreign conception of international law.[75] If Germany were to escape this subordination, then it had to formulate a distinctive, indigenous conception of international law. The tension between these two approaches was linked to other choices. Thus, attempts to exploit such principles as the equality of states tended to appeal to those inclined to adopt a statist perspective more generally. Attempts to emphasise a distinctive National Socialist approach tended to appeal to those inclined to adopt a *völkisch* perspective. As in other areas of political thought in the Third Reich, indeed even more so, uncertainty about the final goals of the regime, compounded in this case by tactical considerations, left scope for divergent interpretations and mutual recriminations.

Especially in the earlier years, relatively orthodox assertions were still possible. Friedrich Wilhelm von Rauchhaupt bluntly stated: 'The subject and object of international relations are fundamentally the states recognised in international law'.[76] The fact that Rauchhaupt asserted that states without arms and honour do not qualify as subjects of international law amounted to little more than a reformulation of this basic principle, though the emphasis on arms and honour clearly reflected the continuing resentment of the impositions of the Versailles Treaty.[77] Gustav Walz defended the same principle as the foundation of international law. He explicitly rejected 'monistic' arguments that gave primacy to either domestic law or international law in favour of a 'pluralistic' conception of international order. This emphasis upon pluralism was, he claimed, wholly consistent with National Socialist principles. It entailed a rejection of any form of imperialism as well as the assumption that individuals or the 'totality of individuals', that is, mankind, counted as subjects in international law. The only subjects of international law, he claimed, are 'national [*völkisch*] communities organised into states'.[78]

Hans Keller was not convinced that the full significance of the National Socialist emphasis upon the *Volk* had been truly grasped.

Walz had come close but failed at the last hurdle because he allowed the state to speak in the name of the *Volk*.[79] Just as Höhn had attacked the concept of the state in general in the name of *völkisch* principles, so too Keller attacked its use in international law. The idea of the territorially defined state divorced from the *Volk* is, he argued, an un-Germanic concept derived from the Italian renaissance and Roman law and refined by French absolutism and the idea of the nation state as developed in nineteenth-century France.[80] From this perspective, insofar as international law exists, it does so on the basis of the conception of law held by the various nations. As such, it extends so far as these peoples share the same conception of law. According to Nicolai, an exponent of an overtly racial approach to law, such conceptions are rooted in the racial characteristics of peoples. From this, he concluded that there can be no universally valid international law, but only a law shared by those of similar racial stock, In the case of Germany, that meant an international community coextensive with Nordic peoples.[81] Best's deductions from the *völkisch* principle did not even allow for this. The overriding priority of the *Volk* is compatible with a degree of 'regularity' but no more. Law is rooted in the *Volk*, and there is nothing beneath the *Volk* and nothing above the *Volk* in which law can be rooted.[82]

The starkness of Best's position took no account of the lingering conviction, which Heinrich Triepel still expressed, that the persistence of power could only be ensured by some form of law.[83] Nor did it take account of the need to challenge alternative conceptions of international law that might appeal to neutral powers in the event of war. It was this that continued to concern Schmitt. Schmitt was still haunted by Germany's defeat by the sea powers, that is, the British and the Americans, in the First World War. Indeed, he sought to deploy his assumptions about the role of myth in politics to create a myth of sea power through which he could discredit those aspects of international law that he saw as a threat to Germany. The sea powers, he claimed, are inherently imperialistic and reject tradition rooted in the experience of continental European land power whereby war is treated as a duel between two states, neither of whom need be presumed to be unjust by third parties who can remain neutral. It is typical that sea power discriminates in the event of war, defining one of the parties as unjust, as an enemy of mankind, who can, therefore, be pursued with all ferocity.[84] Behind all this lay Schmitt's fear that America would intervene in a European war as it had done in the First World War.

Schmitt's search for a new form of international law, his search for an alternative concept of political unity to that of the state and his continuing hostility to the sea powers came together in his *Völkerrechtliche Grossraumordnung* (The Order of Large Spaces in International Law), first published in 1939. There, Schmitt noted that in the autumn of 1937 he had not been able to specify what he wanted to put in the place of the old concepts of international law. Now, however, he had found an answer, without having to 'yield to the concepts of the western democracies', namely the *Reich*.[85] Each *Grossraum*, or large region, would consist of a leading power, the *Reich*, as well as several nations. The *Reiche*, Schmitt explained, 'are the leading powers, whose political idea radiates through a specific *Grossraum* and who specifically exclude the intervention of alien powers into this *Grossraum*'.[86] With this principle of non-intervention by powers alien to the *Grossraum*, Schmitt sought to turn the ideas of the western democracies against them, for this principle is, he claimed, that of the American Monroe doctrine.

Schmitt's vision raised a number of awkward questions. Huber, who was generally supportive, worried that it might look too much like a ' "superstate" '.[87] Best, ever suspicious that Schmitt had not taken the *völkisch* principle to heart, was concerned that Schmitt had conceded too much to those nations subject to German hegemony – for, if the *Grossraumordnung* was a system of international law, it was possible that they might claim the right to negotiate treaties with the hegemonic power or even the right to renounce their 'international legal ties with the leading nation'.[88] Höhn raised a host of objections, including the idea that the principle of non-intervention was itself associated with the 'individualistic state', that is, the liberal state.[89] Such responses were reflections of more general differences of emphasis as well as continuing animosities. They were also bound up with persistent uncertainty about the final destination and shape of a Europe dominated by National Socialist Germany and the difficulty that supporters of that hegemony had in conceiving of some structure and order without at least fragments of the liberal discourse which they competed to disparage.

Political thought in the Third Reich was driven forward by this competition to reject the concepts of the past, which were recognised as part of the German past, if only to be disparaged as foreign implants. Yet the peculiar lack of system, the proliferation of competing agencies, the emergence of policies driven forward by those 'working towards the *Führer*' still left room for dispute and for greater or lesser adaptation to the racial visions for which the Third Reich, and with it part of German political thought, would be condemned.

Notes

1. Jeremy Noakes and Geoffrey Pridham (eds), *Nazism*, vol. 2 (Exeter: Exeter University Press, 1984), p. 207. For the wider significance of this, see Ian Kershaw, 'Working towards the Führer', *Contemporary European History* 2 (1993), pp. 103–18.

2. Gottfried Neesze, 'Verfassungsrechtliches Schrifttum', *Zeitschrift für die gesamte Staatswissenschaft* 96 (1936), p. 388.

3. Ibid., p. 395.

4. Karen Schönwälder, *Historiker und Politik* (Frankfurt am Main: Campus, 1992), pp. 23, 80–1.

5. The conflict between the soldier and the state was the theme of Carl Schmitt, *Staatsgefüge und Zusammenbruch des Zweiten Reiches* (Hamburg: Hanseatische Verlagsanstalt, 1934). It was still possible to argue that this was simplistic history. See Fritz Hartung, 'Staatsgefüge und Zusammenbruch des Zweiten Reiches', *Historische Zeitschrift* 151 (1935), pp. 528–44.

6. Carl Schmitt, *Staat, Bewegung, Volk* (Hamburg: Hanseatische Verlagsanstalt, 1933), p. 14.

7. Michael Stolleis, *Geschichte des öffentlichen Rechts in Deutschland*, vol. 3 (Munich: C. H. Beck, 1999), p. 319.

8. Michael Geyer, 'The state in National Socialist Germany', in Charles Bright and Susan Harding (eds), *Statemaking and Social Movements* (Ann Arbor: University of Michigan Press, 1984), p. 196.

9. Ibid., p. 206.

10. Wilhelm Stuckart, 'Zentralgewalt, Dezentralisation, Verwaltungseinheit', in Wilhelm Stuckart et al., *Festgabe für Heinrich Himmler* (Darmstadt: Wittich, 1941), p. 24.

11. Otto Koellreutter, 'Der nationale Rechtsstaat', *Deutsche Juristen-Zeitung*, 38 (1933), p. 522.

12. See Christian Hilger, *Rechtsstaatsbegriffe im Dritten Reich* (Tübingen: Mohr, 2003).

13. G. Walz, 'Autoritärer Staat, nationaler Rechtsstaat oder völkischer Rechtsstaat?', *Deutsche Juristen-Zeitung*, 38 (1933), pp. 1,338–9.

14. Herbert Krüger, 'Das neue Staatsrecht des dritten Reiches', *Fischers Zeitschrift* 70 (1934), p. 291.

15. Walz, 'Autoritärer Staat, nationaler Rechtsstaat oder völkischer Rechtsstaat?', p. 1,338.

16. Werner Sombart, 'Das Wesen der ständischen Gliederung mit besonderer Berücksichtigung Deutschlands', *Deutsche Juristen-Zeitung* 39 (1934), pp. 502–11.

17. Walz, 'Autoritärer Staat, nationaler Rechtsstaat oder völkischer Rechtsstaat?', p. 1,340.

18. Ernst Forsthoff, *Der totale Staat* (Hamburg: Hanseatische Verlagsanstalt, 1933), p. 31.

19. Arnold Köttgen, 'Die Stellung des Beamtentums im völkischen Führer-staat', *Jahrbuch des öffentlichen Rechts der Gegenwart* 25 (1938), pp. 59–60.
20. Schmitt, *Staat, Bewegung, Volk.*
21. Ibid., p. 12.
22. Ibid.
23. Ibid., pp. 16–17, 21.
24. Ibid., p. 21.
25. Reinhard Höhn, 'Staat und Rechtsgemeinschaft', *Zeitschrift für die gesamte Staatswissenschaft* 95 (1935), p. 656.
26. Ibid., p. 662.
27. Quoted in Michael Stolleis, 'Community and national community (Volksgemeinschaft): reflections on legal terminology under National Socialism', in Michael Stolleis, *The Law under the Swastika* (Chicago: University of Chicago Press, 1998), p. 75.
28. Neesze, 'Verfassungsrechtliches Schrifttum', p. 396.
29. Ernst Rudolf Huber, 'Einheit und Gliederung des völkischen Rechts', *Zeitschrift für die gesamte Staatswissenschaft* 98 (1938), p. 331. For other critics, see Stolleis, *Geschichte des öffentlichen Rechts in Deutschland*, vol. 3, pp. 328–30.
30. Ernst Rudolf Huber, *Verfassungsrecht des Grossdeutschen Reiches* (Hamburg: Hanseatische Verlagsanstalt, 1939), pp. 163–7.
31. Carl Schmitt, 'Staat als ein konkreter, an eine geschichtliche Epoche gebundener Begriff' [1941], in Carl Schmitt, *Verfassungsrechtliche Aufsätze aus den Jahren 1924–1954* (Berlin: Duncker & Humblot, 1958), p. 379.
32. Carl Schmitt, 'Politik' [1936], in Carl Schmitt, *Staat, Grossraum, Nomos* (Berlin: Duncker & Humblot, 1995), p. 133.
33. Schmitt, *Staat, Bewegung, Volk*, p. 15.
34. Schmitt, 'Politik', p. 135.
35. Schmitt, *Staat, Bewegung, Volk*, pp. 36–41.
36. Ibid., p. 42. On the translation of *Artgleichheit*, see Peter Caldwell, 'National Socialism and constitutional law', *Cardozo Law Review* 16 (1995), p. 408.
37. Schmitt, *Staat, Bewegung, Volk*, p. 42.
38. Ernst Rudolf Huber, 'Die deutsche Staatswissenschaft', *Zeitschrift für die gesamte Staatswissenschaft* 95 (1934–35), p. 29.
39. Ibid., p. 30.
40. Ibid., p. 41.
41. Helmut Schelsky, 'Die Totaliät des Staates bei Hobbes', *Archiv für Rechts- und Sozialphilosophie* 31 (1937–8), p. 185.
42. Ibid.
43. See Gerwin Klinger, 'Die Modernisierung des NS-Staates aus dem Geist der Anthropologie', in Wolfgang Bialas and Manfred Gangl (eds),

Intellektuelle im Nationalsozialismus (Frankfurt am Main: Peter Lang, 2000), pp. 299–324.

44. Hans Peter Ipsen, *Politik und Justiz* (Hamburg: Hanseatische Verlagsanstalt, 1937), p. 82.
45. Ibid., pp. 283–4.
46. Ibid., p. 276.
47. Ibid., pp. 303–10.
48. See Ebergard Laux, 'Führung und Verwaltung in der Rechtslehre des Nationalsozialismus', in Dieter Rebentisch and Karl Teppe (eds), *Verwaltung contra Menschenführung im Staat Hitlers* (Göttingen: Vandenhoeck & Ruprecht, 1986), p. 52.
49. Ibid., p. 60.
50. Huber, 'Einheit und Gliederung des völkischen Rechts', p. 333.
51. Johannes Heckel, *Wehrverfassung und Wehrrecht des Grossdeutschen Reiches* (Hamburg: Hanseatische Verlagsanstalt, 1939), p. 37.
52. Huber, *Verfassungsrecht des Grossdeutschen Reiches*, p. 199.
53. Stolleis, *Geschichte des öffentlichen Rechts in Deutschland*, pp. 351–80.
54. Ernst Forsthoff, *Die Verwaltung als Leistungsträger* (Stuttgart: Kohlhammer, 1938), p. 47.
55. Ibid., p. 13.
56. Ibid., pp. 17–18.
57. Werner Best, 'Grundfragen einer deutschen Grossraum-Verwaltung', in Stuckart et al., *Festgabe für Heinrich Himmler*, pp. 36–7.
58. Reinhard Höhn, 'Volk, Staat, Reich', *Volk im Werden* 4 (1936), p. 372. For Laband's argument, see above, Chapter 1.
59. Höhn, 'Staat und Rechtsgemeinschaft', p. 662.
60. Thus Huber, *Verfassungsrecht des Grossdeutschen Reiches*, p. 361.
61. Wilhelm Sauer, 'Schöpferisches Volkstum als nationales und weltpolitisches Prinzip', *Archiv für Rechts- und Sozialphilosophie* 27 (1933), pp. 19, 17, 6.
62. Ibid., p. 6.
63. Huber, *Verfassungsrecht des Grossdeutschen Reiches*, pp. 153–4.
64. Arnold Köttgen, 'Vom deutschen Staatsleben', *Jahrbuch des öffentlichen Rechts der Genewart*, 24 (1937), p. 63.
65. Quoted in Horst Dreier, 'Die deutsche Staatsrechtslehre in der Zeit des Nationalsozialismus', *Veröffentlichungen der Vereinigung der deutschen Staatsrechtslehrer* 60 (2001), p. 42.
66. Walter Sommer, 'Die NSDAP als Verwaltungsträger', in Hans Frank (ed.), *Deutsches Verwaltungsrecht* (Munich: Eher, 1937), p. 169.
67. Hilger, *Rechtsstaatsbegriffe im Dritten Reich*, pp. 83–4.
68. Carl Schmitt, *Über die drei Arten des Rechtswissenschaftlichen Denkens* (Hamburg: Hanseatische Verlagsanstalt, 1934), p. 32.
69. Ibid., pp. 63–4.
70. Ibid., pp. 58–9.

71. On Schmitt's rejection of the concept of the *Rechtsstaat*, see 'Was bedeutet der Streit um den "Rechtsstaat"?', *Zeitschrift für die gesamte Staatswissenschaft* 95 (1935), pp. 189–201.

72. Werner Best, 'Die politische Polizei des Dritten Reiches', in Frank (ed.), *Deutsches Verwaltungsrecht*, p. 424.

73. See the comments of Ernst Wolgast quoted in Eduard Bristler, *National-sozialistische Völkerrecht* (Zurich: Europa, 1938), pp. 66–7.

74. Hermann Jahrreis, 'Wandel der Weltordnung', *Zeitschrift für Öffentliches Recht* 21 (1942), p. 519.

75. See also: 'But we will not subject ourselves spiritually to the coercive fictions of a dead positivism'. Carl Schmitt, *Nationalsozialismus und Völkerrecht* (Berlin: Duncker & Dünnhaupt, 1934), p. 29.

76. Fr. von Rauchhaupt, *Völkerrecht* (Munich: Voglrieder, 1936), p. 33.

77. Ibid., p. 124.

78. Gustav Adolf Walz, 'Das Verhältnis von Völkerrecht und staatlicher Recht nach nationalsozialistischer Rechtsauffassung', *Zeitschrift für Völkerrecht*, 18 (1934), pp. 146–7.

79. Hans Keller, *Das Recht der Völker* (Berlin: Franz Vahlen, 1938), pp. 124–5.

80. Ibid., pp. 105–15.

81. As Lawrence Preuss noted, such theorists had no explanation for the failure of Scandinavians to share this view: 'National Socialist conceptions of international law', *American Political Science Review* 29 (1935), p. 606.

82. Werner Best, 'Rechtsbegriff und "Völkerrecht"', *Deutsches Recht* 9 (1939), pp. 1,347–8.

83. Carl Heinrich Triepel, *Die Hegemonie* (Stuttgart: Kohlhammer, 1943), p. 202.

84. Carl Schmitt, *Die Wendung zum diskriminierenden Kriegsbegriff* (Berlin: Duncker & Humblot, 1938).

85. Carl Schmitt, *Völkerrechtliche Grossraumordnung*, 4th edn (Berlin: Deutscher Rechtsverlag, 1941), p. 49.

86. Ibid., p. 36.

87. Ernst Rudolf Huber, 'Positionen und Begriffe', *Zeitschrift für die gesamte Staatswissenschaft* 101 (1941), p. 43.

88. Werner Best, 'Nochmals: Völkische Grossraumordnung statt "Völkerrechtliche" Grossraumordnung', *Deutsches Recht* 11 (1941), p. 1,534.

89. Reinhard Höhn, 'Grossraumordnung und völkisches Rechtsdenken', *Reich – Volksordnung – Lebensraum* 1 (1941), pp. 279–81.

4

The Political Thought of the Exiles

The experience of exile, especially exile to the USA, formed part of the 'Great Migration' that H. Stuart Hughes has called the 'the most important cultural event – or series of events – of the second quarter of the twentieth century'.[1] Exile was far from being a purely German experience. It was a European-wide phenomenon, but Germans and Austrians accounted for about two-thirds of those who left Europe for America. Some of those who remained in continental Europe fell within the grip of National Socialism or its allies for a second time, and some of these did not survive. Others found refuge in the handful of countries that managed to remain neutral throughout the war, as did Wilhelm Röpke in Switzerland, or in England, as did Gerhard Leibholz, or even in New Zealand, as did Karl Popper.

That exile was a 'series of events' reflected the combination of external events – whether individuals were dismissed in the initial wave of persecution at the beginning of the Third Reich, or whether they sought refuge in France, as did Hannah Arendt, or in Spain, as did Hans Morgenthau, before being driven to seek refuge elsewhere – and their perceptions about the immediacy of the threat. Again, the difficulty of grasping the true nature of the Third Reich played a part in shaping decisions about whether, and when, to take the step of exile with all its attendant uncertainties in a world still in the grip of economic depression. The core members of the Institute for Social Research were unusual in grasping the degree of the threat early and making preparations for exile. Leo Löwenthal later recalled that the day after the September 1930 election in which the National Socialists made their first electoral breakthrough, the Instiutute began preparing for exile.[2] Others hesitated for varying reasons. Theodor Adorno delayed his departure until 1934 in the expectation that a military coup would end the National Socialists' domination.[3] Ernst Fraenkel delayed his departure until 1938 using the remaining and shrinking legal scope to protect the victims of the regime while engaging in illegal activity, the utility of which was increasingly questioned.[4] Family ties

107

and worry about the prospects for a German jurist in a foreign country also made Leibholz hesitate until 1938, which he later admitted was a mistake.[5]

Exile meant being deprived of German citizenship and, for German Jews, being exposed to the anti-semitic prejudices of the police and immigration officials across Europe and in the new world. Exile meant becoming part of what Hannah Arendt described as the 'most important product of recent history', as a 'completely new class of men': the stateless.[6] The condition of statelessness inevitably coloured perceptions of the meaning of politics, the nature of the state and the rule of law. The impact was enhanced by the fact that their exclusion from their home state took place at a time when migration, and international commerce, faced greater barriers than before the First World War. From the perspective of the end of the Second World War, the previous thirty years appeared as a period of international 'disintegration'. Nations not only imposed new restrictions on immigration, they also legislated to increase the reasons for non-voluntary loss of citizenship. The first major study of this phenomenon, published in 1937, noted: 'Today, there is still no principle of international law that generally prohibits expatriation leading to statelessness'.[7]

Culturally, the exiles were suspended between two worlds. Commitment to their native culture and to the principle that the National Socialists should not be the only ones allowed to speak for German culture in the German language induced the Institute for Social Research to continue to publish its journal in German, despite repeated warnings from its supporters that this unnecessarily restricted the impact of its ideas in America. It was only in 1940, after the German invasion of France, that the journal appeared in English under the title *Studies in Philosophy and Social Science* and only in 1941 that an issue of the journal was explicitly dedicated to 'specifically American subject matter'.[8] Yet it is misleading to portray the experience as a purely negative one. America was a relatively egalitarian society in the sense of lacking the more hierarchical social traditions of European societies. Some adapted to this society so well that they became part of the American intellectual tradition and culture. John Herz, for example, recalled returning to this 'new homeland' at the end of a brief visit to Germany after the war and added: 'For me, as for many others, it had not been exile but emigration'.[9] Herz and the even more influential Hans J. Morgenthau are examples of those who became so much a part of American political thought that the significance of their German origins for their ideas had to be subsequently rediscovered at a much later date.[10]

For many, the period of exile, whether it ended with a return to Germany or turned into emigration, meant reflection on the forces that had driven them into exile and especially on the nature of the Third Reich. Some looked to distinctive characteristics of the German political tradition in order to explain events and the nature of the state in the Third Reich. Many were influenced by more or less sophisticated Marxist accounts that related the German experience and forms of fascism to the development of the capitalist economic order.[11] Others were so shaken by the barbarity of the regime, especially as information about the Holocaust began to seep through, that they could account for what had happened only in terms of a more deep-rooted collapse of civilisation that called into question the entire tradition of western thought. A few already held that the totalitarian form of government was a product of socialism and hence prepared the ground for the identification of National Socialist Germany and the Soviet Union as totalitarian regimes.

These differences were bound up with their positions in the debates that took place in the Weimar Republic and the Austrian Republic and with their estimation of the prospects of democratic forms of government. For much of the period of exile, this appeared to be at best an open question. In the contest between democracy and autocracy, as Karl Loewenstein presented it, one of the factors strengthening the cause of autocracy was the 'assumption that autocracy has entrenched itself as the definite form of modern government'.[12] For Loewenstein, writing in the mid-1930s, this presumption was not necessarily correct. Loewenstein's cautious optimism was still evident in the first edition of his *Hitler's Germany*, in which he considered the regime to be an 'experiment' that would be defeated in war; but, in the second edition, in 1940, he considered that it 'may well become the blueprint for the political society of the future'.[13] The embattled position of systems of government based on parliamentary party systems, and the sense that they belonged to an era that was coming to an end, took such a firm grip in some minds that not even the defeat of Germany shook it loose. Thus Herbert Marcuse could still write in 1947: 'the world is dividing into a neo-fascist and a Soviet camp. What still remains of democratic-liberal forms will be crushed between the two camps or absorbed by them.'[14]

The comparatively clear division of the world into competing camps, whether construed as a competition that still left hope for democratic forms of government, or not, did not necessarily make sense of the international order. The road to the heterogeneous coalition that finally defeated Germany was a long and tortuous one. Appeasement, American isolationism, the alliance between Germany and the Soviet Union and the subsequent German invasion of the Soviet Union formed the backcloth for an interpretation of the international order as one governed by suspicion and uncertainty. That the interdependence of states discerned by German theorists before the First World War and the hopes for a less violent world embodied in the League of Nations had failed to prevent an even worse outbreak of international disorder induced in some of the exiles scepticism about the faith that had been invested in international law. The state, not law, returned to the centre of the stage.

The state and statelessness

To some extent, the problem that confronted the exiles resembled the problem that confronted those within the regime, namely: how could one reconcile the façade of unity and coherence with the dynamism and anarchic traits? Although constrained by neither the need nor the desire to justify the regime, the concentration of power seemed overwhelming to some. Shortly before agreeing to return to Germany, Carl J. Friedrich gave a paper on 'The unique character of totalitarian society', in which category he included the Third Reich and the Soviet Union. There, he argued that the totalitarian society is defined by five sets of characteristics, namely an 'official ideology . . . covering all vital aspects of man's existence', a 'single mass party . . . organized in a strictly hierarchical, oligarchical manner, usually under a single leader', a 'technologically conditioned near complete' monopoly of armed force, a similar monopoly of mass communications and a 'system of terroristic police control'.[15] This model of totalitarianism became extremely influential in the western world, yet its image of control, coherence and hierarchy glossed over the ambiguities that had bothered many of the exiles.

Leibholz was also struck by the unconstrained power that the regime exercised. For him, the key feature was the compulsive intolerance of any rights, institutions or groups with which the totalitarian state might have to compromise. Compromise and the totalitarian state are mutually exclusive: 'A totalitarian state always has the alternative: to be a total state or *not* to exist'.[16] Compromise, which

Kelsen had seen as the core of the democratic order and as the inevitable conclusion to be drawn from the acceptance of a relativistic stance, is excluded. This suggested to Loewenstein that Hitler's position within the state and his relationship to his followers could only be explained by 'evaluating the Third Reich less in terms of political science than of political theology'.[17] Both Leibholz and Loewenstein were struggling to find the appropriate formulation for a state whose reality was self-defined to the point that any other definition of reality, any institution or group that might challenge that reality, was simply incompatible with its existence.

This peculiar quality of the regime was dealt with at greater length by Hannah Arendt. She argued that the root cause lies in the nature of ideologies. Ideologies, she claimed, are comprehensive explanations orientated towards past and future as well as the present, all of which they explain by reference to a single idea – race in the case of National Socialism. Secondly, they are 'emancipated from the reality that we perceive with our five senses' and insist 'on a "truer" reality concealed behind all perceptible things'. Thirdly, they compensate for their neglect of experience by substituting a 'kind of logical deduction' for it.[18] The key point, however, is that totalitarianism is an attempt to shape the world around it in accordance with this ideological vision. For Arendt, totalitarianism is frighteningly novel, but not in the content of its ideology. It is the fact that totalitarian movements act on the basis of the ideology that matters:

> the Nazis *acted* as thought the world were dominated by the Jews and needed a counter-conspiracy to defend itself. Racism for them was no longer a debatable theory of dubious scientific value, but was being realized every day in the functioning hierarchy of a political organization in whose framework it would have been very 'unrealistic' to question it.[19]

The fact that the world as construed by the ideology is, as Arendt put it, 'fictitious' makes no difference.[20]

While Arendt's account of totalitarianism was formulated after the war, other exiles had been troubled by the peculiar features of the National Socialist state from the outset. This is evident in Loewenstein's comments on Hitler's position. He noted that 'if one tries to understand it in terms of constitutional law' then it is possible to refer to his appointment as Chancellor and various provisions formally enhancing his power. But he realised that such constitutional provisions had little bearing on Hitler's role in either his own eyes or those of his followers.[21] Again, Arendt pushed this point much further. It is significant here that her comments on the totalitarian state appear under the heading 'The So-called Totalitarian State'. She claimed there that it was not 'monolithic' and that many had recognised the 'peculiar "shapelessness"' of totalitarian government. Laws were no guide to how the state and its agencies acted, because laws formally remained in place when they were clearly obsolete, and regulations that informed actual behaviour were not made public. In both Soviet Russia and the Third Reich, the only reliable assumption was that 'the more visible government agencies are, the less power they carry'.[22]

In a work drafted before fleeing the Third Reich, but not published in revised form until 1941, Fraenkel sought to capture the ambiguity of the Third Reich under the title *The Dual State*. While Fraenkel traced certain features of the Third Reich back to fragments of Prussian history, primarily the sense of permanent military mobilisation, he drew a significant distinction between the dualistic structure of the nineteenth-century constitutional state and the dual or double state (*Doppelstaat*) of the Third Reich: 'While in the dualistic [*dualistischen*] state two independent powers – prince and estates, monarch and people – have to work together before a legally effective act of state can appear, the double state [*Doppelstaat*] is characterised by the organisational unity of the state leadership'.[23] In Fraenkel's account, the double state is not characterised by the duality of party and state that struck most, including Arendt and Loewenstein,[24] since both were instances of the same dictatorship.[25] The duality is that between the decree state (*Massnahmestaat*) and the norm state (*Normenstaat*) which, he claimed, had first been noticed during the First World War by Emil Lederer.[26] The decree state designated the unrestrained use of decree power that makes the state of siege a permanent and potentially all-encompassing feature of the regime. Yet the regime did not rely purely upon this arbitrary decree power. Certain aspects of life, primarily the capitalist economy upon which the regime depended, could be, and were, regulated by norms, but there were no spheres that were immune to the decree state. Fraenkel's choice of the term double or dual state is clearly not intended to refer to competing agencies or complementary agencies: '*The norm state and the decree state are two competing systems of order and not two complementary powers*'.[27]

For Franz Neumann in his aptly titled book *Behemoth*, even this conceded too much, for it did not do justice to the complete absence of anything warranting the name 'law'. But this induced him to ask whether the Third Reich counted as a state at all. If, he argued, the rule of law defines the state, then the answer is clearly no. He considered an alternative definition of states as 'rationally operating machineries disposing of the monopoly of coercive power'.[28] This, however, presumed that there was a unified political power in the Third Reich. Neumann rejected this too; for Germany, he wrote, 'is organized in four solid, centralized groups, each operating under the leadership principle, each with a legislative, administrative, and judicial power of its own'.[29] In effect, each of these four groups, the Party, the army, the bureaucracy and industry, resembled a state. Neumann's point, of course, is that there cannot be four states within a state. Quite consistently, Neumann concluded that the Third Reich was not a state at all. That left him with the problem of explaining what it was: 'I venture to suggest that we are confronted with a form of society in which the ruling groups control the rest of the population directly, without the mediation of that rational though coercive apparatus hitherto known as the state'.[30]

Max Horkheimer, the Director of the Institute of Social Research to which Neumann belonged, sought to use the analogy of rackets to capture this phenomenon, though he also extended it into a more general account of domination. Reference to racketeering in America helped to suggest this more extensive usage which culminated in the blunt assertion: 'The basic form of domination is the racket'.[31] It also fitted in with the Marxist approach that he shared with Neumann insofar as rackets are a form of exploitation, though his model of rackets had little else in common with Marx's account of capitalist exploitation. Like Neumann's organised groups, in Horkheimer's rackets domination is direct, unmediated by law or the state. The analogy of rackets has a host of other connotations. The archetypal form of racket is the protection racket in which, on the one hand, protection against harm is offered while, on the other hand, tribute is extracted under the threat of inflicting harm. Horkheimer also emphasised the parasitic nature of rackets, which he claimed corresponds to the way in which all forms of social domination involve the monopolisation of socially necessary functions in order to assert the domination of the ruling group over the subordinate classes as well as the competition between different ruling groups.[32] Horkheimer pushed the analogy too far when he suggested that beneath the façade of unity in the Third Reich there was a vicious struggle for power which 'is so great that Germany could dissolve overnight into a chaos of gangster battles'.[33] This neglected the ability of the competing groups within the Third Reich to reach at least informal compromises at least so long as expansion by conquest opened up new opportunities for the various agencies, which was better grasped by Neumann and another member of the Institute, Otto Kirchheimer.[34] Yet Horkheimer's fragmentary theory of rackets does mark the opposite end of the spectrum from Friedrich's emphasis upon coherence and coordination, without losing sight of the impotence of the individual within the Third Reich.

One of the motives for Horkheimer's dissolution of the concept of the state into that of the protection racket lay in his own experience as a Jewish refugee: 'The greatest error of the Jews is this: that for millennia they have not exercised any kind of domination, they were always forced to rely on protection, however rich they might be'.[35] That exiled Jews and the stateless more widely were devoid even of any protection symbolised for Arendt, who disliked Horkheimer's Institute, a general crisis of the nation state. Just as Neumann saw 'security, order, law and equality before the law' as part of the tradition of the western state, so Arendt saw the state as an 'instrument of the law'.[36] According to Arendt, the triumph of the concept of the nation, which was not peculiar to Germany, represented a crisis for the nation state. The state principle rests on the idea of equality before the law; and, once this has broken down, 'the nation dissolves into an anarchic mass of over- and underprivileged individuals'.[37] The archetype of the underprivileged individual is the stateless person, bereft of protection by any government. All that the stateless person has to fall back on is his supposed rights as a mere human being. Yet, Arendt argued, the experience of the stateless revealed the fragility of precisely those rights. For the stateless, even the 'prolongation of their lives is due to charity and not to right, for no law exists which could force the nations to feed them'.[38] Loss of any and all political status, the condition of the stateless, amounts in Arendt's explanation to 'expulsion from humanity altogether'.[39] Compulsory deprivation of citizenship in a world of nation states leaves the stateless in a void in which the stateless individual has fewer rights than a convicted criminal, who is at least left with some rights as opposed to none at all. There is in Arendt's account a curious parallel between the disintegration of the state within the Third Reich and the deprivation of statehood in the figure of the exile.

The concept of politics

Looking back on the relationship between economics and politics in the first half of the twentieth century, Neumann concluded: 'The primacy of politics was always a fact, which was at times glossed over, at times openly recognized. In the structure of totalitarian states the circumstances are so clear that one need not waste many words.'[40] Neumann and his colleagues in the Institute for Social Research had begun as Marxists and in some respects remained so. The link between the capitalist economy and the major political phenomena of the first half of the twentieth century was summed up in Horkheimer's assertion that 'whoever is not willing to talk about capitalism should also keep quiet about fascism'.[41] This had not led them into a simple correspondence theory relating political phenomena to economic development in an unmediated way. Yet they were all agreed that National Socialism and fascism more generally were of epochal significance. It was this that induced Neumann to assert the primacy of politics and Horkheimer to proclaim: 'Once Fascism had developed in European society, we are now able to find its hallmarks in earlier stages of history, but it would be an error to say that because of those traces the development was a necessary one'.[42] Recognition of the primacy of politics meant a change of perspective that affected their assessment of the pre-fascist era, indeed of the entire western tradition.

In the work of Horkheimer and Adorno, the principle of the primacy of politics found expression in a theory of domination that embraced philosophical arguments reaching back to the very beginning of European enlightenment with the ancient Greeks. Enlightenment was construed as an attempt to escape from the fear embodied in myths, an attempt already evident in those myths. Yet the culmination of this was, they wrote, that:

> Since it exposes substantial goals as the power of nature over mind, as the erosion of its self-legislation, reason is – by virtue of its very formality – at the service of any natural interest. Thinking becomes an organic medium pure and simple, and reverts to nature . . . After the short intermezzo of liberalism, in which the bourgeois kept one another in check, domination appears as archaic terror in a fascistically rationalized form.[43]

By interpreting fascism as the culmination of a cultural process in which all substantive goals, whether of humanity or political community, were revealed as mere products of nature, Horkheimer and Adorno left little space in which they could articulate an alternative. The primacy of politics as domination was too pervasive. Horkheimer did glimpse an alternative when he wrote to Adorno suggesting that:

To address someone ultimately means to recognize him as the future possible member of an association of free men. Speech posits a common relation to truth, therefore to the innermost affirmation of the alien existence which is addressed . . . The speech of an overseer in a concentration camp is in itself a fearful nonsense completely regardless of its content.[44]

This insight was, however, left undeveloped. Despite the pessimism of the overarching argument, they were still able to expose the irrationality of, for example, the persecution and murder of the Jews in the sense that it was economically irrational, though that too served to emphasise the primacy of politics as domination.[45]

Fear, myth and the irrational were prominent in several other approaches to politics despite the fact that their authors shared little or none of the Marxian and Hegelian philosophy that lay behind the arguments of Adorno and Horkheimer and their colleagues in the Institute for Social Research. Indeed, it is only a slight exaggeration to say that insight into the primacy of politics led to insistence on the primacy of fear. That is evident, for example, in a study of Hobbes by Leo Strauss which was critically reviewed for the Institute, though his emphasis upon fear received approval.[46] According to Strauss, Hobbes's justification for the law and state lies in an account of human reason and passion in which fear of death is decisive. Strauss wrote that he found it 'striking' that Hobbes used the expression 'avoiding death' in preference to 'preserving life'. He continued by arguing that it was not merely death as an inevitable natural fact that mattered, nor even the possibility of an 'agonizing' death that might be alleviated through some medical intervention. What concerned Hobbes, so Strauss argued, is the fear of 'violent death at the hands of other men'. Without the state and law, there can be no escape from this fear, for the attempt to do so through killing an enemy would still leave the fear of all those who remained. In Strauss's words: 'This fear is a mutual fear, i.e. it is the fear each man has of every other man as his potential murderer'.[47]

For Herz, it was not Hobbes but an Italian, Guglielmo Ferrero, whose words crystallised the centrality of fear: 'Power is the supreme manifestation of the fear that man has created for himself by his efforts to liberate himself. It is perhaps the most profound and obscure secret of history.'[48] Herz's elaboration of this insight did not involve the reference to human passions that played an important part in Strauss's interpretation of Hobbes. In fact, Herz explicitly severed his explanation from any assumptions about human nature. He relied simply on the idea that each individual or state, fearful of the uncertain intentions of others, will seek to enhance its own security. The others, whether individuals or states, cannot be sure of the intentions of this individual or state and will be fearful of the preparations that the first makes for its own defence, which could equally become means of aggression. They too will take precautions which will further enhance the fear of the first. The ensuing 'security dilemma', as Herz came to call it, is a vicious circle driven forward not by malign intent but by uncertainty and the precautions that each takes to secure its own security. Herz did not transfigure this security dilemma into the essence of politics in the way that Carl Schmitt had done with the distinction between friend and foe. Nor did he abandon hope of mitigating its vicious nature. He did see it as an inescapable backcloth that political calculation is foolish to ignore. That such otherwise diverse theorists should converge in making fear the key to their understanding of the political condition is, of course, hardly surprising in the light of what they witnessed and what they had to fear.

It is not difficult to see how the emergence of the National Socialist and fascist regimes informed and consolidated other understandings of politics. The quasi-religious nature of these regimes was widely noted. It was this that was taken up by Eric Voegelin in his *Die politischen Religionen* (The Political Religions).[49] Near the beginning of the book, Voegelin invoked Georg Jellinek's definition of the state, albeit without naming him, and focused on Jellinek's reference to an 'original' power of domination. This has to refer, Voegelin claimed, to an absolute power, and such a power can only be understood ultimately as a divine power.[50] Although Voegelin briefly examined an ultimately unsuccessful attempt to establish a political religion in ancient Egypt, it was Christian Europe that provided him with the elements that structured his concept of political religions, namely a hierarchy of offices construed as part of a hierarchy culminating in God, the ecclesia or community construed as the *corpus mysticum* of the Christians united with Christ, and the vision of the apocalypse. All these, he continued, had been given a this-worldly reference point with what he described as the 'decapitation of God'.[51] More specifically, once severed from any relation to God, the hierarchy of offices became available for any movement that could effectively mobilise the religious symbols of a mystic community and an apocalyptic vision, which is exactly what the political religions of the twentieth century had done. Underlying this point was the conviction that political community is also a religious order and that the attempt to understand the political as something 'in which we only have to deal with questions of the organisation of law and power' is misguided.[52] The claim that National Socialism was one kind of response to genuine religious needs exposed him to the charge of supporting National Socialism, a charge that he bitterly rejected from his American exile. Nor did he did retract any of his arguments, insisting that: 'One cannot fight a satanic force with ethics and humanity alone'.[53]

One difficulty with Voegelin's assessment was that the contrast between the 'religious and philosophical transcendentalists' on the one hand and the 'immanentist sectarians' on the other made the distinctions between liberals and totalitarians seem secondary.[54] That was a mistake to which Arendt did not succumb. She saw totalitarianism not just as a political phenomenon but as an attempt to abolish the human capacity for political action, an attempt at 'the transformation of human nature itself'.[55] Here, political action means the ability to begin something new which presupposes 'recognition of my fellow men or our fellow nations as subjects, as builders of worlds or co-builders of a common world'.[56] A political framework, whose creation is a political act, requires a political status. Spontaneity is innate but meaningless without some political framework in which it can be recognised. All this totalitarianism seeks to destroy, in archetypal fashion in the concentration camps that Arendt described as the laboratories of totalitarianism. Consequently, she claimed that the 'first step on the road to total domination is to kill the juridical person in man'.[57] The death of the 'juridical person' is also the fate of the stateless person who, unlike the inmate of the concentration camp, may enjoy physical safety by virtue of some charitable act and may enjoy freedom of movement and opinion. But, for Arendt, this did not change the fate of the stateless, for they 'are deprived, not of the right of freedom, but of the right to action'.[58] Just as she sought to salvage the significance of the state from the experience of statelessness, so too she sought to salvage the significance of politics from what she saw as the National Socialist attempt to suppress its very existence.

Collective identity and tribal nationalism

The assertive nationalism of the Third Reich and the phenomenon of statelessness inevitably focused attention on nationalism. This, however, presented the exiles with two dilemmas. The first was whether to emphasise the peculiar character of nationalism as it developed in Germany or the broader characteristics of nationalism. The second was how to reconcile the power of the nationalism embodied in the Third Reich with insight into its artificiality. Both Arendt and Karl Popper believed that they were faced with a form of nationalism that could be described as tribal, though their accounts of tribal nationalism differed significantly. For Popper, the phenomenon with which he was confronted in the middle of the twentieth century was essentially the same as that which emerged among the ancient Greeks. Tribal nationalism was an attempt to reassert the authority of a 'tribal or "closed society"', with its submission to magical forces against what was seen as the corrosive effects of the 'open society' that dispensed with belief in magic and gods and placed its faith in the critical faculties of mankind and the democratic order.[59] Popper located the origins of his open society in fifth-century BC Athens where, he claimed, seafaring and commerce shook the bonds of tribal society and opened up the way for democracy. That seafaring and commerce were the foundations of Athenian imperialism did not concern him greatly. Indeed, he wrote that 'it is necessary, I believe, to see that tribalist exclusiveness and self-sufficiency could be superseded only by some form of imperialism'.[60]

Popper's hostility to nationalism and sympathy for empire were rooted in his own origins as a citizen of the multi-ethnic Habsburg Empire and the fact that he found refuge in the British Commonwealth.[61] He argued that, ever since the empire of Alexander the Great, tribal nationalism had been displaced by empire and multi-ethnic communities.[62] There is, in fact, nothing natural about nationalism at all: 'the idea that there exist natural units like nations, or linguistic or racial groups is entirely fictitious'.[63] Given his account of the apparent triumph of empire over the closed society and his assertion that political theories of nationalism had disappeared for two millennia, it is not surprising that he had some difficulty accounting for its re-emergence, especially in central Europe. He wrote that the rise of German nationalism was 'a rather strange story', for central Europe was one of the most ethnically mixed and diverse parts of Europe. Popper effectively relied upon the idea that German reaction to the impact of revolutionary France, including Napoleon's invasion of Germany, was the proximate cause, though he described this as 'something like an historical accident'.[64] He struggled to account for the modern resurgence of tribal nationalism because he held it be so thoroughly artificial as well as destructive of all that he regarded as valuable, especially democracy, cosmopolitanism and equalitarianism, as well as empire because he believed that imperialism had fostered all of these things.

Popper's account was extremely wide-ranging and highly selective. So too was that of Hannah Arendt, albeit in a different and much more nuanced way. She too showed some sympathy for ancient empires, or at least for the Roman Empire. Since the latter defined itself in terms of law, it could integrate conquered peoples simply by imposing upon them the same law. This, however, was increasingly problematic in the modern world of nation states, for:

> The nation-state, however, based upon a homogenous population's active consent to its government . . . lacked such a unifying principle and would, in the case of conquest, have to assimilate rather than to integrate, to enforce consent rather than justice, that is, to degenerate into tyranny.[65]

She knew that, in fact, this is not what empires built by modern nation states had done, but her point is that modern nation states are unsuited to empire insofar as they cannot extend the principle upon which they are founded onto their imperial possessions. The Romans could.

For Arendt, tribal nationalism is inherently related to modern imperialism, for neither accepted the limitations imposed by the limited extent of the nation state. As long as nationalism remained confined to the modern nation state, it was 'bound to a defined national territory and controlled by pride in a limited nation-state'.[66] The nation state, at least as it was favoured by Arendt, is based upon the idea of citizenship, that is, of membership of the nation defined in terms of a common and equal possession of rights whose infringement is an affront to all, not just to those immediately affected by the violation of a right. Tribal nationalism, as defined by Arendt, is radically different to this. Tribal nationalism involves a 'concept of nationhood as something independent of state and territory'.[67] She found it embodied in diverse forms, in the Boers in the British Empire whose great trek from one part of territory to another prefigured, she thought, the rootlessness that was definitive of tribal nationalism, in which she included the pan-Slav and pan-German movements of the nineteenth and twentieth centuries. She illustrated what she meant by a quote from an Austrian pan-German, Georg von Schoenerer, who had proclaimed: 'It is our distinction . . . that we do not gravitate toward Vienna but gravitate to whatever place Germans may live in'.[68] This idea of a nation existing without any necessary relation to a specific state or to any specific delimited territory was also embodied, as Arendt emphasised, in the existence of the Jewish people: 'the Jews were a perfect model of a nation without a state and without visible institutions'.[69] They were also dependent upon the state for protection from the anti-semitism of people like Schoenerer. The triumph of the nation over the state, of tribal nationalism over the limited nationalism of the nation state, exposed the Jews to the anti-semites who regarded the state as entirely secondary. Arendt did not find any answer to this vulnerability that she found fully satisfactory, but her account of it is consistent with her support for a Jewish army that would fight alongside the Allies, that is, for a visible institution that could be recognised by Jews as their own and could be recognised by the Allied states.[70]

The members of the Institute for Social Research had little in common with Popper and stoutly defended the reputation of Hegel, whom Popper condemned for supposedly providing a philosophical justification for the new tribal nationalism. They had, however, a strong sense of the artificiality of the nation to which the National Socialists sacrificed both the concept of the state and the individual. Thus, for Herbert Marcuse, the national community in the Third Reich was essentially bogus. The mythological veneration of the natural existence of the community compensated for the absence of any true community of interests.[71] The studies of demagogic techniques by several members of the Institute, including those deployed by anti-semitic agitators in their American exile, encouraged them to focus on the ways in which collective identity can serve as a substitute for identity of interests. Thus, Löwenthal noted that the success of the demagogue has little to do with reason or interests. He simply sidesteps the issue of interests and 'depicts himself as one of the plain-folk, who thinks, lives and feels like them. In agitation this suggestion of proximity and intimacy takes the place of identification of interests.'[72] They extended this judgement to cover nationalism. They claimed that the more the egoistic individual is supposed to suppress his own interests the more the egoistic assertion of interest is encouraged at the level of the nation. The recurrent emphasis in their assessment of nationalism is, however, that there is something not quite genuine in the nationalist fervour. In this spirit, Horkheimer wrote of the 'Nazi blood community' as a 'racial racket'.[73] There is already a sense of underestimation of National Socialist ideology in Horkheimer's comments. This underestimation was also evident in Neumann's claim that the Jews were too useful as a scapegoat for the National Socialists to 'allow a complete extermination of the Jews'.[74] In the case of both Horkheimer and Neumann, insight into the manipulative dimension of national identity blinded them to the anti-semitic convictions that had threatened their own existence.

Neumann had sought to give an account of the intellectual history of German developments. He portrayed the political concept of the nation, culminating in the Jacobin vision of the nation as a community of free and equal citizens, as alien to the German tradition. Yet this account, deeply unsatisfactory in the eyes of Horkheimer, was not central to the Institute's, and Neumann's, emphasis upon the economic functions of nationalism and anti-semitism. Arendt, Popper and the members of the Institute were all aware of German precursors of the kind of nationalism they were confronted with, though they disagreed about who they were, and specifically German traditions formed only part, and in the case of Popper and the Institute a minor part, of their explanations. A specifically German tradition is much more central to Helmut Plesssner's *Die verspätete Nation* (The Belated Nation).[75] According to Plessner, 'Germany is the only country in Europe that is still on the road to becoming a nation state because the boundaries of the German nation do not coincide with the boundaries of the new *Reich*.'[76] The tortuous German road to a nation state had been aggravated by a number of factors. Plessner was well aware of the trauma of the First World War, defeat and Versailles, yet he insisted that German reactions had to be set in a much longer historical perspective. He dated German alienation from the west, which took such sharp form during and after the war, back to the sixteenth and seventeenth centuries.[77] Failure to connect the idea of the state to any sense of humanistic mission, whether this took the form of the English 'Common-wealth' or the French 'nation', formed part of the problem. So too did the 'alliance of politically indifferent Lutheranism and princely grandeur' which inhibited the formation of more radical religious movements capable of helping to create a vibrant public realm independent of political authority.[78] This specifically Prussian phenomenon accounted, however, for only part of Germany's traditions. Indeed, Plessner saw the problem in the very proliferation of German traditions that the belated nation had been unable to fuse together. There was no ideal behind which Germans could rally, and hence the only basis for the desired unity lay in 'a natural-historical foundation in the fact of the German nation'.[79] At the end of the day, Plessner too saw that there was something fake about the nationalism of the Third Reich.

The National Socialist movement versus militant democracy

Plessner had noted that in some cases the problem was a lack of traditions, for example in the absence of a tradition of autonomous and radical religious movements. The same suspicion that the novelty of the National Socialist movement lay in the rejection of tradition, in rootlessness and the weakness of previous, democratic, institutions was prominent in accounts of the National Socialist movement. Fraenkel sought to capture the peculiarity of the movement by developing suggestions that there was a discrepancy between Max Weber's tripartite model of forms of authority – traditional, rational and charismatic – and his dualistic distinction between society and community. It is clear, Fraenkel argued, that prominence of community and traditional forms of authority can be correlated. So too, the prominence of society can be correlated with a preference for rational, procedural forms of authority. There seemed, however, to be no point of correlation for charismatic authority of the kind operative in the Third Reich. Yet, he claimed, it did exist in the idea of the league (*Bund*). The point of this suggestion had less to do with clearing up perceived discrepancies in Weber's sociology and much more to do with accounting for the nature of the National Socialist movement in a way that disputed the National Socialists' rhetoric of community. In Fraenkel's words:

> The followers of the charismatic leader, the league, is not a community. Its members come together not on the basis of traditional customs, but on the basis of emotional experiences. The individual is born into the community, he enters the league by his own decision. The community intends to preserve traditional values [whereas] the uprooted individual joins up with the league.[80]

Several other exiles struggled to grasp the dynamics of the National Socialist movement in the light of its apparent lack of institutional stability, its novelty and the difficulty of relating it to stable and identifiable interests whether construed as rational or traditional. Horkeimer drew a distinction between reactionary movements whose membership might be characterised as a 'mob' and the 'staging of a bourgeois pseudo revolution with radical populist trappings, wholly contrary to any possible reorganization of society'.[81] Although slightly hesitant, he suggested that recent phenomena were probably better characterised as deformed versions of the 'bourgeois pseudo revolution'. He explored these through a wide-ranging survey including Cola di Rienzo and Gerolamo Savonarola, who he said had led such revolts in fourteenth- and fifteenth-century Italy, and Maximilien Robespierre. Despite the diversity of his examples, Horkheimer discerned a similar pattern in which the interests of the mobilised masses could be met to only a limited extent. Faced with this constraint, the leaders had resorted to an array of devices, including a cult of their own personality, the manipulation of the historical symbols of their country or state in carefully staged ceremonies and processions and the invocation of religion in one form of another. For Horkheimer, such techniques were not arbitrary or purely reflections of the psychological character of the leaders but responses to the social conditions in which these men found themselves.

Whereas Horkheimer looked to interests, for Arendt any relationship to interests, however conflictual, was impossible where the 'chief characteristic' of the masses

> is that they belong to no social or political body, and who therefore present a veritable chaos of individual interests. The fanaticism of members of totalitarian movements, so clearly different in quality from the greatest loyalty of members of ordinary parties, is produced by the lack of self-interest of masses who are quite prepared to sacrifice themselves.[82]

This willingness to sacrifice themselves did not arise, she argued, from the fact that they had been persuaded by totalitarian propaganda. The novelty of the totalitarian movements did not lie in their ideologies, nor were their successes to be ascribed to the oratorical skills of their leaders. Hitler's skill as an orator simply misled his opponents into believing that he was nothing more than a skilled orator. The novelty of totalitarianism lay not in its ideas or oratory but in its organisation, especially the development of front organisations. In Arendt's account, these organisations had several functions within both the rise to power of the totalitarian movement and the so-called totalitarian state. One key function was the paralysis or undermining of existing institutions.[83]

Despite their considerable and evident differences, both Horkheimer and Arendt argued that the techniques of the political movements that concerned them were important in explaining their relative success. Loewenstein turned this into a definition: '*Fascism is not an*

Ideology but a Political Technique.[84] It was a technique that had ruthlessly exploited the democracies' commitment to tolerate any form of opinion so long as it outwardly conformed to the rules of the democratic order. Fascism exploited all the freedoms and institutions of the democratic order, freedom of speech and assembly, elections and parliamentary activity, in order to build up a coercive apparatus intended to destroy democracy. In a much-used metaphor, Loewenstein denounced those who 'were unwilling to recognize that the mechanism of democracy is the Trojan horse by which the enemy enters the city'.[85] His answer to this problem was that democracy had to become militant, that is, it had to deploy a set of techniques that would cut the ground from under the fascist movements even at the expense of curtailing some of the fundamental rights associated with democracy. His conviction that this was possible was based upon an empirical survey of measures adopted by various governments in the 1930s. While militant democracy allowed for optimism in this sense, Loewenstein conceded that this would be, at least for some unspecified period, at the expense of understanding democracy as 'the application of disciplined authority, by liberal-minded men, for the ultimate ends of liberal government'.[86] The need for a militant democracy would be recalled when it came to re-establishing democracy in Germany.

Planning and the rule of law

One of the relatively widespread assumptions among those looking forward to the restoration of a democratic order was that it could not be founded on the model of the nineteenth-century laissez-faire state.[87] Within the Institute for Social Research, Frederick Pollock sketched a model of state capitalism on the assumption that free trade and free enterprise were being consigned to the past with no more prospect of revival than there had been for the residues of feudalism in post-Napoleonic France. Although he made provision for both democratic and totalitarian versions, he stressed that it was National Socialist Germany that had made most progress towards the model. The model itself specified that the market no longer served to coordinate production and consumption, this function being taken over by the state, which employed a series of methods including a 'pseudo-market' and recognised none of the previous limits on the scope of its activity. The totalitarian and democratic versions differ in that in the former the state is in the hands of a 'new ruling group, which has resulted from the merger of the most powerful vested interests', whereas in the latter the state remains sufficiently under the control of the people to 'prevent the bureaucracy from transforming its administrative position into an instrument of power'.[88] Economic laws, as they were known in the nineteenth century, no longer operate. The problems with which state capitalism is confronted are 'mere problems of administration'.[89] Even within the Institute, Pollock's model was disputed. Neumann was dismissive of both the coherence of the very idea of state capitalism, which he denied, and Pollock's judgement of developments in Germany.[90]

Despite the strength of Neumann's dispute with Pollock, the Marxist perspective shared by the Institute's members, now being seriously challenged by Pollock, had led both of them to regard the model of competitive capitalism as obsolete. For Neumann and Kirchheimer, that also meant a challenge to the function of law in the post-liberal economic world. They agreed that law as general law had arisen in what they described as essentially competitive capitalist economic systems, and that such law, intended to apply equally to a large number of enterprises, makes little sense where the state is confronted with a monopoly. Here, wrote Neumann, 'the individual measure is the only appropriate expression of the sovereign power'.[91] They agreed that natural law had been deployed to restrict progressive social legislation in the Weimar republic and that law in the Third Reich had become no more than an administrative technique. The real question was whether anything could be salvaged from these trends. Neumann gave the clearest answer, insisting that it is necessary to distinguish between the different functions fulfilled by general laws, not all of which are reducible to economic functions:

> If one does not draw these distinctions and sees in the generality of law nothing but a requirement of capitalist economy, then, of course, one must infer with Carl Schmitt that the general law, the independence of judges, and the separation of powers, must be abolished when capitalism dies.[92]

Fraenkel's attempt to deal with the prospects of the rule of law was orientated towards the specific post-war context that he anticipated in Germany, namely that some form of planned economy was inevitable. He looked to English and American experience for resources that might help but found none. English practices were too deeply rooted in the historical traditions of that country to be imitated. State intervention in America was organised through ad-hoc regulatory commissions that did not form part of an hierarchical bureaucracy.[93] They were not well placed to convert their administrative functions into a political power base in a way that continental bureaucracies were, but their characteristics were no more transferable than English legal culture. He did find one aspect of German traditions that he thought might help. This was that 'The idea of the *Rechtsstaat* is not opposed to state activity in the economic and social realms but signifies rather that state intervention must rest on written law'. He then repeated his judgement at the end of the Weimar Republic to the effect that the *Rechtsstaat* had been undermined not by an excess of legislative activity but by the crippling of the legislature.[94]

The conviction that some form of planning was inevitable and desirable as well as capable of reconciliation with the *Rechtsstaat* and militant democracy was widespread but not undisputed. For Friedrich Hayek, planning is inherently inimical to the rule of law. He wrote his book, *The Road to Serfdom*, to warn the England to which he had emigrated against the temptation of unwittingly following the path that had led Germany to Hitler and away from the principles of the nineteenth century. Although he insisted that prior to 1914 the German people had been 'more varied in its views than any other', he did agree that Germany had never truly shared these nineteenth-century beliefs, including laissez-faire economic principles.[95] Whereas Fraenkel thought that planning could be guided by legislation, Hayek argued that parliaments entrusted with planning will degenerate into 'talking shops' while the real activity will be carried out by administrative agencies.[96] Germans, he claimed, had been tempted down this road in the name of socialism and the reconciliation of socialism and nationalism, for which, among others, Oswald Spengler served as an example.[97] Indeed, Hayek naively accepted Spengler's account of the development of German political thought.

International law and power politics

If law was threatened by economic change and policy at the domestic level, the fragility of law in the international order was all too evident. Hans Kelsen continued to advocate the development of international law, but it is notable that others, including former pupils of Kelsen, who had espoused the cause of international law, entered increasingly strong reservations, albeit without abandoning the cause of international law entirely. The challenge posed by the Third Reich and other revisionist powers obviously played a strong part in this development. The most sustained analysis of ideas about the international order emerging from the Third Reich came from Herz. He distinguished two broad approaches, one based upon an appeal to natural law, the other based more firmly upon National Socialist racial theory.[98] He noted that both the National Socialists and the Soviet Union proclaimed that they would inaugurate a new form of international law in accordance with their respective philosophies. Neither, however, had succeeded: 'the actual international situation of Germany and also of Russia – their belonging to an existing state system has necessarily developed, in their foreign policies, "nationalistic" features which allowed only such theoretical "systems" to be practised as did not contradict political necessities'. Indeed, Germany had been even less successful than Russia.[99]

It is consistent with this rejection of German and Russian claims to have developed a new and distinctive form of international law that could serve as a guide to the actual practice of foreign policy that Herz increasingly focused on the structure of the state system. From this perspective, states appear both as the subjects of international law and as competing powers whose very existence is by no means guaranteed. They are dependent for their existence upon 'relations of power which prepare for their end at any moment and thereby pull the ground from under the rules applying to them'.[100] A similar pessimism was evident in the title of an article by Georg Schwarzenberger: 'The rule of law and the disintegration of international society'. Schwarzenberger drew a distinction between community and society according to whether any sense of solidarity can be detected. Summarising the distinction, he wrote that: 'Whereas the members of a community are united in spite of their individual existence, the members of a society are isolated in spite of their association'.[101] In fact, community was in catastrophic decline, and even international society, understood as the minimal prevention of a *bellum omnium contra omnes*, was under threat. The very presumption of the 'normality of peace' or even the possibility of clearly distinguishing between peace and war seemed questionable.[102] It also seemed questionable to Herz. Technical advances merely aggravated the problem. Indeed, well before the detonation of atomic weapons, Herz had already come to the dark speculation that:

> Unable to escape the vicious circle of mutual fear, insecurity, and conflict for power and to eliminate the life-and-death struggle from the societies formed by his own kind, the 'victor over Nature' may turn out to have been but another among Nature's abortive attempts to create a species capable of survival.[103]

Herz and Schwarzenberger did not abandon international law, and Herz held out some hope, albeit highly qualified, for a revival of the idea of collective security. Hans J. Morgenthau sought to salvage what he could after mounting an attack on the positivist approach to international law, understood as a 'logically coherent system'. International law, he argued, was nothing of the kind. Much of it did not even take the form of general law but consisted of 'individualised rules' whose meaning and significance is evident only by considering the specific context in which they are formulated.[104] He conceded that it had been true that states had been guided by their own interests, only abiding by international law while it served those interests; nevertheless, they had generally respected the 'fundamental rights of other states'.[105] He added that there is only an apparent paradox here. The restraint of states arose not from the force of law but from the fact that the moral principles behind these basic rights had filtered into the minds of statesmen, shaping and limiting what they could conceive of as being in the interests of their states. Now, however, all such constraint had been swept away by the example and practices of the totalitarian powers.[106]

The political ideas of the exiles were not constrained by the façade of unity to which those in the Third Reich usually had to pay obeisance, though some of the exiles were more adept at seeing through it than others. They also differed in the extent to which they perceived the emergence of totalitarian states, especially the Third Reich, as a more or less inevitable outcome of either German history or western civilisation. Attempting to account for these states affected their understanding of key political concepts, usually – but not inevitably – giving them a darker pessimistic tone. For some, that pessimism never truly evaporated. Yet it also forced them to confront the exercise of power without the comfort enjoyed by those who venerated power.

Notes

1. H. Stuart Hughes, *The Sea Change* [1973], p. 1 in H. Stuart Hughes, *Between Commitment and Disillusion* (Middletown, CT: Wesleyan University Press, 1987).
2. Leo Löwenthal, *Mitmachen wollte ich nie* (Frankfurt am Main: Suhrkamp, 1980), p. 67.
3. See his letter to Löwenthal of 6 July 1934 in ibid., p. 256.
4. See his 'Der Sinn illegaler Arbeit' [1935], in Ernst Fraenkel, *Gesammelte Schriften*, vol. 3 (Baden-Baden: Nomos, 1999), pp. 491–7.
5. Manfred H. Wiegandt, *Norm und Wirklichkeit* (Baden-Baden: Nomos, 1995), pp. 41–2.

6. Hannah Arendt, 'Zur Minderheitenfrage' [1940], in Hannah Arendt, *Vor Antisemitismus ist man nur noch auf dem Monde sicher* (Munich: Piper, 2000), p. 228.

7. H. Lessing, *Das Recht der Staatsangehörigkeit und die Aberkennung der Staatsangehörigkeit zu Straf- und Sicherungszwecken* (Leiden: Brill, 1937), p. 78.

8. Max Horkheimer, 'Preface', *Studies in Philosophy and Social Science* 9 (1941), p. 1. The previous title was *Zeitschrift für Sozialforschung*.

9. John H. Herz, *Vom Überleben* (Düsseldorf: Droste, 1984), p. 142.

10. For Morgenthau, see William Scheuerman, *Carl Schmitt: The End of Law* (Lanham: Rowan & Littlefield, 1999), pp. 225–51. For Herz, see Peter Stirk, 'John H. Herz: realism and the fragility of the international order', *Review of International Studies* 31 (2005), pp. 285–306.

11. See the recollections of Ferdinand Hermens, 'Die deutschen Emigranten in den Vereinigten Staaten und die alliierte Kriegsdiplomatie' [1967], in Ferdinand Hermens, *Zwischen Politik und Vernunft* (Berlin: Duncker & Humblot, 1969), pp. 225–8.

12. Karl Loewenstein, 'Autocracy versus democracy in contemporary Europe, II', *American Political Science Review* 29 (1935), p. 784.

13. Karl Loewenstein, 'Preface to the second edition', *Hitler's Germany*, 3rd edn (New York: Macmillan, 1944), p. xi.

14. Herbert Marcuse, '33 theses' [1947], in Herbert Marcuse, *Technology, War and Fascism* (London: Routledge, 1998), p. 217.

15. Carl J. Friedrich, 'The unique character of totalitarian society', in Carl J. Friedrich (ed.), *Totalitarianism* (New York: Grosset & Dunlap, 1953), pp. 52–3.

16. Gerhard Leibholz, 'Das Phänomen des totalen Staates' [1946], in Gerhard Leibholz, *Strukturprobleme der modernen Demokratie*, 3rd edn (Karlsruhe: Müller, 1967), p. 227.

17. Loewenstein, *Hitler's Germany*, p. 35.

18. Hannah Arendt, *The Origins of Totalitarianism*, 3rd edn (London: Allen & Unwin, 1967), pp. 470–1.

19. Ibid., p. 362.

20. Ibid., p. 391.

21. Loewenstein, *Hitler's Germany*, pp. 37–8.

22. Arendt, *The Origins of Totalitarianism*, p. 403.

23. Ernst Fraenkel, 'Der Urdoppelstaat' [1938], in *Gesammelte Schriften*, vol. 2, p. 421. The entire sentence is italicised in the original.

24. Arendt, *The Origins of Totalitarianism*, p. 395; Loewenstein, *Hitler's Germany*, p. 101.

25. Fraenkel, 'Der Urdoppelstaat', p. 276.

26. Ibid., pp. 436–7. On Lederer, see Chapter 1 above.

27. Fraenkel, 'Der Urdoppelstaat', p. 316.

28. Franz Neumann, *Behemoth* (London: Gollancz, 1942), p. 382.

29. Ibid., pp. 382–3.
30. Ibid., pp. 383–4.
31. Max Horkheimer, 'Die Rackets und der Geist' [1939–42], in Max Horkheimer, *Gesammelte Schriften*, vol. 12 (Frankfurt am Main: Fischer, 1985), p. 287.
32. Max Horkheimer, 'Zur Soziologie der Klassenverhältnisse' [1943], in Horkheimer, *Gesammelte Schriften*, vol. 12, pp. 101–2.
33. Max Horkheimer, 'The Jews and Europe' [1939], in Stephen Bronner and Douglas Kellner (eds), *Critical Theory and Society* (London: Routledge, 1989), p. 85.
34. Neumann, *Behemoth*, p. 383; Otto Kirchheimer, 'Changes in the structure of political compromise', *Studies in Philosophy and Social Sciences* 9 (1941), pp. 273–89.
35. Max Horkheimer, 'Jüdischer Charakter' [1939–40], in Horkheimer, *Gesammelte Schriften*, vol. 12, p. 263.
36. Neumann, *Behemoth*, p. 48; Arendt, *The Origins of Totalitarianism*, p. 275.
37. Ibid., p. 290.
38. Ibid., p. 296.
39. Ibid., p. 297.
40. Franz Neumann, 'Economics and politics in the twentieth century' [1951], in Franz Neumann, *The Democratic and the Authoritarian State* (New York: Free Press, 1957), p. 268.
41. Horkheimer, 'The Jews and Europe', p. 78.
42. Max Horkheimer, 'The authoritarian state' [1940], in Andrew Arato and Eike Gebhardt (eds), *The Essential Frankfurt School Reader* (Oxford: Blackwell, 1978), p. 101.
43. Max Horkheimer and Theodor W. Adorno, *Dialectic of Enlightenment* [1947] (London: Allen Lane, 1973), p. 87.
44. Max Horkheimer, *Gesammelte Schriften*, vol. 17 (Frankfurt am Main: Fischer, 1996), p. 172.
45. See Horkheimer and Adorno, *Dialectic of Enlightenment*, pp. 170–2.
46. By Herbert Marcuse, *Zeitschrift für Sozialforschung* 6 (1937), pp. 426–7.
47. Leo Strauss, *The Political Philosophy of Hobbes* [1936] (Chicago: University of Chicago Press, 1952), pp. 15–21. On this and Strauss's relationship with Schmitt, see John P. McCormick, 'Fear, technology and the state: Carl Schmitt, Leo Strauss and the revival of Hobbes in Weimar and National Socialist Germany', *Political Theory* 22 (1994), pp. 619–52.
48. John H. Herz, 'Power politics and world organization', *American Political Science Review* 36 (1942), p. 1,039.
49. Eric Voegelin, *Die politischen Religionen* [1938] (Munich: Fink, 1996). Although this was first published shortly before Voegelin's flight into exile from Austria, I include it under the heading of political ideas of the exiles.

50. Ibid., pp. 12–15.
51. Ibid., p. 31.
52. Ibid., p. 63.
53. 'Vorwort' (Christmas 1938), ibid., p. 6.
54. See Michael Henkel, *Eric Voegelin* (Hamburg: Junius, 1998), p. 116.
55. Arendt, *The Origins of Totalitarianism*, p. 458.
56. Ibid.
57. Ibid., p. 447.
58. Ibid., p. 296.
59. Karl Popper, *The Open Society and its Enemies*, vol. 1, 4th edn (London: Routledge & Kegan Paul, 1962), p. 1. As Popper explained in the Preface to the second edition, the book was finished while the outcome of the war was uncertain: ibid., p. vii.
60. Ibid., p. 181.
61. See the excellent account in Malachai Haim Hacohen, 'Dilemmas of cosmopolitanism: Karl Popper, Jewish identity, and "Central European culture"', *Journal of Modern History* 71 (1999), pp. 105–49.
62. Popper, *The Open Society and its Enemies*, vol. 2, p. 50.
63. Popper, *The Open Society and its Enemies*, vol. 1, p. 288.
64. Ibid., pp. 49–51.
65. Arendt, *The Origins of Totalitarianism*, p. 125.
66. Ibid., p. 228.
67. Ibid., p. 45.
68. Ibid., p. 232.
69. Ibid., pp. 239–40.
70. See Hannah Arendt, 'Von der Armee zur Brigade' [1944], in Arendt, *Vor Antisemitismus ist man nur noch auf dem Monde sicher*, pp. 165–8.
71. Herbert Marcuse, *Reason and Revolution* (London: Routledge, 1955), p. 414. The main part of the text was first published in 1941.
72. Leo Löwenthal, 'Prophets of deceit' [1949], in Leo Löwenthal, *False Prophets* (New Brunswick, NJ: Transaction, 1987), p. 129.
73. Max Horkheimer, 'Draft letter' [1942], in Horkheimer, *Gesammelte Schriften*, vol. 17, p. 295.
74. Neumann, *Behemoth*, p. 107.
75. This was originally published in 1935 under the title *Das Schicksal deutschen Geistes im Ausgang seiner bürgerliche Epoche* (The Fate of the German Spirit at the End of its Bourgeois Epoch). Marcuse wrote a dismissive review in *Zeitschrift für Sozialforschung* 6 (1937), pp. 184–5.
76. Helmuth Plessner, *Die verspätete Nation* [1959] (Frankfurt am Main: Suhrkamp, 1974), p. 38.
77. Ibid., pp. 41, 46.
78. Ibid., pp. 45–6.
79. Ibid., p. 96.
80. Fraenkel, 'Der Urdoppelstaat', p. 454.

81. Max Horkheimer, 'Egoism and freedom movements' [1936], in Max Horkheimer, *Between Philosophy and Social Science* (Cambridge, MA: MIT, 1993), p. 97.
82. Arendt, *The Origins of Totalitarianism*, p. 348.
83. Ibid., pp. 361, 364–72.
84. Karl Loewenstein, 'Militant democracy and fundamental rights I', *American Political Science Review* 31 (1937), p. 423.
85. Ibid., p. 424.
86. Karl Loewenstein, 'Militant democracy and fundamental rights II', *American Political Science Review* 31 (1937), p. 658.
87. For a combination of advocacy of planning and militant democracy, see Karl Mannheim, *Diagnosis of Our Time* (London: Kegan Paul, 1943), pp. 4–8.
88. Frederick Pollock, 'State capitalism', *Studies in Philosophy and Social Science* 9 (1941), pp. 201–2.
89. Ibid., p. 217.
90. Neumann, *Behemoth*, pp. 181–7.
91. Franz Neumann, 'The change in the function of law in modern society' [1937], in Neumann, *The Democratic and the Authoritarian State*, p. 52.
92. Franz Neumann, *The Rule of Law* [1935] (Leamington Spa: Berg, 1986), p. 257, and, more weakly, in Neumann, 'The change in the function of law in modern society', p. 66.
93. Ernst Fraenkel, ' "Rule of law" in einer sich wandelnden Welt' [1943–4], in Ernst Fraenkel, *Gesammelte Schriften*, vol. 3 (Baden-Baden: Nomos, 1999), p. 66.
94. Ibid., p. 67.
95. F. A. Hayek, *The Road to Serfdom* (London: Routledge, 1943), pp. 124, 140.
96. Ibid., p. 46.
97. Ibid., pp. 131–3.
98. Eduard Bristler [John H. Herz], *Die Völkerrechtlehre des National-sozialismus* (Zurich: Europa, 1938).
99. Joseph Florin and John H. Herz, 'Bolshevist and National Socialist doctrines of international law', *Social Research* 1:3 (1940), pp. 5–6.
100. Hans Herz [John H. Herz], 'Einige Bemerkungen zur Grundlegung des Völkerrechts', *Internationale Zeitschrift für Theorie des Rechts* 13 (1939), p. 283.
101. Georg Schwarzenberger, 'The rule of law and the disintegration of international society', *American Journal of International Law* 33 (1939), p. 60, and *Power Politics* (London: Cape, 1941), p. 35.
102. Georg Schwarzenberger, 'Jus pacis ac belli', *American Journal of International Law* 37 (1943), pp. 466, 468–9, 471, 479.
103. Herz, 'Power politics and world organization', p. 1042.

104. Hans J. Morgenthau, 'Positivism, functionalism and international law', *American Journal of International Law* 34 (1940), pp. 262, 271–2.
105. Hans J. Morgenthau, 'The resurrection of neutrality', *American Political Science Review* 33 (1939), p. 483.
106. Ibid., pp. 483–4.

5

Refounding the Democratic Order

The unconditional surrender of Germany and Allied assumption of full sovereign power raised the question of whether Germany had ceased to exist as a state. According to the old international concept of *debellatio* or subjugation, total defeat and the disintegration of all indigenous political institutions entitled the victor to assume full sovereignty and to annex the defeated nation. Although the Allied powers explicitly disavowed any intent to annex Germany, they acted in other respects as if the doctrine of subjugation was applicable. They recognised no principled limit on their authority, not even Hague Regulations governing the law of occupation, for those Regulations enjoined respect for existing laws, and the Allies obviously did not intend to respect the laws of the Third Reich. They assigned some parts of German territory to other states and eventually established two separate states on the bulk of German territory.[1] It is not surprising that most German legal and political theorists reacted to this situation by asserting the continuity of a German state in the hope that this might give them some leverage vis-à-vis the occupying powers. After the effective division of Germany, it served as part of the basis for the desire for reunification.[2]

Occupation, revelations about the crimes of the Third Reich, and division also inevitably raised questions about the nature of German identity. Reservations about the supposed deficient national self-consciousness of Germans surfaced in opinion polls. The politician Ernst Reuter asked: 'Have we Germans really been a true nation?'[3] National identity and the issue of the continuity of the German state were brought together in 1958 by the philosopher Karl Jaspers when he proclaimed:

> We had a Prussian *Kleindeutschland*, the Bismarck state that falsely appealed, as the second *Reich*, to the first, medieval *Reich* . . . Today . . . the Bismarck state belongs entirely to the past. If we live as if it could become real once again, we allow ghosts to drink the blood of the present and prevent ourselves from grasping the real dangers and the great possibilities of the future.[4]

This renunciation of the goal of reunification clashed with the official policy of the Federal Republic of Germany, though Chancellor Konrad Adenauer, whose long grip on political power stamped the character of the first phase of the Federal Republic's history, left no doubt about his commitment to western political systems and values. Freedom, and anti-communism, took priority over the desire for national unity.

The political system of the Federal Republic was regulated by a Basic Law, a term chosen in preference to the more obvious word, constitution, in order to emphasise the provisional character of the west German state. It was drafted amid the emergence of the Cold War but was shaped by the need to avoid what were seen as the flaws of the Weimar constitution, especially a strong presidential authority and plebiscitarian elements. It committed the Federal Republic to being a *Rechtsstaat* and to being a 'democratic and social federal state'.[5] Of these three characteristics, only the idea of the social state (*Sozialstaat*) proved contentious, though what was meant by a *Rechtsstaat* and whether it was compatible with the social state formed part of the dispute. The Basic Law also explicitly sanctioned the role of political parties, though whether those who framed the Basic Law saw this as the foundation of what became known as the party state (*Parteienstaat*) has been questioned. It is clear, however, that the expansive interpretation of Article 21 had much to do with Gerhard Leibholz, who favoured such an interpretation, and his position as a member of the Federal Constitutional Court.[6] The Court itself came to play a central role in the definition of key political concepts, including that of the party state.[7] Interpretation of the constitution, or so it seemed to some, had finally taken priority over the general theory of the state.

In contrast to the troubled years of the Weimar Constitution, the stability of the Federal Republic was striking. Yet contemporaries were not always reassured. In 1951, two years after the Basic Law came into effect, Franz Neumann still expressed 'grave doubts that, first, German society is stable and, second, that the political power centres in German society are committed to democracy'.[8] Only six years after the end of the war, and so soon after the foundation of the Federal Republic, that is an understandable reservation, especially from the perspective of someone who had been driven into exile. Yet even the demonstrable success of the Federal Republic did not suffice to shake off underlying concerns. Indeed, as Otto-Heinrich von der Gablentz put it:

The domestic order leaves nothing to be desired: coherent administration, correct adjudication, parties that loyally support the democratic order of the Basic Law, elections in which ninety per cent of those entitled to vote freely participate and which turn out to the benefit of unimpeachably democratic parties, an extremely stable government, a condition which our large neighbouring countries envy. And yet a dull uneasiness of the masses, a deep concern of the initiated about the character and condition of this state.[9]

Despite the strength of Cold War anti-communism in the Federal Republic, which took on added sharpness because of the embodiment of the ideology in the German Democratic Republic, German political thought in this period was affected by the emphasis upon economic reconstruction and the so-called economic miracle of the 1950s. Economic success suggested that the problems of hyper-inflation and unemployment that had repeatedly wracked German society were soluble. Advanced industrial society seemed amenable to various forms of planning without having to abandon the capitalist form of economy. Technocracy, shrinking ideological divisions within the Federal Republic and the popular focus on private life all fitted into a picture of a less politicised form of existence. It was, as Max Horkheimer put it, a world characterised by 'administration, progress and order'.[10] By the same token, it was a world which had left behind the more revolutionary ambitions once favoured by Horkheimer. While Horkheimer wrote of the administered world in a spirit of resignation in which his opposition to the existing order was still visible, Helmut Schelsky, an opponent of Horkheimer's Insititute for Social Research, welcomed the stability represented by what he described as a 'sceptical generation', alienated from the ill-understood complexities of a modern democratic order, lacking ideals, disinclined to engage in active politics, and ultimately unpolitical.[11]

When Schelsky surveyed the sceptical generation, he was in part projecting his own disillusion with political activism onto a younger generation, though he shared that with many who had experienced the years of the Third Reich. A focus on reconstruction, whether economic or intellectual, and a certain reserve about the career of individuals before zero hour, as 1945 came to be known, served to moderate disputes between political theorists, though the differences between them remained strong. One point of disagreement concerned the extent to which German political and social thought had to undergo a process of westernisation, if not Americanisation. Here, Schelsky warned against wholesale adaptation.[12] The new political-science discipline, supported by people like Fraenkel and von Gablentz, was more likely to contain advocates of westernisation as part of a process of democratisation, though that still left room for significant disagreement about what part of the west might provide the appropriate model.[13]

Some form of intellectual westernisation went hand in hand with the foreign-policy orientation of the Federal Republic. In this realm, the new Federal Republic began life as a state subject to an Occupation Statute that reserved extensive powers to the western Allies, so much so that the lack of provision for a state of emergency in the Basic Law could initially be regarded as a simple acknowledgement of those reserved powers. The Federal Republic initially existed in fact under a system of dual sovereignty. That constraint was greatly reduced in 1955 as part of the process of political and economic integration, in which the Federal Republic took part during the 1950s. Even before the Rome Treaties of 1957 added the European Economic Community and EURATOM to the European Coal and Steel Community, Wilhelm Grewe was sufficiently impressed by the trend to refer to a 'power of integration' (*Integrationsgewalt*) alongside the traditional 'treaty-making power'.[14] Western integration took place against the background of the Cold War division of Europe and the world. It was clear to German observers that both processes had put an end to the old system of the European balance of power. It was also clear that nowhere was this fundamental change in the international order clearer than in the case of Germany itself. The visible symbol of the Cold War was the wall that ran through Berlin. Although most were inclined to approve of the turn from the power politics that had led to what Friedrich Meinecke described as *Die deutsche Katastrophe* (The German Catastrophe), some interpreted the precariousness of the global order and its dualistic character as the embodiment of a civil war, justified, albeit inappropriately, in moral categories. By comparison, the old state-centric European order appeared as a political system that had offered some stability.

The concept of politics

The influential vision of a technocratic society, whether defended by Schelsky and Arnold Gehlen or denounced by Max Horkheimer and Theodor Adorno, constricted the scope for any meaningful conception of political action. Schelsky made the point forcefully:

> Political norms and laws are replaced by objective exigencies of scientific-
> technical civilization, which are not posited as political decisions and
> cannot be understood as norms of conviction or *Weltanschauung*. Hence
> the idea of democracy loses its classical substance, so to speak. In place of
> the political will of the people emerges an objective exigency, which man
> produces as science and labour.[15]

From this perspective, political institutions serve to 'unburden' people
from the need to take decisions. Institutions as stabilising factors had,
he noted, been emphasised by Gehlen in the revised edition of his
Der Mensch (Man).[16] Institutions, Schelsky argued, provide stability
by satisfying social needs and have to adapt to those needs as they
change. Abrupt institutional transformation risks leaving significant
sections of the population bereft of guidance. Illustrating his point by
reference to German history, Schelsky claimed that this is precisely
what had happened in the Weimar Republic. The sudden introduction
of an 'abstract-democratic' system had overburdened those sectors of
the population who still longed for 'patriarchal' political forms,
pushing them in a direction that finally 'exploded in the call for
the strong man'.[17] The moral is clear. Political activism, especially
insofar as it is guided by abstract, rational models, threatens to tip
over into irrational political behaviour whose consequences were all
too familiar to his readers. This also allowed him to invoke both
Bismarck's political system, which supposedly catered for the diverse
needs of German society through its combination of monarchical,
federal and parliamentary elements, and Anglo-Saxon political systems that emphasised tradition, in contrast to a French, Rousseauian,
model with an 'emotionally laden veneration of a dark will of the
people' that issued in revolution.[18]

This kind of technocratic approach to politics, bolstered by the
careful invocation of divergent national traditions and trajectories,
was challenged from diverse perspectives. On the one hand, Carl
Schmitt and those influenced by him insisted that although the scope
for genuine political action was increasingly under threat it was still
possible, and indeed inescapable. On the other hand, several theorists
sought to formulate a conception of politics that did not succumb to
technocratic constriction but also did not reduce politics purely to
considerations of power, let alone Schmitt's distinction between friend
and foe. When Schmitt republished his *Der Begriff des Politischen*
(The Concept of the Political) in 1963, he asserted its continuing
relevance but conceded that its main limitation was the failure to
adequately distinguish between 'different kinds of enemy – the

conventional, the real or absolute enemy'.[19] He then sought to deploy these distinctions in order to show how genuine political decisions, in the sense of drawing the distinction between friend and foe, were still possible without slipping into absolute enmity with the associated moral discrimination and lack of all restraint in the conduct of warfare. His *Theorie des Partisanen* (Theory of the Partisan) served as an illustration of this. The choice of the figure of the partisan reflected the prevalence of partisan or guerrilla warfare amid the anti-colonial conflicts of the day but also elements of European history, including German resistance to Napoleonic hegemony. The partisan fitted Schmitt's requirements insofar as the enmity displayed by the partisan was genuine and political. The partisan, Schmitt argued, is not like the pirate or the blockade-runner with whom he had, he acknowledged, once mistakenly identified the partisan. The partisan was not like a pirate because the pirate is unpolitical and motivated by profit. He is not like the blockade-runner because he risks his life and not just his cargo. The partisan's enmity, though real, is also limited, for he fights to expel the invader from his homeland. Schmitt conceded that this form of partisan could be swept up into the ideological conflicts that would undermine his autochthonous character, turning him into an instrument of global ideological causes that issued in absolute enmity.[20] Schmitt's attempt to rescue his concept of the political by invoking the partisan was not without influence, or indeed relevance to the dynamics of guerrilla warfare in the post-war world; but a concept of the political illustrated through the figure of the partisan had peripheral relevance for Adenauer's Federal Republic.

It was possible, however, to adapt some of Schmitt's ideas both to fend off the challenge from the technocratic vision and to do so from the standpoint of a commitment to liberal parliamentary democracy that Schmitt had never shared. Hermann Lübbe is a prime example. He noted that the attraction of the technocratic vision is that it promises to replace the 'force of the decision' by the much less demanding resolve simply to do what is objectively required.[21] Antagonistic relationships are supposed to evaporate amid a general process of the decline of ideologies and of the depoliticisation of life. Lübbe found none of this convincing. As the utilisation of technocracy by the two ideologically opposed superpowers proved, the technocratic vision was all too easily incorporated into ideological visions. The technocratic vision then, so argued Lübbe, was inadequate as a description of the political condition at the time. Yet he had another argument against the technocratic vision, one that was more normative in character. The technocratic vision is 'structurally un-democratic', not in the sense that it is inherently dictatorial but in the sense that it substitutes the decision of the expert for the conflict of opinion among the citizens. The technocratic vision, which he described as a 'system of silence', puts an end to democratic debate, that is, an end to politics, that properly ought to be ended only by majority votes.[22] The decisionistic theme in Lübbe is reminiscent of Schmitt, but the purpose is radically different.

Dolf Sternberger, Ulrich Scheuner and the younger Wilhelm Hennis all directly challenged Schmitt's underlying premise and also challenged the technocratic vision. All three argued that politics is concerned with the establishment of peace and is not orientated towards the ever-present possibility of the distinction between friend and enemy. Scheuner even claimed that this is evident in warfare: 'The aim of war is not the destruction of the enemy but overcoming him and thereby incorporating him into one's own political system or the aim is a genuine settlement, therefore at the end a peaceful order'.[23] Sternberger agreed, defining peace as the 'object and goal' or as the 'basis, the characteristic and the norm' of politics.[24] Schmitt's attempt to extract the essence of the state from prescription and civil war is, he suggested, like trying to extract the essence of marriage from divorce.[25] Scheuner worried that Sternberger had gone too far, failing to recognise the positive functional role of political conflict and the distinctive function of the state, rather than politics per se, in the creation of a peaceful order.[26] Yet Sternberger in fact praised the Romans for not only recognising the existence of conflicts of interest inherent in their society but also giving them institutional expression. He also appealed to the prominent place given to the state by classical authors as evidence of wider recognition that a peaceful order is indeed the goal of politics.[27]

The normative understanding of politics that animated the comments of Sternberger and Scheuner was shared by Hennis. Hennis set his account in the context of a general stagnation as he saw it of political science as a discipline, its reduction to a study of causal factors and of the concept of politics itself to a struggle for power. Politics as the struggle for power, he complained, had supposedly been discredited after the war, but had become the commonplace assumption once again. According to Hennis, the advocates of this conception failed to grasp the extent to which its popularity was tied to the peculiar conditions of the era of competing nation states and im-perialism on the one hand, and the associated class-divided societies on the other hand.[28] Nor was Hennis any more sympathetic to the technocratic vision or any elision of politics to sciences that deal with necessities. Whereas Schelsky had referred to the 'objective exigencies of scientific-technical civilization', Hennis insisted that politics is a practical science that deals with possibilities and probabilities between which people choose in the light of what they deem to be a well-ordered commonwealth.[29] This is a concept of politics that explicitly invoked Aristotle against what Hennis saw as the constriction of politics by the technocratic vision.

Hennis, however, knew that such deliberation was threatened not only by technocratic visions but also by the manipulation of public opinion by the mass media. In fact, this compounded an old problem, for government, so Hennis believed, had always required trust in the judgement of those of those who governed. In the context of modern, parliamentary systems, that means that 'Parliamentarianism . . . loses its legitimacy if its representatives are no longer regarded as more intelligent, better informed and more insightful observers of political questions'.[30] Jürgen Habermas, who carried on the tradition of the Institute for Social Research, albeit in innovative ways, approached the same problem from a much more radical perspective. He too invoked Aristotle in the name of a concept of politics that now 'seems hopelessly old-fashioned to us'. Politics, 'understood to be the doctrine of the good and the just life', politics not as a skill but as 'cultivation of character', politics as prudential judgement rather than an exact science, was precisely what Habermas wanted to defend.[31] He sought to determine the sociological and political conditions that might make such a defence seem plausible in the modern world rather than in the Greek city states of the fifth century BC. His model lay in eighteenth-century England and France. Here he found the emergence of a 'bourgeois public sphere' that

> may be conceived above all as the sphere of private people come together as a public; they soon claimed the public sphere regulated from above against the authorities themselves, to engage them in a debate over the general rules governing the relations in the basically privatized but publicly relevant sphere of commodity exchange and social labor.[32]

This public sphere did not entail a claim to rule, nor, at least initially, did it engage with the 'properly political tasks of a citizenry acting in common'.[33] Yet, Habermas claimed, it 'was intended to change domination as such'.[34] The equivocal status of this forum in which politics might be practised only at the expense of renouncing some of the features that are most evidently political is clear. This conceptual problem is complicated by the fact that Habermas also argued that the conditions that had made it possible had given way in the class-divided societies of the nineteenth century and consumer societies of the twentieth to conditions in which it was increasingly difficult to see how there was still scope for the force of the better argument, which stood at the heart of Habermas's model of the public sphere, to prevail. It is clear, however, that Habermas's model had a critical and radical potential that marked it out from Hennis's more cautious position.[35]

Political parties and democracy

These concepts of politics were linked to assessments of the role of political parties and related conceptions of parliamentary democracy. The stability of the party system, the importance of parties and party membership in areas of life beyond elections and parliamentary debate, provided a striking contrast to the contested republics of the inter-war era. The critical strategies of the Weimar years, outright rejection of political parties in favour of corporatist models and the open or implicit attempt to discredit political parties in the name of a true democracy were largely absent. Echoes of this part of the past were evident, however, in the work of Werner Weber, a pupil of Schmitt.[36] Weber acknowledged that it was not plausible to speak of the persistence of the structures of the constitutional monarchy in the Bonn Republic as it had been in the Weimar Republic and that it was necessary to come to terms with the reality of party-based mass democracy. These concessions were, however, a prelude to the assertion of an 'authority vacuum' behind which lay a *'multitude of oligarchic action communities and influence groups'*, among which he counted the political parties.[37] The description of political parties as mere pressure groups that distort or form a substitute for the will of the people was an old one. Gablentz replied that Weber's assimilation of parties and pressure groups was based on a failure to grasp the public functions that parties fulfil and which differentiate them from other associations, namely their key role in the formation of the public will. Nor did he hesitate to denounce what he saw as standing behind Weber's account: 'Whoever believes with Hegel that the common good is already provided as the reason of state, or with Rousseau that it is already provided as the general will, represents – consciously or unconsciously – a totalitarian, but not a free, democratic conception of the state'.[38]

Gablentz's insistence that the common good or will is something that has to be shaped rather than something that already exists in some objective form is consistent with the Basic Law (Article 21). It was also central to Konrad Hesse's attempt to elaborate on the distinctive status of political parties in the public realm. Hesse was part of a younger generation whose ideas took shape in the post-war world. What matters, according to Hesse, is not only that parties are a legitimate element of the political order and that they seek to influence the citizenry as a whole but also that they make these attempts to exert influence in the public realm and, above all, that they accept public responsibility for these efforts.[39] Hesse was wary of the idea that this made political parties into 'constitutional organs' or 'organs of the state' as was suggested, with varying degrees of precision, by Gerhard Leibholz and several judgements of the Federal Constitutional Court. Yet Leibholz's intent was to break down what he saw as the damaging traditional nineteenth-century view that contrasted state and society and relegated parties firmly to the latter category, as more conservative theorists like Herbert Krüger were still inclined to do.[40]

The constitutionally anchored position of political parties in general was but one perceived novelty of the Federal Republic. Sternberger identified another and used it as an opportunity for challenging the heart of Schmitt's concept of the political. There was, he said, a 'completely new phenomenon' in German parliamentary life, namely a 'strong, coherent, even firmly organised, steady opposition' of which one could say that it was '*the* Opposition'.[41] What was important, however, was that this Opposition understood itself as a government-in-waiting and that it thought in terms of a contrast not between government and parliament but between governing majority and opposition minority. Sternberger saw the former contrast as a traditional vice of German parliamentary life and was not wholly convinced that it had been replaced by the more desirable contrast. Equally important, he insisted that the contrast between governing majority and opposition minority was incompatible with Schmitt's concept of the political. It is incompatible with Schmitt's friend–foe relationship, in the light of which it would be necessary to see the parties as at best existing in a state of a 'persistent Cold War'.[42] Furthermore, he argued that the contrast is 'historically astonishing', for it means that a ruling group allows the existence of an organised opposition with which it sits in the same chamber and whose purpose is to displace the ruling group.

These disputes between those who retained an abiding suspicion of, if not scarcely concealed antipathy to, parliamentary party democracy and the advocates of the new political order of the Federal Republic formed only one element of the debate. There was also a deep division between some of the most fervent advocates. As indicated above, Leibholz, partly through his position on the Federal Constitutional Court, was able to exert considerable public influence, even if his arguments met with extensive, and often harsh, criticism among political and legal theorists.[43] Elaborating on ideas already formed in the Weimar Republic, Leibholz insisted upon a principled distinction between the 'traditional, liberal-representative parliamentary democracy' and the 'modern democratic party state'.[44] The former presumed, as Edmund Burke had argued, that, once elected, the parliamentary representative was bound only by his own conscience and his commitment to represent the entire notion. It is consistent with this that any idea of an imperative mandate was firmly rejected and that political parties were at best loose associations. The same conception of liberal representation explained, Leibholz argued, why political parties, as they became more coherent, were initially treated with such suspicion. The battle against parties had, however, been lost. They are, he argued, a sociological reality as well as now being constitutionally recognised. Parliamentary deputies are members of parties whose collective decisions they represent. With this development, the autonomy of the parliamentarian is exposed as a fiction. In place of the now discredited liberal-representative parliamentarianism, so Leibholz claimed, it was necessary to put a different conception, according to which modern party democracy is 'nothing other than a rationalised form of appearance of plebiscitarian democracy or – if one wants – a surrogate for direct democracy'.[45] Political parties shape the 'general will' of the people, or rather, the will of the actual majority of active citizens is 'identified' with the 'general will of the people'.[46]

This idea of the identity of the rulers and rules was dismissed by Ernst Fraenkel with undisguised scorn as a 'vulgar-democratic theory' that made it impossible to accord parliament the dignity it deserves.[47] Although Fraenkel was well aware of the manipulation of the idea of a national tradition in the shape of the 'ideas of 1914', he indulged in a sometimes indiscriminate attack on what he saw as the abject failure of Germans to comprehend the nature of English parliamentarianism.[48] The source of this deficiency was, he claimed, the fact that Germany had taken its constitutional law and reality from the English model but its constitutional ideology from revolutionary France.[49]

The problem lay in the presumption of the existence of a general will which parliamentarians were supposed to embody and the consequent perception of the representation of particular interests as a threat to this pristine unity. Fraenkel located this in the French model of 1973, though he also traced it back to the 'subaltern position' of the German parliament in the *Obrigkeitsstaat*.[50] His comments on contemporary attitudes were even more scathing. Parliamentarians in Bonn acted under the 'compulsory neurosis' of the belief in a general will and then had to represent the particular interests of the electorate with a 'bad conscience'. Popular criticism of parliamentarians, condemning them for any governmental crisis but then mocking them for following the party whip, was 'reactionary and schizophrenic'.[51] Parliamentary democracy is not, for Fraenkel, government by the people in another form; it is not a surrogate for direct democracy. It is, if it is to function, based on recognition of the inescapable plurality of society, the open acknowledgement of the representation of diverse interests and the establishment of an accommodation between them. In substance and in the ferocity of his criticism, Fraenkel, in fact, is not far removed from Kelsen's comments during the Weimar Republic.

Although Leibholz and Fraenkel differed on the fundamental nature of parliamentary party democracy, both sought to legitimate the role of political parties. Fraenkel's account was ultimately more realistic and more influential, but the disagreement was about how to best understand, and legitimise, the democratic order of the Federal Republic. Legitimising the role of political parties was understood, in part at least, as overcoming a dualistic vision which alienated political parties from the state and relegated them to the role of opposition and the uneasy combination of ideological commitment and de facto representation of narrow interest that had long been criticised by some German political theorists. The decline of the old party commitment to 'opposition of principle' was not, however, regarded as an unmixed blessing by Otto Kirchheimer. As 'part channel of protest, part source of protection, part purveyors of the future', they had encouraged more vigorous participation in party life than the emerging pragmatic 'catch-all' parties.[52] Nor was this the only threat to the vitality of political parties. With explicit reference to the fate of German social democracy in the Weimar era, Kirchheimer warned that premature identification with the state could 'amount to democratic parties existing under the protection of the state's symbols, while yet lacking the strength and the will to fashion this same state according to their own image'.[53] Behind this warning lay the belief that the socialists had failed to grasp the opportunity at the beginning of the Weimar Republic to radically transform the political order.

The state and the constitution

The more successful transformation of the political order in the Federal Republic also gradually led to increasing consideration of whether a transformation of key political concepts was desirable, of whether the concept of the state, especially as formulated around the turn of the century, was still a useful guide to the reality of political life and whether it had been flawed all along. This was reinforced in Hennis's mind by what he described as the 'as good as completely dying out of the so-called "theory of the state"'. Hermann Heller's *Staatslehre* now appeared as the 'swan song' of the tradition of writing books entitled *Allgemeine Staatslehre*. According to Hennis, apart from one little-observed text, there was only Hans Nawiasky's *Allgemeine Staatslehre*, whose first volume appeared in 1945 – and that did not move beyond the debates of the Weimar Republic.[54]

That was true, though, given the date of publication, not surprising. Nawiasky offered a pragmatic approach to the state. Its purpose, in contrast, for example, to religious communities, is the fulfilment of strictly temporal purposes and more specifically to meet those needs that cannot be met by individuals alone or other associations of individuals. In other words, the principle of subsidiarity takes on a key role in the definition of the state.[55] He repeatedly insisted that the state has no purpose or existence apart from the individual citizens of the state. He dismissed any definition of the purpose of the state in terms of power or self-preservation – for, he argued, this fails to distinguish the state from a band of robbers and leads to the supposed justification of any means deployed by the state in pursuit of this goal.[56] Nor did he accept that the state is a necessary function of human existence. Some form of social ties and frameworks are necessary, but the phenomenon of the modern state as such is not.[57] Yet Nawiasky's style of theory fitted in neither with those who wanted to emphasise the authority of the state rather than its ethical purposes, nor with those who took a more critical approach to concept of the state in general.

Hennis can be described as part of a group centred on Rudolf Smend, who increasingly questioned the concept of the state.[58] Whereas most critics of the concept of the state described its vices as a product of the insufficient modernity of German political thought, usually in the late nineteenth century, Hennis took a different view: 'We Germans are not an especially conservative, tradition-bound people; rather, Germany – at least intellectual Germany – stands for the most radically modern since the beginning of the nineteenth century'.[59] The state, understood as a 'machine' or 'apparatus' that could be deployed for any arbitrary purpose so long as it has the power to pursue that purpose, could emerge only at the price of the 'forced dumping' of a common European tradition. In seeking to reassert this tradition, Hennis could pull together his concept of politics, his concept of democracy and his critique of the concept of the state. The key concept here is that of the 'office' (*Amt*) understood as a 'trust'. Hennis conceded that the theory of the state understood in terms of will had repressed this common tradition more strongly in German lands than elsewhere, but it is nevertheless part of a common European tradition. The concept of an office is bound here to an understanding of government as 'a task bound to justice and the common good', that is, bound to what Hennis said politics is. It entails a responsibility to fulfil that task which cannot be subordinated to any kind of democratic imperative mandate. German development, he continued, went astray insofar as it lost sight of the political nature of the concept of office, and hence those 'who are and should be nothing more than functionaries, civil servants, have been able to decorate themselves, almost exclusively, with the dignity of [the concept of] an office'.[60] From this perspective, Hennis denounced the definition of the state in terms of the monopoly of legitimate violence as a distortion of the empirical reality of the task of governing and as an 'authoritarian delusion'.[61] The reference point for this attack on the state as 'machine', 'apparatus' and monopoly of legitimate violence is, of course, Max Weber.[62]

Others sought to distance themselves from a more general characteristic of what they held to be the traditional view of the state, namely the separation of state and society. In 1949, Leibholz invoked an Anglo-Saxon model in contrast to a continental European model in order to argue for a concept of society that was not depoliticised. It was not the case, he argued, that Anglo-Saxon literature was unfamiliar with a depoliticised conception of society; but a different conception had survived alongside, namely the idea of '*civil society*' as a category that embraced the political and unpolitical. From this perspective, he claimed, the state appears as but one function of this wider category.[63] Horst Ehmke later took up this theme on a broader front, under the heading 'Staat und Gesellschaft als verfassungstheoretisches Problem' (State and society as a theoretical constitutional problem). The problem, he argued, is the distinction itself. He had to qualify this – for, he noted, in the light of the experience of the Third Reich, it would be unwise to dismiss the contrast between state and society as mere liberal ideology.[64] He suggested, therefore, recasting constitutional terminology by drawing on Anglo-Saxon traditions that spoke of 'government' and 'civil society' where the relationship of the former to the latter is one of 'trust'. In fact, Ehmke wanted to dispense with the contrast between state and society entirely: 'It is a matter of *a* human association; there is no need for its duplication into "state" and "society"'.[65] The difficulty was how to avoid this distinction without sweeping away all distinctions. The answer, he claimed, lies in the terms 'political community' and 'government', both of which are looser than state and society. That is precisely their virtue. For Ehmke, they avoided the stark traditional contrast that could only classify political parties as part of the state, which alienates them from the community, or part of society, which denies their political character or disparages them as the product of contingent, sectional interest and hence passes over their integrative function.[66]

Those who resisted such interpretations did so with a certain amount of resignation, partly because the Federal Republic did not display all of the characteristics they thought proper to a state. Hence they were tempted to deny it the title of state. On the other hand, they were reluctant to concede the field to their opponents and were inclined to assert that the Federal Republic had to be a state, whether other political theorists wished to see it as such or not. Both sentiments were evident in Ernst Forsthoff. He noted that many observers were proclaiming an end to the era of the state as traditionally understood, but retorted: 'In any case, politics, or better the political, will not disappear from the world with the state and it is not yet evident what new form of the political will replace the state'.[67] Within a few sentences, he then proclaimed: 'Nevertheless, the Federal Republic can and will do nothing other than step forward with the claim to be a state'.[68] In terms of international relations this was true, but Forsthoff also referred to the real issue that divided political and legal theorists, namely: how was the Federal Republic's power to be justified?

For Forsthoff, this was all the more important in the as yet unencountered case of a state of emergency. This, in fact, concerned many who did not share Forsthoff's vision of the state, especially in the continuing absence of constitutional provision for a state of emergency or emergency-powers legislation. Werner Weber, who did share Forsthoff's conception of the state, alluded to this kind of crisis when he referred to the balance of power in contemporary mass democracies as 'exceptionally unstable and precarious'.[69] Equally important, he asserted that a balance between the various social groups would have been better assured by a 'powerful authority [*Obrigkeit*]', and warned that with the 'evaporation of authoritative [*obrigkeitlich*] force' the sovereignty of the state along with the responsibility and dignity of the state were threatened.[70] Nor did Weber neglect to specify where he thought the appropriate authority should be located: namely in the executive and the civil service (*Beamtentum*).[71]

This emphasis upon the administrative aspect of the state, to the point of almost identifying it with the state, was shared by Forsthoff and Krüger as well. In 1964, the year after Hennis had proclaimed the death of the *Allgemeine Staatslehre*, Krüger published a massive exemplar of that genre. It was intended, as he emphasised in the opening sentence of the Preface, '*to be truly a theory of the state*'. He did not intend to follow the widespread practice of simply assuming the concept of the state in order to set about showing how it should be limited and weakened by basic rights and the division of powers.[72] According to Krüger, the state is a 'community of an existential bond' born out of the insight into the sheer fact that men could not exist without it, though he conceded that the threat to existence was no longer widely grasped, despite the threat from atomic weapons.[73] The modern state, he argued, is the administrative state, something demonstrated negatively by the failure of those German territories that neglected to develop administrative agencies in the face of Napoleon's onslaught.[74] He concluded the book with a consideration of the 'renewal of the willingness to obey', though with more than a little resignation about the prospects.[75] Although Forsthoff praised Krüger's book, the general response was highly critical. The concept of the state, it seemed, was on the defensive.

The Rechtsstaat *and the* Sozialstaat

This was true of the concept of the state as such but not of the concept of the state as qualified by the appropriate adjective. That prominence was given to the concept of the *Rechtsstaat* and to the nature of law in general followed naturally as a response to the perversion of law in the Third Reich. In a highly influential assessment of 1946, Gustav

Radbruch reflected critically on the legal positivism that he himself had espoused. His judgement was damning: 'Positivism in fact, with its conviction "law is law" ["*Gesetz ist Gesetz*"], made the German judiciary defenceless in the face of laws with arbitrary and criminal content'.[76] It is now increasingly recognised that this was a highly misleading claim. It was not procedurally correct law combined with relativism but substantive values of a specific kind that weakened the commitment of the judiciary to the democratic order and the rule of law. It was not positivists but their critics who stood at the intellectual forefront of the assault on Weimar. Yet Radbruch's impeccable credentials as a democrat and jurist helped to make his judgement authoritative for a long time.

The conclusion that Radbruch drew was that it is possible for there to be an unjust law and consequently that there is a form of law and justice beyond statutory law. In the negative formulation that Radbruch used, 'where justice is not even sought, where equality, which constitutes the core of justice, is consciously denied in the issuing of positive law, there the law is not only an "unlawful law" but rather it lacks entirely the nature of law'.[77] Radbruch did not in fact discard positivism. The legal certainty that it provided is, he claimed, part of justice. Only the exceptional explicit disavowal of equality condemned the law in the light of 'supra-statutory law'.[78] Nevertheless, Radbruch's explicit invocation of natural law, that is of a law valid at all times and in all places and accessible to human reason regardless of statutory provision, formed part of a wider assertion of natural law and a condemnation of the supposed dominance of the positivist model.[79]

The assertion of the importance of values to the understanding of the *Rechtsstaat* was not restricted to the revival of natural law. Indeed, several factors converged in promoting such a trend. The theorists allied to Smend drew on his earlier work as well as his post-war texts to argue for the role of values. The greater activism of the Federal Constitutional Court, with the explicit reference to values in its judgements, pointed in the same direction. So too did the constitutional anchoring of the concept of the *Sozialstaat* in the Basic Law. A key dispute centred on the extent to which the *Sozialstaat* and the *Rechtsstaat* are compatible conceptual principles or whether there is an ineradicable tension between them. Ernst Rudolf Huber identified the conflicting aims between the two concepts as well as their distinctive historical locations before claiming that there is a common core that allows one to reconcile the two and hence to come to terms with the fact that in modern society the *Rechtsstaat* can only exist insofar as it is also a *Sozialstaat*. Both concepts, he wrote, were products of the nineteenth century, but they were products of significantly different historical problems. The *Rechtsstaat* was the product of tension between the state and civil society. It promised not just a set of formal procedures, including the division of powers and the independence of courts, but also substantive justice in the sense of the security of life, liberty and property. Life, liberty and property were valued insofar as they were held to be preconditions of the development of the individual person, or, in the language of the Basic Law, human dignity.[80] By contrast, the concept of the *Sozialstaat* arose from the tension between state and industrial society. It promised '*security of existence, full employment* and *preservation of labour power*' in the interests of the integration of the working classes. The *Rechtsstaat* restricted the state's right to intervene in society. The *Sozialstaat* demanded that the state intervene. Huber, however, sought to dilute the contrast by claiming that what the concept of the *Sozialstaat* was meant to secure is not bare existence but a life worth living, which amounts, he argued, to protecting the 'personality' of all from the ravages of industrial society.[81] The two concepts, despite their historical and analytic differences, ultimately converge.

Forsthoff was less conciliatory. He too traced the concept of the *Rechtsstaat* back to the nineteenth century but in order to assert that the concept could not be divorced from its origins in 'civil [*bürgerlich*] society'.[82] Forsthoff recognised the reality and legality of the *Sozialstaat* as the interventionist state orientated to the 'provision of existence [*Daseinsvorsorge*]', but he claimed that the concepts of the *Rechtsstaat* and the *Sozialstaat* belonged on different levels. The former is central to constitutional law, the latter to administrative law.[83] Behind this distinction lay the intent of accepting the reality and legality of the interventionist state but without endowing it with the same constitutional status as the *Rechtsstaat*. That in turn was intended to curtail what Forsthoff regarded as a worrying trend, namely the appeal to a set of values that required a level of interpretative activism on the part of judges that Forsthoff found unacceptable. He was especially concerned by the extension of constitutional basic rights from norms governing the relationship between the state and the citizen, primarily restricting the state's right to intervene in the affairs of the citizen, into norms governing the relationship between citizens themselves that imposed positive duties on citizens amounting to the prescription of a system of values.[84] He complained that at the heart of this expansive and indeterminate vision stood the judiciary, especially the Federal Constitutional Court. Here, warned Forsthoff, is the transition from the *Rechtsstaat* to the state of the judiciary (*Justizstaat*).[85]

Behind Forsthoff's arguments, Alexander Hollerbach discerned the old value relativism and an inability to conceive the state in any form other than as a rationalised machine equipped with a monopoly of physical violence. Forsthoff stood in the tradition identified with Max Weber. Hollerbach conceded that this tradition was not without its virtues in a world now stripped of ideology and myth, but, he concluded, 'it does not strike the right road towards the "normative power of the constitution" '.[86] The normative power of the constitution was a theme to which Hesse devoted much energy.[87] The phrase symbolises opposition to the idea of the state as a machine and acceptance that values are not an alien factor potentially dangerous to the state but are precisely the mechanism through which the state derives its legitimacy. Indeed, it is not inappropriate to suggest that theorists like Hesse were less interested in developing a theory of the state as such and more interested in a 'contemporary, consensual, material constitutional theory'.[88] The *Sozialstaat* formed part of that consensus.

Commitment to the *Sozialstaat* did not necessarily mean subscribing to the idea of an activist judiciary, let alone to a judicial state, as Forsthoff suggested. Indeed, one of the strongest condemnations of judicial activism came from the radical democrat Helmut Ridder, who even took exception to the description of the judiciary as a 'third power'. According to Ridder, there is 'no "judicial *power*" in the democracy of the Basic Law, but *a state* power, which arises from the people, one of whose functional aspects is the administration of justice'.[89] This was no mere terminological quibble. Ridder's denial that the judiciary constituted a separate 'power' went with an assertion of primacy of parliamentary activity in fulfilling the tasks established by the constitution, one of which was the creation of the *Sozialstaat*. Ridder expressed his opposition to the ambitions of the German judiciary, especially the Federal Constitutional Court, with unusual sharpness. Yet even those who were less suspicious of the courts were often wary of assigning them an unrestricted power of interpretation. Thus, Ehmke noted that to deny the possibility of a clash between natural law or 'elementary legal principles' and constitutional provisions would be to relapse into positivism. The problem, however, was that the courts enjoyed, by virtue of constitutional provisions, a monopoly of adjudication; but, he argued, there can be no such monopoly in the interpretation of natural law.[90] For Ehmke, that suggested that the Federal Constitutional Court should base its decisions on the constitution, not natural law. Yet he also acknowledged that, even here, logically compelling decisions are rare. Compelling judicial argument relies upon the existence of a consensus. The question is: who determines that consensus? Ehmke's answer was that it was not the Federal Constitutional Court but rather 'all right and just thinking people', a category that potentially extended to the entire political community.[91]

Relying on the 'normative power of the constitution' or the consensus of 'all right and just thinking people' presumes, of course, as Hesse and Ehmke well knew, that such a consensus exists. More conservative theorists never tired of invoking the possibility of the state of emergency that would expose the absence of such a consensus. It was a possibility that Hesse was clearly aware of, for it was on precisely this issue that he concluded his plea for the 'normative power of the constitution'.[92]

Identity and international order in a divided world

When Hesse reflected on the prospects of a state of emergency, he did so in the light of the fact that the Federal Republic had still not legislated for this eventuality and that, therefore, the Allied Powers still retained a right of intervention in such cases. The competence of the state and international relations were clearly interwoven in a distinctive way, as too were more general questions about national identity and the nature of the state. Hans Kelsen's answer was that Germany had simply ceased to exist as a state with the Allied assumption of 'supreme authority'. The fact that the Allies had not annexed Germany made no difference. According to Kelsen, international law held that a state exists 'if, and as long as, a certain population is living on a definite territory under an independent government'.[93] Since the latter had been abolished, the state had ceased to exist, and since the territory could not be 'no state's land' it had to be under the sovereignty of the Allied Powers.[94] Though supported by some, including Nawiasky, most political and legal theorists refused to accept this conclusion. The persistence of the state had to be asserted in order to preserve the conceptual possibility of national unity and at least some form of constitutional order. The tension of conceiving of national unity and constitutional order in the face of de facto division and Allied authority was evident in the assertion that 'Germany persists as a state because we want it to persist as a state'.[95]

The identity of this 'we' was also problematic. In the immediate aftermath of war, Meinecke considered the argument that in the light of foreign occupation, all should rally behind the nation and forget the preceding internal divisions. This, however, he rejected:

> Only he who has made quite clear to himself that the era of external, alien domination, which has now broken over us, was preceded by an era of internal alien domination, the domination by a criminal club, will find a way to a solution of the national problem of duty.[96]

The fatalistic language with which Meinecke presented the German predicament was well suited to the time. Yet, alongside such laments ran a different vocabulary that sought to deal with the experience of the Third Reich in terms of varying degrees of guilt or responsibility. Jaspers distinguished between no fewer than four types of guilt, including the political guilt that 'results in my having to bear the consequences of the deeds of the state whose power governs me and under whose order I live'.[97] Yet even the language of guilt was susceptible to surprising nuances. Over a decade after Meinecke's and Jaspers's accounts, Adorno gave a lecture on 'coming to terms with the past' in which he focused on the rhetoric of the guilt complex from which it was said that Germans suffered. Adorno was not convinced by this, for, he argued, the very idea of a 'guilt complex' suggested that the sense of guilt was disproportionate to the events that had caused it. The implication was that 'the murdered should be cheated out of the only thing which our impotence can give them: remembrance'.[98]

Even before the establishment of the Federal Republic, Sternberger had offered a different approach which was to reclaim the concept of the patriotism from the right wing and especially from the anti-democratic stream in German political thought. Turning to the French political theorist Montesquieu, Sternberger invoked the Frenchman's definition of patriotism as love of laws and country. For Sternberger, love of country is not identical with a relationship to a physical fact, nor is it be confused with the mysticism that is invoked in association with it. Patriotism requires the existence of laws, of a constitution with which its citizens can freely identify. So far is this the case, he asserted, that '[t]here is no fatherland amid despotism'.[99] Yet the Basic Law that provided a constitution fit for Sternberger's concept of patriotism did not solve the dilemma presented by the fact that only some Germans belonged to it. Indeed, the problem was aggravated by the fact that the Basic Law included as Germans millions who did not reside within the Federal Republic. It was, as Sternberger noted, 'a very remarkable situation'.[100]

If the issue of national identity continued to be problematic albeit under new conditions, so too did the international order that divided Germans. For all the apparent rigidity of the Cold War division of Europe and the promise of European integration, the general trends in the international order did not seem clear-cut. It was evident that in some respects the old European order had passed away, though how that order should be judged was another matter. In Ludwig Dehio's 'result of an autopsy', as he described it, the European order was treated as a series of bids for hegemony barely held in check by the balance of power, until the final triumph of the European system of states 'cost the system its life, just as the *Reich*, the assailant, paid for its defeat with its existence'.[101] Looking back from the perspective of the death of the European order Dehio pointed to the failure of the nineteenth-century historian Leopold Ranke to grasp the significance for the European order of the then 'flanking powers', that is, Russia and Britain.[102] That the flanking powers, or at least the sea powers to the west, were of great significance had always been clear to Schmitt. His *Der Nomos der Erde* (The Nomos of the Earth) was both a lament for the European order, which was presented as the precondition for the limitation of warfare, at least within Europe itself, and a continuation of his denunciation of the sea powers, first Britain and then the USA, as prophets of a concept of discriminating war in which the enemy was treated from the outset as a criminal.[103] Schmitt still held that the only choice was between a world of continental blocs that recognised each other as such, and a 'global civil war'.[104] The image of civil war was taken up by several of his students. They traced the current crisis of the international order back to the eighteenth century and more specifically to the ideas of the French Revolutionaries. The common theme was that the contrast of morality and politics had led to the attempt to subordinate the political to the moral and to repress the aporia of politics through utopian projections.[105] The outcome was that 'the idea of a total, global peace necessarily had as a consequence total global civil war'.[106] The existence of two superpowers each of which claimed to embody the principles of progress and to represent the higher values of the human race seemed to lend some credence to such images.[107]

Despite the proliferation of regional cooperation and the existence of the United Nations, general assessments of the international trends were often marked by ambivalence. Ulrich Scheuner, for example, agreed that the nineteenth-century predominance of European great powers had brought a hierarchical order to the international arena, but neither the League of Nations nor the United Nations had been able to provide a stable substitute. The outcome was that international law appeared to be in a condition of 'chaotic decomposition and tension'.[108] There was, as Wilhelm Grewe argued, a tendency towards the moderation of assertions of sovereignty. Moreover, Germany's constitutional provision expressly permitting the transfer of sovereign powers to international organisations was not unique.[109] It was here that Grewe suggested that the relevant article of the Basic Law should be construed not as a mere declaration of policy but as the basis of a distinctive 'power of integration' analogous to but distinct from the traditional 'treaty-making power'.[110] Yet Grewe recognised limits to this trend towards a strengthening of the international community. In terms of power politics, only states of continental scope would have a role in the future – and they, especially the Soviet Union and the USA, showed little inclination to follow this trend towards a limitation of their sovereignty.[111] Scheuner pointed to a reassertion of the doctrine of sovereignty in the wider world as the end of European empires brought with it a proliferation of new states.[112]

Despite this ambiguous picture, Scheuner argued for reconsidering the traditional nineteenth-century doctrine that international law is the creation of states and regulates the relationship between states. This, he said, was challenged by the fact that international organisations and even individuals were in practice being acknowledged as subjects in international law. More importantly, he sought to root international law in the ancient conception of *ius gentium*, that is, a set of laws held to be common to all peoples rather than a set of laws regulating relations between states.[113] In arguing thus, Scheuner was suggesting that not only had the factual basis of the European order of the nineteenth century disappeared but also its intellectual foundation was no longer plausible.

The refoundation of the democratic order took place in the context of the shadow of the Third Reich, the division of Germany and the end of European dominance of the international order. Despite the reservations about its stability, it was remarkably successful. The desire for reconstruction, intellectual as well as political and economic, exerted a moderating influence. Forsthoff's complaint that polemic had become rare reflected not just this pressure but also his feeling that the kind of position which he represented was being marginalised.[114] That was true, but his complaint was also an old polemical strategy in its own right. The real constraint was not the intellectual hegemony of Forsthoff's critics but the political reality of the Federal Republic. Nor was the consensus as strong or widespread as Forsthoff implied. That was evident in the continuing deployment of models of the German tradition of political thought, as well as Anglo-Saxon, French and wider European models as polemical weapons.

Notes

1. For a critique of the concept of *debellatio*, see Eyal Benvenisti, *The International Law of Occupation* (Princeton NJ: Princeton University Press, 1993), pp. 91–6.
2. See Bernhard Diestelkamp, 'Rechtsgeschichte als Zeitgeschichte', *Zeitschrift für neuere Rechtsgeschichte* 7 (1985), pp. 181–207.
3. Jörg Echternkamp, '"Verwirrung im Vaterländischen"?', in Jörg Echternkamp and Sven Oliver Müller (eds), *Die Politik der Nation* (Munich: Oldenbourg, 2002), pp. 223–4.
4. Quoted in Heinrich August Winkler, *Der lange Weg nach Westen*, vol. 2 (Munich: Beck, 2002), p. 174.
5. Article 20 (1).
6. Wilhelm Hennis, 'Der "Parteienstaat" des Grundgesetzes' [1992], in Wilhelm Hennis, *Auf dem Weg in den Parteienstaat* (Stuttgart: Reclam, 1998), pp. 107–35.
7. Bernhard Schlink, 'Die Enthronung der Staatsrechtswissenschaft durch die Verfassungsgerichtsbarkeit', *Der Staat* 28 (1989), pp. 161–72.
8. Franz Neumann, 'The labor movement in Germany', in Hans J. Morgenthau (ed.), *Germany and the Future of Europe* (Chicago: University of Chicago Press, 1951), p. 103.
9. Otto-Heinrich von der Gablentz, 'Autorität und Legitimität im heutigen Staat', *Zeitschrift für Politik* 5 (1958), p. 5.
10. Max Horkheimer, 'Soziologie und Philosophie' [1959], in Max Horkheimer, *Gesammelte Schriften*, vol. 7 (Frankfurt am Main: Fischer, 1985), p. 111.
11. Helmut Schelsky, *Die skeptische Generation* (Düsseldorf: Eugen Diederichs, 1963), especially pp. 351–63. The first edition appeared in 1957. On the limitations of Schelsky's account, see A. D. Moses, 'The Forty Fivers', *German Politics and Society* 17 (1999), pp. 95–127.
12. Helmut Schelsky, *Ortsbestimmung der deutschen Soziologie*, 3rd edn (Düsseldorf: Eugen Diederichs, 1967).
13. See chapter 8, 'Politologie als Demokratiewissenschaft', of Wilhelm

Bleek, *Geschichte der Politikwissenschaft in Deutschland* (Munich: Beck, 2001) for the linkage.

14. Wilhelm Grewe 'Die auswärtige Gewalt der Bundesrepublik', *Veröffent-lichungen der Vereinigung der deutschen Staatsrechtslehrer* 12 (1954), p. 143.

15. Quoted in Jürgen Habermas, 'Vom sozialen Wandel akademischer Bildung' [1963], in Jürgen Habermas, *Kleine Politische Schriften* (Frankfurt am Main: Suhrkamp, 1981), p. 113.

16. Helmut Schelsky, 'Über die Stabilität von Institutionen, besondere Verfassungen', *Jahrbuch für Sozialwissenschaften* 3 (1952), p. 17. For Gehlen's change of emphasis, see his *Der Mensch* [1950] (Wiebelsheim: Aula, 2004), pp. 382–4.

17. Schelsky, 'Über die Stabilität von Institutionen, besondere Verfassungen', p. 16.

18. Ibid., p. 19; Kurt Lenk, *Deutscher Konservatismus* (Frankfurt am Main: Campus, 1989), pp. 198–9.

19. Carl Schmitt , 'Vorwort' [1963], in Carl Schmitt, *Der Begriff des Politischen* (Duncker & Humblot, 1996), p. 17. For a careful consideration of the distinctions see Hasso Hofmann, 'Feindschaft – Grundbegriff des Politischen?', *Zeitschrift für Politik* 1 (1965), pp. 17–39.

20. Carl Schmitt, *Theorie des Partisanen* (Berlin: Duncker & Humblot, 1963).

21. Hermann Lübbe, 'Zur politischen Theorie der Technokratie', *Der Staat* 1 (1961), p. 20.

22. Ibid., p. 38.

23. Ulrich Scheuner, 'Der Bereich der Regierung' [1952], in Ulrich Scheuner, *Staatstheorie und Staatsrecht* (Berlin: Duncker & Humblot, 1978), p. 473.

24. Dolf Sternberger, 'Begriff des Politischen' [1960], in Dolf Sternberger, *Staatsfreundschaft* (Frankfurt am Main: Insel, 1980), pp. 304–5.

25. Ibid., p. 307.

26. Ulrich Scheuner, 'Das Wesen des Staates und der Begriff des Politischen in der neueren Staatslehre', in Konrad Hesse, Siegfried Reicke and Ulrich Scheuner (eds), *Staatsverfassung und Kirchenordnung* (Tübingen: Mohr, 1962), p. 258.

27. Sternberger, 'Begriff des Politischen', pp. 306–7, 309.

28. Wilhelm Hennis, 'Politik und praktische Philosophie' [1963], in Wilhelm Hennis, *Politikwissenschaft und politisches Denken* (Tübingen: Mohr, 2000), p. 9.

29. Ibid., p. 16.

30. Wilhelm Hennis, 'Meinungsforschung und repräsentative Demokratie' [1957], in Wilhelm Hennis, *Regieren im modernen Staat* (Tübingen: Mohr, 1999), p. 82.

31. Jürgen Habermas, 'The classical doctrine of politics in relation to social

philosophy' [1963], in Jürgen Habermas, *Theory and Practice* (London: Heinemann, 1974), pp. 41–2.

32. Jürgen Habermas, *The Structural Transformation of the Public Sphere* [1962] (Cambridge: Polity, 1992), p. 27.

33. Ibid., p. 52.

34. Ibid., p. 28.

35. For Habermas's rejection of Hennis's solution, see ibid., p. 238.

36. On Werner Weber, see William E. Scheuerman, 'Unsolved paradoxes: conservative political thought in Adenauer's Germany', in John P. McCormick (ed.), *Confronting Mass Democracy and Industrial Technology* (Durham, NC: Duke University Press, 2002), pp. 221–8.

37. Werner Weber, 'Gewaltenteilung als Gegenwartsproblem', in Hans Barion, Ernst Forsthoff and Werner Weber (eds), *Festschrift für Carl Schmitt* (Berlin: Duncker & Humblot 1959), p. 261. Weber deployed a series of arguments, not wholly consistent, in order to discredit political parties. See Birgit von Bülow, *Die Staatsrechtslehre der Nachkriegszeit (1945–1952)* (Berlin: Berlin Verlag, 1996), pp. 38–43.

38. Gablentz, 'Autorität und Legitimität im heutigen Staat', p. 17.

39. Konrad Hesse, 'Die verfassungsrechtliche Stellung der politischen Parteien im modernen Staat' [1959], in Peter Häberle and Alexander Hollerbach (eds), *Konrad Hesse. Ausgewählte Schriften* (Heidelberg: Müller, 1984), pp. 85–6.

40. See Gerhard Leibholz, *Strukturprobleme der modernen Demokratie*, 3rd edn (Karlsruhe: Müller, 1967), pp. viii–x; Herbert Krüger, *Allgemeine Staatslehre* (Stuttgart: Kohlhammer, 1964), pp. 371–3.

41. Dolf Sternberger, 'Opposition des Parlaments und parlamentarischer Opposition' [1955], in Dolf Sternberger, *Herrschaft und Vereinbarung* (Frankfurt am Main: Insel, 1980), p. 343.

42. Ibid., p. 362.

43. See Jan Hecker, 'Die Parteienstaatslehre von Gerhard Leibholz in der wissenschaftlichen Diskussion', *Der Staat* 34 (1995), pp. 286–311.

44. Gerhard Leibholz, 'Der Strukturwandel der modernen Demokratie' [1952], in Leibholz, *Strukturprobleme der modernen Demokratie*, p. 93. The key Weimar work is Leibholz, *Das Wesen der Repräsentation* [1929], 3rd edn (Berlin: de Gruyter, 1966).

45. Leibholz, 'Der Strukturwandel der modernen Demokratie', p. 93.

46. Ibid., p. 94.

47. Ernst Fraenkel, 'Historische Vorbelastungen der parlamentarischen Demokratie in Deutschland' [1959], in Ernst Fraenkel, *Deutschland und die westlichen Demokratien*, 7th edn (Stuttgart: Kohlhammer, 1979), p. 20.

48. Ernst Fraenkel, 'Deutschland und die westlichen Demokratien' [1960], in Fraenkel, *Deutschland und die westlichen Demokratien*, pp. 35–6. On the impact of the 'ideas of 1914', see above, Chapter 1.

49. Ernst Fraenkel, 'Strukturdefekte der Demokratie und deren Über-windung' [1963], in Fraenkel, *Deutschland und die westlichen Demokratien*, p. 53.

50. Ibid., pp. 59–62; 'Die repräsentative und die plebiszitäre Komponente im demokratischen Verfassungsstaat' [1958], in Fraenkel, *Deutschland und die westlichen Demokratien*, pp. 139–40.

51. Fraenkel, 'Historische Vorbelastungen der parlamentarischen Demokratie in Deutschland', pp. 20–1, 'Strukturdefekte der Demokratie und deren Überwindung', p. 55.

52. Otto Kirchheimer, 'The waning of opposition in parliamentary regimes' [1966], in Frederic S. Burin and Kurt L. Shell (eds), *Politics, Law and Social Change* (New York: Columbia University Press, 1969), p. 370.

53. Otto Kirchheimer, 'Party structure and mass democracy in Europe' [1954], in ibid., p. 267.

54. Hennis, 'Politik und praktische Philosophie', p. 5.

55. Hans Nawiasky, *Allgemeine Staatslehre*, vol. 1 (Einsiedeln: Benziger, 1945), pp. 33–4, 146–7.

56. Hans Nawiasky, *Allgemeine Staatslehre*, vol. 2 (Einsiedeln: Benziger, 1952), pp. 199–200.

57. Ibid., p. 11.

58. On the Smend 'school', see Frieder Günther, *Denken vom Staat her* (Munich: Oldenbourg, 2004).

59. Wilhelm Hennis, 'Zum Problem der deutschen Staatsanschauung', *Vierteljahreshefte für Zeitgeschichte* 7 (1959), p. 4.

60. Wilhelm Hennis, 'Amtsgedanke und Demokratiebegriff', in Hesse, et al. (eds), *Staatsverfassung und Kirchenordnung*, pp. 54–5, 62. See also Scheuner, 'Das Wesen des Staates und der Begriff des Politischen in der modernen Staatslehre', p. 230.

61. Wilhelm Hennis, 'Aufgaben einer modernen Regierungslehre' [1965], in Hennis, *Regieren in modernen Staat*, p. 154.

62. On Hennis's changing interpretation of Weber, see Lothar R. Waas, 'Politikwissenschaft als "praktische Wissenschaft" in der Nachfolge Max Webers: Wilhelm Hennis', in Hans J. Lietzmann (ed.), *Moderne Politik* (Opladen: Leske & Budrich, 2001), pp. 263–85.

63. Gerhard Leibholz, 'Staat und Gesellschaft in England' [1949], in Leibholz, *Strukturprobleme der modernen Demokratie*, p. 209.

64. Horst Ehmke, 'Staat und Gesellschaft als verfassssungstheoretisches Problem', in Hesse, et al. (eds), *Staatsverfassung und Kirchenordnung*, p. 25.

65. Ibid., p. 44.

66. Ibid., pp. 46–7.

67. Ernst Forsthoff, 'Der introvertierte Rechtsstaat und seine Verortung', *Der Staat* 2 (1963), p. 395.

68. Ibid.

69. Weber, 'Gewaltenteilung als Gegenwartsproblem', p. 265.
70. Ibid., pp. 268–9.
71. Ibid., pp. 271–2.
72. Krüger, *Allgemeine Staatslehre*, p. v.
73. Ibid., p. 191.
74. Ibid., pp. 80–1.
75. Ibid., pp. 983–8.
76. Gustav Radbruch, 'Gesetzliches Unrecht und übergesetzliches Recht', [1946] in Gustav Radbruch, *Gesamtausgabe*, Vol. 3 (Heidelberg: Müller, 1990), p. 88.
77. Ibid., p. 89.
78. See Gustav Radbruch, 'Gesetz und Recht' [1947], in Radbruch, *Gesamtausgabe*, vol. 3, pp. 99–100, and 'Vorschule der Rechtsphilosophie' [1948], in ibid., p. 150.
79. See, for example, Ulfried Neumann, 'Rechtsphilosophie in Deutschland seit 1945', in Dieter Simon (ed.), *Rechtswissenschaft in der Bonner Republik* (Frankfurt am Main: Suhrkamp, 1994), pp. 145–64.
80. Ernst Rudolf Huber, 'Rechtsstaat und Sozialstaat in der modernen Industriegesellschaft', in Ernst Rudolf Huber, *Nationalstaat und Verfassungsstaat* (Stuttgart: Kohlhammer, 1965), p. 253.
81. Ibid., p. 271.
82. Forsthoff, 'Der introvertierte Rechtsstaat und seine Verortung', p. 389.
83. Ernst Forsthoff, 'Begriff und Wesen des sozialen Rechtsstaates', *Veröffentlichungen der Vereinigung der deutschen Staatsrechtslehrer* 12 (1954), pp. 13–15.
84. Ernst Forsthoff, 'Die Umbildung des Verfassungsgesetzes', in Barion, et al. (eds), *Festschrift für Carl Schmitt*, pp. 45–8.
85. Ibid., p. 59.
86. Alexander Hollerbach, 'Auflösung der rechtsstaatlichen Verfassung?', *Archiv des öffentlichen Rechts* 85 (1960), p. 270.
87. Konrad Hesse, 'Die normative Kraft der Verfassung' [1959], in Häberle and Hollerbach (eds), *Konrad Hesse*, pp. 3–18.
88. Thus Günther, *Denken vom Staat her*, p. 169.
89. Helmut Ridder, 'Empfiehlt es sich, die vollständige Selbstverwaltung aller Gerichte im Rahmen des Grundgesetzes gesetzlich einzuführen?', *Verhandlungen des 40. Deutschen Juristentages* 1 (1953), p. 109.
90. Horst Ehmke, 'Prinzipien der Verfassungsinterpretation', *Veröffentlichungen der Vereinigung der deutschen Staatsrechtslehrer* 20 (1963), p. 79.
91. Ibid., pp. 71–2.
92. Hesse, 'Die normative Kraft der Verfassung', pp. 17–18.
93. Hans Kelsen, 'Is a peace treaty with Germany legally possible and politically desirable?', *American Political Science Review* 41 (1947), p. 1,188.

94. Hans Kelsen, 'The legal status of Germany according to the declaration of Berlin', *American Journal of International Law* 39 (1945), p. 521.
95. Thus Günter Dürig, quoted in Michael Stolleis, 'Besatzungsherrschaft und Wiederaufbau deutscher Staatlichkeit 1945–1949', in Josef Isensee and Paul Kirchhof (eds), *Handbuch des Staatsrechts der Bundesrepublik Deutschland*, vol. 1 (Heidelberg: Müller, 2003), p. 285.
96. Friedrich Meinecke, *Die deutsche Katastrophe* (Wiesbaden: Brockhaus, 1946), pp. 151–2. See also the dilemma of ruthless self-criticism or obstinate defiance presented by Gerhard Ritter, *Europa und die deutsche Frage* (Munich: Münchner, 1948), p. 8.
97. Karl Jaspers, *The Question of German Guilt* [1947] (New York: Fordham, 2000), p. 25.
98. Theodor W. Adorno, 'Aufarbeitung der Vergangenheit' [1959], in Theodor W. Adorno, *Erziehung zur Mündigkeit* (Frankfurt am Main: Suhrkamp, 1970), p. 12.
99. Dolf Sternberger, 'Begriff des Vaterlands' [1947], in Dolf Sternberger, *Staatsfreundschaft* (Frankfurt am Main: Insel, 1980), pp. 20–1.
100. Dolf Sternberger, 'Das Problem der Loyalität' [1956], in Dolf Sternberger, *Verfassungspatriotismus* (Frankfurt am Main: Insel, 1990), p. 88.
101. Ludwig Dehio, *The Precarious Balance* [1948] (London: Chatto & Windus, 1963), p. 264. The reference to an autopsy is from the 1960 Epilogue, ibid., p. 269.
102. Ibid., p. 8.
103. Carl Schmitt, *Der Nomos der Erde* [1950] (Berlin: Duncker & Humblot, 1997).
104. Ibid., p. 271.
105. Reinhard Koselleck, *Kritik und Krise* [1959] (Frankfurt am Main: Suhrkamp, 1973), pp. 8–9.
106. Roman Schnur, 'Weltfriedensidee und Weltbürgerkrieg 1791/92', *Der Staat* 2 (1963), p. 316.
107. For a critique, see Jürgen Habermas, 'Verrufener Fortschritt – verkanntes Jahrhundert', *Merkur* 5 (1960), pp. 468–77.
108. Ulrich Scheuner, 'Die Entwicklung des Völkerrechts im 20. Jahrhundert' [1962], in Ulrich Scheuner, *Schriften zum Völkerrecht* (Berlin: Duncker & Humblot, 1984), p. 190. See also Rudolf L. Bindschiedler, 'Illusion und Wirklichkeit', *Jahrbuch für internationales Recht* 8 (1957–8), p. 1.
109. Wilhelm Grewe, 'Die auswärtige Gewalt der Bundesrepublik', *Veröffentlichungen der Vereinigung der deutschen Staatsrechtslehrer* 12 (1954), pp. 137, 146.
110. Ibid., p. 143.
111. Ibid., p. 142.
112. Scheuner, 'Die Entwicklung des Völkerrechts im 20. Jahrhundert', pp. 188–9.

113. Ulrich Scheuner, 'Ius gentium and the present development of international law' [1962], in Scheuner, *Schriften zum Völkerrecht*, pp. 169–83.
114. Forsthoff, 'Der introvertierte Rechtsstaat', p. 396.

6

From 1968 to the Eve of Reunification

The year 1968, with its student radicalism, seemed in retrospect to mark a turning point in the intellectual history of the Federal Republic. The students indicted everything from the structure of higher education to the failure to come to terms with the past. Existing democratic institutions were denounced as façades behind which lay a potentially authoritarian, if not fascist, state. The symbol of 1968 is now regarded by some as myth rather than reality.[1] Nevertheless, it was a powerful symbol for discontent and protests that, according to Karl-Dietrich Bracher, 'led to a renaissance of the sense of crisis, which put in question anew the successful politics of reconstruction – but now in the global context of a world civilisation, of the north–south conflict and a worldwide renewal of ideologies'.[2] Marxism of varying kinds was one of those ideologies that fed into the student protests. Yet their radicalism was not only unsettling in the eyes of established figures but also seemed suspect. Indeed, the call for direct democracy seemed to invoke visions of identitarian models of democracy that were regarded as one of the flaws in German political thought.[3] Even those in principle more sympathetic to the students, including members of the Frankfurt School from whom the students initially claimed to draw inspiration, were concerned by their political activism, so much so that Jürgen Habermas accused the most radical of 'left-wing fascism', a charge from which he later distanced himself.[4]

There was, then, some irony in the fact, that as a small group of the radicals turned to terrorism, especially in the 1970s, conservative politicians accused the Frankfurt School of intellectual responsibility for the violence. The accusation, however, was taken seriously enough for Horst Ehmke to feel that it was necessary to refute it in a debate in the *Bundestag*.[5] That was in 1977 amid a series of terrorist attacks that were grouped together under the name 'the German autumn'. Anti-terrorist measures, including the exclusion of those deemed ideologically suspect from the civil service, a wide category of employees in German law, were variously perceived as a test, and demonstration, of 'militant democracy', that is, a democracy able and willing to defend itself, or as a massive challenge to the integrity of the *Rechtsstaat*. Again, Habermas expressed the latter sentiment forcefully when he spoke of a 'pogrom atmosphere' and 'totally repugnant malice'.[6]

Nor was this the only case in which the language of crisis seemed appropriate. All the western economies experienced increasing difficulty in the 1970s, aggravated by dislocation of financial and currency markets as well as increases in global oil prices. Institutional political weaknesses and changing social expectations led to talk about ungovernability. Habermas caught the mood in the title of his book *Crisis of Legitimacy*. Yet this was not the return of that crisis mood at the beginning of the 1930s in which nothing save the stars seemed stable, and Otto Kirchheimer's question 'Weimar – and what then?' was an urgent one. At the end of the 1970s, the conservative Rüdiger Altmann observed that one could not avoid the 'ironic suspicion' that for Habermas crisis seemed to be 'normal, that is, the characteristic situation of late capitalism'.[7]

Despite the terrorism and the language of crisis, the Federal Republic proved once again that Bonn is not Weimar. The problem was rather that the institutions and policies that had been the basis of the achievements of the years of reconstruction appeared to be dysfunctional rather than in imminent danger of collapse. Similarly, ideas that had been attacked as dangerous relics of a former era or even, in the case of natural law, as something that had to be recovered urgently in the light of the horrors of the past, seemed simply less relevant to the complexities of modern societies. The enthusiasm for democratisation and emancipation also faded, giving way to a change of mood, the *Tendenzwende*, which signalled a turn to a more conservative intellectual climate. For Habermas, this was an unwelcome trend, as was evident in his introduction to a collection entitled *Observations on 'The Spiritual Situation of the Age'* in which he presented the authors of the collection as members of a generation that 'has developed an awareness that our republic, even in the thirtieth year of its existence, still stands on feet of clay and must be defended against those who are no longer too timid to complain openly of a surfeit of democracy'.[8]

These transitions, whether symbolised by 1968 or by the *Tendenzwende*, did not mean that old problems disappeared. Concern about the gap between constitutional provisions and political reality, or concern about the objectivity of adjudication by the courts, both of which went back to the Wilhelmine era, continued to call for answers, even if the answer was that the concern was misconceived. Even the idea that modern societies suffer from a process of social acceleration, evident in technological development, but not only there, whereby areas of life governed by tradition are subordinated to the imperatives of abstract processes at an accelerating rate, went back to the same era.[9] From this perspective, traditional political structures appeared to be inflexible in an increasingly complex environment. Such impressions were inevitably enhanced by concern about the marginalisation of disadvantaged social groups, ecological threats and the dangers of atomic energy. It was precisely such issues that encouraged new forms of political activism and the resort to protests outside the traditional political institutions and channels.

Economic globalisation and the continuing uncertainties of the Cold War division of Europe compounded those concerns. The increased room for manoeuvre which the Federal Republic seemed to enjoy at the end of the 1960s and during the détente of the 1970s gave way to the more ideologically charged atmosphere of the second Cold War of the 1980s. For some, that reconfirmed the sense of living through a European civil war that had its roots in the First World War or even earlier. That in turn meant the perpetuation of the division of Germany and the persistence of the problem of construing German identity. As the accusations by the radical students showed, increasing distance from the Nazi era, including the emergence of a generation with no personal experience of that era, had not lessened the difficulty of how to relate to that part of Germany's past. The point had been put clearly by Chancellor Willy Brandt at the beginning of the 1970s: 'no one is free from the history that he has inherited'.[10]

By the 1980s, however, the significance of Germany's history was in dispute. Periodic attempts to draw up a balance sheet that took into account the idea of a German nation which stretched across two states proved only that the problem was intractable. Attitudes ranged from stubborn insistence upon the reality of the nation as an ethnic category, mixed with resentment against what was presented as an enforced division in the wake of a lost war, through a hypothetical acceptance of the obsolescence of Bismarck's *kleindeutsch* solution, on the condition that East Germans identified with their state to the extent that citizens of the Federal Republic did with theirs, to more or less unqualified acceptance of the status quo, which effectively wanted to shrug off the burden of the aspiration for reunification. The so-called 'historians' dispute' (*Historikerstreit*) of the mid-1980s was an especially bitter episode, in which the historian Ernst Nolte fused historical interpretation, understanding of national identity and the rhetoric of a European civil war, provoking a fierce response from Habermas.[11]

These judgements were inextricable from a wider understanding of the international order, though as in other countries of the west, other factors, including European integration and economic globalisation, played a part. In academic circles concerned with the study of the international order, the process of westernisation, or rather American-isation, was especially strong. American models, even when these were shaped by German exiles such as Hans Morgenthau in the case of realist approaches, predominated.[12] Whatever the merits of realism as a general approach to the international order were, and they were disputed, the realist approach with its emphasis upon the state, national interest and power could appear peculiarly inappropriate to the Federal Republic. That was evident when Hans-Peter Schwarz complained that Germans had moved from an obsession with power (*Machtbesessenheit*) to a neglect of power (*Machtvergessenheit*).[13]

Politics and power

That politics is about power (*Macht*) and domination (*Herrschaft*) was what made it suspect in the eyes of the student radicals. Against this they set a kind of counter-politics that did not shrink from the resort to violence in the interests of emancipation from what was seen as the institutionalised coercion of a repressive society. In this they believed, as noted above, that they could draw on the ideas of the Frankfurt School, whose members, in varying degrees, had empha-sised emancipation as the defining goal of their 'critical theory'. In the case of Habermas, this emancipatory intent had been prominent in his earliest major work. Among his critics, this led to the accusation that he was engaged in the pursuit of a utopia, to use the title of an essay by Robert Spaemann, of 'Die Utopie der Herrschaftsfreiheit' (The utopia of the freedom from domination). For Spaemann, this utopia was simply unpolitical because it does not address the basic problem that had concerned all political philosophy, namely 'the problem of the legitimation of domination'.[14] Recognition of this does not mean, he argued, sanctioning naked force. Legitimacy is the key, not, for example, fear, for fear is what motivates the obedience of the slave: 'Domination over slaves is . . . as Aristotle says, the opposite of political domination'.[15]

Moreover, Spaemann claimed that Habermas, albeit contrary to his intent, effectively sanctioned a claim to unrestricted power by those who claimed to be enlightened over those whom they deemed to be unemancipated. The goal of discourse leading to consent might be appropriate in the classroom, but it is not appropriate to the polity: 'To take political decisions means: to put through a "closure of the debate", thus to "exercise domination"'.[16] Helmut Schelsky joined in the attack, accusing Habermas and others of offering a quasi-religious doctrine of salvation behind which lay the pretensions of a new priesthood. Going back to Max Weber, he noted that *political domination* by the state was but one form of domination. Domination could also take the form of the 'hierocratic' domination of the priesthood, whose power lay in the monopoly of interpretation of sacred texts and symbols.[17]

It can be argued that Habermas had opened himself up to such attacks by seeking to deploy psychoanalytic theory as a model for a critical social theory orientated towards the removal of hidden constraints upon human action. Among the numerous problems with the analogy was the authoritarian asymmetry between the analyst and the patient. Habermas sought to defend the analogy but, in a letter to Spaemann, conceded that it had its limits.[18] Even before Spaemann's criticism, he had drawn a distinction between processes of enlightenment and decisions about political action. The core of the argument is that processes of enlightenment entail making people aware of ideological constraints that have constricted their self-understanding but that these processes are not a substitute for decisions about what political actions to take. The asymmetry, presupposed by the idea that some are enlightened and others are not, cannot be carried over into decisions about how to act. The reason for this is that political action entails risks and only those who are potentially exposed to the risks, are entitled to judge whether or not they are willing to accept them.[19] Habermas's argument clearly reflects the debates about political activism of the time, as well as long-standing debates about the relationship between theory and practice in the Marxist tradition. Yet it also has a wider significance, insofar as it is informed by an understanding of politics from the perspective of citizens considering whether, and how, to act rather than from the perspective of the state.

The clamour for the dissolution of domination seemed misguided to both Dolf Sternberger and Wilhelm Hennis, though they generally avoided the polemical excesses of Spaemann and Schelsky. Hennis, however, could not resist adding to his complaint that Habermas lacked 'any sense of the institutional moment of all political domination' the criticism that Habermas could not free himself from his 'messianic rhetoric'.[20] Hennis's objection, like Sternberger's, was that the condemnation of domination was too indiscriminate. What matters, they argued, is what kind of domination is legitimate and what kind is not legitimate. Denouncing all forms of domination as equally objectionable, or as Sternberger put it sinful, can only lead to a rage against the world that claimed to justify the murder of a state official not because he was himself a tyrant but because he embodied a system that was tyrannical.[21]

Both relied upon the contrast between rule over slaves, or paternalistic power, as understood in ancient Greece, and rule over free men. It had, they argued, been clear to the ancient Greeks that these two forms of domination are very different things. It was precisely this distinction that absolutist theories of government had lost sight of and that John Locke had sought to retain.[22] It was this distinction that led Sternberger to the apparently surprising claim that a supposed classic text about politics, Niccolò Machiavelli's *The Prince*, is not in fact about politics at all. It is, rather, about the arts of state that the ruler must practise in order to maintain a power that is essentially tyrannical in nature because it knows nothing of the free and equal citizens without whom the polis, and hence politics, does not exist.[23] For Hennis and Sternberger, the choice lies between these two forms of domination, not between an undifferentiated concept of domination and the absence of domination.

Hennis and Sternberger tried to revive a concept of politics that provided an alternative to both what they could only see as the denial of the inescapability of domination and the reduction of politics to a technical skill or science. They asserted continuity with the past that reached back to the ancient Greeks, but they knew that what they took to be old insights and distinctions had been lost or glossed over. The alternative response to the discontents of democracy was to accept what were taken to be the consequences of modernity and to remodel the concept of politics accordingly. This was the strategy that was adopted by Niklas Luhmann. For Luhmann, the key factor is the increasing complexity of modern societies and the difficulty those societies face in coping with the range of options and the flood of information that overwhelms actors. Modern societies have responded to this, according to Luhmann, by a differentiation of systems, politics, law and so on, driven by specific codes whose function is to reduce complexity by discriminating between relevant and irrelevant information. Codes are specific to different systems, and none of them provides an overarching model for society as a whole. From this perspective, politics is but one such system alongside others. It has no privileged place but only a function specific to it, namely to generate a 'generalised readiness to accept substantively indeterminate decisions within certain levels of tolerance'.[24] This model is alien to the demand for more participation insofar as other systems, especially the administrative system, are explicitly decoupled from the political system and insofar as participation ceases to be relevant to legitimacy, which is reduced to the 'equality of the chance to receive satisfactory decisions'.[25]

Approaches to politics that reduced the scope for human action were evident elsewhere. Schelsky took up his emphasis upon the struggle for intellectual hegemony and transformed it into the characteristic of politics in an age dominated by the 'global unity of electronic media' whose impact on politics, he claimed, has been even greater than that of the splitting of the atom.[26] Since politicians have to live in the glare of publicity and justify their claims to power as well as their decisions in terms of public opinion, the underlying reality of political compromise has to disappear behind a veil of half-truths and deception. His conclusion was quite simple. So far as possible, political decisions have to be withdrawn into a realm that is protected from publicity and only presented to the citizens for simple affirmation or rejection.[27] The contrast with Habermas's idea of the public sphere is striking. Habermas had been concerned by the deformation of the public sphere by the modern media, but his response had been to look for ways in which it might be opened up rather than sanctioning a withdrawal from the public sphere.

Habermas continued to argue for this, but there were also signs of increased concessions to the constraints of modern, complex societies. That became apparent in his *The Theory of Communicative Action*. As the title suggests, the book's purpose was to explain the conditions under which reaching an understanding that does not entail the kind of duplicity that Schelsky saw as endemic and that can serve as a basis for coordinated action is possible.[28] Yet the displacement of tradition by communicative action thus understood is not an unmixed blessing. According to Habermas:

> Unfettering normative contexts and releasing communicative action from traditionally based institutions . . . loads (and overloads) the mechanism of reaching understanding with a growing need for communication. On the other hand, in two central domains of action, institutions are replaced

by compulsory associations and organizations of a new type; they are formed on the basis of media that uncouple action from processes of reaching understanding and coordinate it via generalized instrumental values such as money and power.[29]

Separating out a political system as something steered by non-normative values analogous to money fits ill with a defence of the public sphere and the right of those who must bear the risks of political action to take part in political decisions. Yet there is also consistency here, for what concerned Habermas was the risk that as traditional consensus evaporates there is no guarantee that a new one will in fact be reached.

The ungovernable state?

According to Hennis, one of the characteristics of the period was that German political science did not want to see itself as the science of the state, at least not the 'state "as such" ', but that the concept of the state had been rehabilitated by the left.[30] The continuing dispute about the concept of the state was not confined to the ranks of political science as an academic discipline. Whatever the disciplinary location of the debate, a key element of disagreement remained the distinction between state and society. To those critical of the distinction, such as Christian Graf von Krockow, its defenders readily appeared as 'apologists for the state' who wanted to derive a crisis of the state from its loss of autonomy vis-à-vis society.[31] Although this was true in some cases, the arguments for retaining the distinction were varied. Horst Ehmke's criticism of the distinction formed the target for Dieter Grimm's claim that Ehmke had missed the point when he claimed that the fact that the members of the state and of society were one and the same group meant that duplicating this group into state and society is superfluous. The point was, rather, that the 'distinction between state and society does not concern persons but rather roles and communications'.[32] Hans Herbert von Arnim used similar language to separate out the role of the citizen (*Staatsbürger*), from whom it was legitimate to expect something more than the naked pursuit of self-interest, and the role of the bourgeois for whom pursuit of self-interest is quite appropriate.[33] It was Grimm, however, who identified the simple but crucial fact that no-one really wanted to fuse state and society. He suggested that opposition to the distinction really arose from a fixation with the nineteenth-century dualism that wanted to ascribe all social phenomena to one sphere or the other.

Ernst-Wolfgang Böckenförde raised the same objection. Ehmke had conflated the state–society distinction with the specific form it took in nineteenth-century constitutional thought and wanted to dismiss the former on the basis of the obsolescence of the latter.[34] The distinction, so Böckenförde argued, still had a significant function. Thus, he objected to the ascription of a 'public' function to radio stations on the grounds that this led to claims for their privileged treatment and the possible extension of such ideas and claims to, for example, churches. The outcome would be a system of privileges that is incompatible with democratic principles as well as leading to natio-nalisation (*Verstaatlichung*) by the back door.[35]

Böckenförde conceded, however, that the boundaries between state and society were far from clear-cut and that this had a bearing on the difficulty facing government in the modern world, namely that the traditional resources of the state, command and prohibition, were no longer adequate to the task.[36] Grimm made exactly the same observation.[37] Even Schelsky conceded that there was no way back to the '*Obrigkeitsstaat* of the monopoly of force'.[38] The modern state is dependent upon mass consent, and that in turn is at the mercy of conditions that the state cannot generate and of processes it can only imperfectly control. The basic problem, according to Grimm, is that the state is dependent upon its ability to steer economic processes but that it can do so only by offering rewards or imposing financial disadvantages. It cannot achieve its goals by command and hence it is reliant upon the decisions of economic actors.[39] Böckenförde added that seeking a solution through enhanced state power would merely overstretch the state. Nor could the situation be improved by trying to democratise powerful economic associations, for this would only provide an illusory legitimacy of their power and would risk a return of corporatist models that belong to an earlier era.[40] The harsh reality is that constitutional rights to private property and freedom of association mean that investors, business associations and trade unions have a decision-making capacity that is so important that it makes sense to speak of them as essential components of the political system although they are not, and cannot be, part of the constitu-tionally organised decision-making apparatus.[41]

Habermas responded to the problem by distinguishing between four different types of crisis: economic crises, rationality crises in the administrative system, legitimation crises and motivation crises. It was, however, the linkages between the different spheres demarcated by these types of crisis that was significant. Thus, Habermas claimed that 'the fundamental contradiction of capitalism is displaced from the economic into the administrative system'.[42] Similarly, in terms of motivational patterns, 'civil privatism', that is, an interest in the benefits conferred by successful state intervention but combined with limited political participation, had historically proved functional for both the state and the economy, but could no longer be guaranteed.[43] The outcome was that the state is faced with an expanded role, requiring more extensive generalised legitimation at the same time as the background, culturally generated motivational patterns that the state could not regenerate threatened to dissipate. The problem was no longer the episodic crisis that Marxists believed would eventually lead to the overthrow of capitalism but, as Habermas conceded, a 'permanent' crisis whose outcome could not be determined.

The abatement of the crisis literature in the 1980s did not put an end to doubts about the capacity of the state to deal with an increasingly complex environment. Indeed, growing concern about environmental threats and the dangers inherent in the accelerated rate of technological development in a global economy made the problem more acute. Ulrich Beck caught the mood with his proclamation of the emergence of the *Risk Society*.[44] The risks in question were not the natural disasters that had bedevilled early societies but man-made risks. For Beck, this entailed a transformation of political goals and structures. Now, the goal of '*eliminating scarcity*' is displaced by the task of '*eliminating risk*'. Equality, he claimed, had been the ambition of class-divided societies, but in the new risk society the ambition is '*safety*'.[45] From this perspective, the state is bypassed as decisions generating indeterminate risks are taken by dispersed actors involved in modernisation and globalisation and in the counter-movements that have emerged in response to them. Even for those not inclined to Beck's vague invocation of epochal change, the difficulty of ascribing to the state a responsibility to prevent risks with multiple causes or expecting it to offer compensation for damage that is potentially incalculable was clear.[46] Ironically, as the language of the risk society proliferated, the concept of the state was beginning to undergo what seemed to be a revival.[47]

Democracy and dissent

Formulating an adequate concept of democracy in this period entailed responding to a series of challenges: the disputed legacy of democratic theory, the challenge from student radicalism and the residual resurgence of nationalist sentiment in the late 1960s and civic initiatives that were sceptical of established political parties. One set of responses involved mounting a defence of the institutions and ideas of the political system of the Federal Republic against challenges that were perceived as utopian or atavistic. At the heart of this response was the idea of a militant democracy that had learned the lessons of Weimar. The alternative was to seek to accommodate new forms of political engagement. At the heart of this response was the fear that a rigid defence of existing ideas and institutions might undermine what it claimed to defend.

Gerhard Ritter was representative of the first set of responses. He defended the kind of pluralism advocated by Ernst Fraenkel and denounced both right-wing and left-wing critics of the political system.[48] His strategy, following Fraenkel, was to expose and undermine what he saw as unduly elevated and hence unachievable assertions of 'true' democracy before which existing practices inevitably appeared deficient. A more nuanced defence of the democratic principle came from Martin Kriele. He too was deeply influenced by the challenge from the left and especially by criticism of the institutional reality of modern democracy in the name of self-determination and true democracy.[49] Both Ritter and Kriele followed Fraenkel in seeing Rousseauian ideas as a key part of the problem. Kriele added that 'Rule by the people in the sense of parliamentary democracy is identical with the rule of law [*Herrschaft des Rechts*] (in the sense of the *rule of law* not of the *Rechtsstaat*)'.[50] He meant this quite literally. Both historically and theoretically, parliamentary democracy has to be seen as a transfer of the judicial procedures of the common-law tradition to the political process. Democracy then appears not as the manifestation of an unmediated will of the people but as a procedurally regulated deliberation that issues in a binding decision. That meant rebutting Carl Schmitt's arguments about the supposed obsolescence of deliberation. Schmitt, in fact, so argued Kriele, had missed the point of deliberation in his enthusiasm for what Kriele described as 'vulgar voluntarism'. The point of deliberation is to focus attention on what the issues are, which is by no means self-evident, and gradually to change the experience (*Erfahrung*) through which we filter immediate impressions (*Erlebnis*).[51]

Kriele's defence of parliamentary democracy as a process characterised by the institutional mediation of the will of people presumed, however, faith in the institutions through which this was to take place. Precisely that was what was lacking in many of the calls for direct democracy. Discontent with political parties (*Parteienverdrossenheit*) joined a similar exasperation with the workings of parliament that refused to go away. This induced a variety of defences. Hennis argued that the error lay in the supposition that the prime task of political parties is to form the political will of the people, which in turn led to an obsession with the internal democratic organisation of political parties that was reflected in the long history of research into party organisation that repeatedly discovered oligarchic traits in political parties. It was, he claimed, one of the legacies of Weimar and pre-Weimar German politics that precedence was given to reflecting the will of the people and to the influence of the party base on its leadership rather than the actual task of governing.[52] Böckenförde also sought to cut the ground from under the feet of the advocates of direct democracy. The argument that representative democracy is a concession to the difficulty of implementing direct democracy in large complex states itself concedes too much. Democratic government is still government. What matters is not that such government should be constrained or reduced to a minimum in favour of authentic democracy but that it is the product of democratic authorisation and is responsible government.[53]

While Kriele, Hennis and Böckenförde took a stand against the clamour for participation and direct democracy, when Michael Stolleis took stock of the debates in the mid-1980s he was more flexible. He acknowledged that the 'longing for a Rousseauian identity and harmony' was part of the legacy of German political culture but denied that this was sufficient to account for the disrepute into which the parties had fallen.[54] Stolleis's concern was that the political energies that were manifest in the citizens' initiative movements and elsewhere might lack adequate channels through which they could be expressed. In part, the problem was not new. The idea that political parties had a monopoly on expressing the will of the people, which was symbolised in Gerhard Leibholz's idea of the parties as the 'loudspeaker' of the people, had never been true. Nor was the demand for direct democracy to be rejected out of hand as unconstitutional. Indeed, he suggested that plebiscitarian elements might have a beneficial effect. By providing an outlet for discontent, they could help 'to neutralise the slow poison of the feeling of impotence vis-à-vis the over-powerful autonomous party apparatus'.[55]

That, however, presumed a certain tolerance of dissent and protest, albeit not of the resort to terror. Even as the 'German autumn' gave way to a period of less extreme forms of opposition, some were worried by what they saw as the inclination to invoke scenarios of civil war, to which Kriele was inclined, in order to condemn any form of protest that did not stay within the strict confines of the law as morally reprehensible, criminal and unconstitutional. According to Habermas, this was the product of a 'German Hobbesianism' that recognised only the state-guaranteed security and public order as a legitimate goal.[56] Yet even some of those who can be ascribed to the étatist camp were concerned by the form that militant democracy had taken. Thus, in the immediate aftermath of the German autumn, Böckenförde expressed concern about the measures taken by the state in response to terrorism, although he also argued for constitutionally anchored emergency powers of a far wider remit than those which had been introduced in the 1960s. He drew widely on Carl Schmitt's arguments to make his case but with the explicit purpose of avoiding resort to an unconstrained and indeterminate right of the state to take whatever powers it deemed fit in an emergency.[57] His reservations about the measures that had been taken centred on the introduction of a principle of 'hostility to the constitution' that, he argued, had no legal basis and effectively condemned a range of actions, including signing petitions, that in themselves were in no way illegal. In effect, they made what the authorities deemed to be 'loyal convictions' rather than specific acts the criteria according to which individuals could be judged in such matters as prospective employment by the state.[58]

In the albeit different, if still tense, climate of the mid-1980s, Habermas sought to defend the idea of 'civil disobedience' against approaches that insisted that 'law is law' with all the vigour of what he presented as a legal positivism discredited by its complicity in the Third Reich.[59] He insisted, however, that civil disobedience has to remain in a state of suspense between legality and legitimacy. More precisely, he argued that civil disobedience has to be a 'morally *based* protest'. Personal interest or privately held convictions do not suffice. Second, it has to be a '*public* act' which is normally announced in advance in order to allow the authorities to take appropriate action. Third, it should involve only the '*provisional violation*' of specific laws and should not challenge the legal order as a whole. Fourth, those engaged in civil disobedience should be prepared to bear the legal consequences that follow from their acts. Indeed, he presented this element of risk as some kind of surety for the moral basis of the disobedience. Finally, disobedience must be of a purely '*symbolic character*', that is, it must not involve any form of violence.[60]

Constitutional state, Rechtsstaat, Sozialstaat

The tension between the static and the dynamic elements of political life that marked discussion of democracy and dissent affected other key concepts. So too did the very success of the ideas and institutions that had played a key role in the Federal Republic, namely the Federal Constitutional Court and the *Sozialstaat*. The disturbances, dissent and reactions which they provoked quickly brought up the idea of a growing divergence between the constitution and constitutional reality, which was a theme that periodically agitated German political theorists throughout the century. Indeed, Hennis saw this as a vice that was peculiar to German constitutional thought. The problem, he claimed, was that German constitutionalism had not set out from the principle of the sovereignty of the people, from which the offices and instruments of government emanated. Instead, it was rooted in the nineteenth century and the existence of monarchical states that granted constitutions that licensed or recognised those social groups that could not be ignored as politically relevant factors. By the same token, whatever was not constitutionally recognised had to appear suspect. Hence, he complained, so long as political parties were not cloaked in the 'ermine of constitutional "recognition"', they were regarded as 'somewhat unpleasant' and even as unconstitutional.[61] He was no less critical of the related tendency to see the constitution as the source of a catalogue of tasks that government and parliament were enjoined to complete.[62]

Behind Hennis's criticisms lay a set of persisting problems, namely of how to construe the relationship between the state and the people, how to understand judicial interpretation and whether the social state should be seen as a constitutionally programmed phenomenon. The problematic relationship between state and people became apparent when the idea of the people as a *pouvoir constituant* was discussed. Böckenförde insisted that this idea had to be retained, yet he knew that it was seen as an idea that had been used to argue that the constitution was the product of some form of essentially arbitrary decision upon the part of the people. His response was that the idea of the people as the *pouvoir constituant* was an eminently democratic one that could be traced from the days of the French Revolution through liberal German constitutional thought of the nineteenth century into the constitution of the Weimar Republic and the Basic Law. In addition to attempting to demonstrate the democratic pedigree of the idea, he also argued that critics of the idea mistakenly assumed that the *pouvoir constituant* is a normatively empty category, whereas the very term itself indicated the desire to create a constitution and hence presumed the existence of a sense of law, political order and so on.[63]

Both Peter Häberle and Sternberger objected to attempts to base the constitution on the concept of the people. For Häberle, it is little more than a 'cryptomonarchical' idea according to which the sovereign people is supposed to fill the role once played by the monarch. The appropriate reference is not the sovereign people but the 'basic right of freedom'.[64] Sternberger took exception to the idea, enshrined in the Basic Law, that 'all state authority emanates from the people' and insisted that the constitutions rest 'not on the collective person, the "people", but on the plural citizenship of the "*civitas*" . . . or of the "*universitas civium*", the totality or community of citizens'.[65] What divided Böckenförde on the one hand and Häberle and Sternberger on the other hand was not commitment to the constitutional order but the connotations of the idea of the sovereignty of the people. Whereas Böckenförde saw a concept with a democratic pedigree that provided the ultimate legitimacy for the constitution, Häberle and Sternberger saw a concept with, in part at least, an authoritarian pedigree that rested on a fiction and encouraged excessive expectations.

Since the Basic Law was in many ways the anchor point of political thought, the role of the Federal Constitutional Court and the nature of adjudication remained key issues of dispute. Although Herbert Krüger continued to insist that subsumption is the core of adjudication, that idea was losing plausibility to the point where it could be asserted that it 'can . . . no longer be seriously maintained that the application of laws involves *no more* than a logical subsumption under abstractly formulated major premises'.[66] If this was accepted, as it was by many, the question arose as to how adjudication should be conceived. Here, Robert Alexy developed an elaborate theory of legal argumentation in order to block the old charge that the only alternative to adjudication as subsumption was the more or less open resort to subjective, and hence arbitrary, values.[67] That in turn fed into a theory of constitutional rights according to which such rights should be construed as principles or '*optimization requirements*', that is, norms that can be satisfied to a greater or lesser extent and which may come into conflict with one another, and hence have to be balanced by courts.[68]

The challenge posed by arguments for an enhanced role for the courts could also be met either by looking to the exercise of discretion by the courts themselves or by straightforward opposition. Häberle continued to argue for some limitation of their power, not by tying them to a narrowly conceived legal positivism with the associated idea of adjudication as subsumption but by setting judicial interpretation into a wider social context. For Häberle, this meant that the courts, especially the Federal Constitutional Court, had to pay special attention to issues that were under constant public discussion and to those which aroused strong dissent. Insufficient sensitivity in the latter case might endanger the integrative function of the constitution. Yet it is not only high-profile or highly contentious issues to which the court should give special consideration. Concerns which are typically not well represented, such as the interests of consumers or ecological issues, also deserve special consideration. The underlying logic of Häberle's position induced him to argue for judicial constraint where participation, in the form of public debate, is widespread or intense, yet for judicial activism where it is diffuse or weak. Judicial control should step into the breach left by deficient public participation.[69]

Others regarded the Court's activities, especially its invocation of value-orientated adjudication, with great suspicion. Both Ulrich Preuss and Ingeborg Maus invoked the judicial activism of the courts in Weimar Germany, which both saw as contributing to the failure of the Republic, as a warning. Indeed, Preuss claimed that in the mid-1970s there was a distinct danger of degrading the constitution into an 'instrument for political and moral expatriation'.[70] Here, it was not only Weimar that served as a warning but also the persecution of German socialists and Catholics in the nineteenth century. Yet this was not the only conclusion that could be drawn from German history. Even those who broadly agreed that judicial activism had become excessive could raise another spectre from the past, namely the value relativism that had supposedly contributed to the demise of the Republic.[71] The analogies on both sides of the argument were dubious insofar as there was no reason to doubt the commitment of the courts to the Bonn Republic, and the old argument that value relativism rendered the German judiciary impotent in the face of the critics of Weimar is misguided. Nevertheless, the power of these images of the failure of Weimar was sufficiently strong to make them seem plausible even in the radically different context of the Federal Republic.

Reflecting on these debates from the viewpoint of the mid-1980s, Grimm too worried about the condition of the *Rechtsstaat* but from a somewhat different perspective. The problem, he thought, lay in the style of political debate and an increasing tendency to present one's own preferences not merely as rational and desirable but as constitutionally required and hence to denounce the opponent's views as not merely inappropriate but as unconstitutional. There was a vicious circle in which political parties sought to use the Court in order to continue to pursue their political preferences, to which the Court too often succumbed. Political parties could also use the decisions of the Court, especially where these might be unpopular, as a screen behind which they could hide.[72] Grimm insisted that the Court neither could nor should be the primary mechanism for securing the underlying social consensus that sustained the Republic. That was the task of the political parties.

Judicial activism could be seen as inevitable and necessary or as excessive and avoidable. So too the implementation of the *Sozialstaat* appeared to have ambiguous consequences. The old debate about the extent to which the principle of the *Sozialstaat* was constitutionally prescribed and hence judicially enforceable continued.[73] Maus discerned an unholy alliance between the judiciary and the administrative agencies, which found its justification in the work of Luhmann. The enhanced autonomy of the judiciary and the assertion of a value-orientated approach went hand in hand with a tendency to assess the relative weight of competing values case by case. That, so argued Maus, facilitated the kind of discretion, exercised according to its own internal imperatives, favoured by the administration.[74] It also left the clients of the welfare state, at least in some cases, subject to that administrative discretion.

Maus was critical of Habermas, to whom she was otherwise much closer than to Luhmann. For Habermas, the modern welfare state was the last in a series of waves of 'juridification', that is, of the extension of the remit of positive law over areas previously regulated by tradition. As with previous waves of juridification, the extension of formal, abstract law to matters of welfare was intended to guarantee freedom. However,

> The *dilemmatic structure of this type of juridification* consists in the fact that, while the welfare-state guarantees are intended to serve the goal of social integration, they nevertheless promote the disintegration of life-relations when these are separated, through legalized social intervention, from the consensual mechanisms that coordinate action and are transferred over to media such as power and money.[75]

For Maus, the problem arises not from the formal, abstract quality of law that tears people from the consensual social contexts within which identities are formed and maintained but a 'de-formalised' type of law that maximises bureaucratic discretion. Despite this important difference, Habermas and Maus were agreed that the development of the *Sozialstaat* was exhibiting negative features, and this was connected with the form taken by the *Rechtsstaat*. The unity of *Rechtsstaat* and *Sozialstaat* had turned out to be problematic in the eyes of theorists who had no desire to retreat to a pre-interventionist idyll or to play off the concepts of the *Rechtsstaat* and the *Sozialstaat* against each other.

National identity and international order

Throughout the countervailing economic global disorder, moves towards further European integration, emergence and fading of the so-called Second Cold War, one thing seemed relatively constant and predictable: the division of Germany. Surveying German foreign policy at the beginning of the 1970s, Waldemar Besson recalled that it was not the first time in the history of the Germans that nation and state failed to coincide in central Europe. To reinforce the inescapability of this fact, he invoked the warning of a nineteenth-century Austrian minister that Bismarck's Germany could aim to unite all Germans only through a bid for European hegemony, a bid that no state had carried off, and that the consequence of failure would be the division of Bismarck's Germany.[76]

Continuity, represented by the persistence of the nation, and discontinuity, represented by the existence of two states, both found justification in the doctrines of international law. Thus, Alfred Verdross could still invoke the continuity of the personality of the state despite a change of government and even despite the temporary disintegration of the state organisation, with explicit reference to Germany after 1945 and Austria after 1938.[77] Continuity as well as the impact of the reality of division was also evident when Ulrich Scheuner quoted international agreements asserting that every state has the right to choose its own political, economic, social and cultural system without interference from other states.[78] That had a wider, global significance but also specific relevance to a Germany whose separate states had chosen, albeit not without external constraints of differing intensity, such radically different systems.

Scheuner was far from oblivious to the novelties of the age, among which, as Hans Peter Ipsen pointed out, Scheuner emphasised Article 24 of the Basic Law that allowed the Federal Republic to 'transfer sovereign powers to international organisations'.[79] In the context of European integration, that meant that citizens could invoke the law of the European Community in national courts against their own state. As Ipsen suggested, the dualistic separation of domestic law and international law and the associated doctrine of the indivisibility of sovereignty had long since been modified as German theorists at the end of the nineteenth century, faced with German unity but also with the persistence of the pre-existing states, continued to designate the latter as states although they were clearly no longer sovereign.[80]

Adaptation to the reality of division and European integration, aided by the recollection of states without sovereignty, was one option. Another was rage against the German predicament, accompanied by more or less resignation. Both were present at the end of the 1960s in Arnold Gehlen's reassertion of self-preservation as the overriding purpose of the state and his lament for Prussia, whose fate he compared to that of Carthage at the end of the third Punic War.[81] Gehlen's main complaint was that Germans had lost sight of this reality as they accepted the 'prescribed moral diet of an invalid'.[82] There was less resignation in Bernhard Willms in the mid-1980s as he called for a reassertion of German idealism as the standard of a revived national consciousness amid what he described as a global civil war. Only thus, he claimed, could Germany's existence be wrung from the hands of the victors of the Second World War, for the 'defeat would only be complete with the destruction of German self-consciousness'.[83]

Willms's intervention came amid the so-called *Historikerstreit* (historians' dispute), although one of the main protagonists, Habermas, was not an historian. At issue was what one side saw as the need to adopt a cooler, more dispassionate assessment of Germany's past and, for some, to re-establish an account of German history with which Germans could identify. According to Michael Stürmer, the alternative was a 'country without memory'. Hence, he continued, 'The search for a lost past is not an abstract striving for culture and education. It is morally legitimate and politically necessary. We are dealing with the inner continuity of the German republic and its predictability in foreign policy terms.'[84] The critics of these revisionists agreed that this was a political issue, though they rejected Stürmer's implication that failure to reassert the kind of memory which he wanted entailed some kind of unpredictability in foreign policy. In fact, the dispute was not about whether Germany should be a country without a memory but what kind of conclusions should be drawn from memory of the past. It was in this context that Habermas made his dramatic assertion and defence of the discontinuity of German history:

> The only patriotism that does not alienate us from the West is a constitutional patriotism. Unfortunately, in the cultural nation of the Germans, a connection to universalist constitutional principles that was anchored in convictions could be formed only after – and through – Auschwitz.[85]

The point was made with less passion by Kurt Sontheimer. The revisionist historians were challenging the consensus that the democracy of the Federal Republic had been built not on the ideas found in German history but in the tradition of western liberal democracy.[86] There was some truth in this, but the consensus had never been complete, and it relied upon a sometimes indiscriminate, monochrome image of the history of German political thought.

Habermas's position found only partial support in the work of Sternberger, who had coined the term 'constitutional patriotism'. This amounted to a restatement of ideas that he had formulated in the immediate aftermath of the Second World War. In the 1970s and 1980s, he emphasised that constitutional patriotism constituted a 'second patriotism' that was founded on the Basic Law and warned against any temptation to draw away from the constitution for the sake of the completeness of the nation.[87] This kind of patriotism is, he argued, the presupposition for cosmopolitanism insofar as people have to belong somewhere before they can expand their horizons. Conversely, echoing Hannah Arendt, he insisted: 'Human rights are only redeemable as civil rights within a state, namely within a constitutional state'.[88] Crucially, he claimed that this patriotism predated 'the entire nation-state organisation of Europe'.[89] It was this that he chose to emphasise in his response to what he took to be some misinterpretation of his ideas in the historians' dispute. The point was not to provide a substitute for a discredited national patriotism but to recall, and advocate, a European conception of patriotism that pre-dated the nationalist tradition.[90]

The challenges to which the Federal Republic was exposed, both domestically and internationally, often induced a bitterness that was coloured by the invocation of a discredited legacy. Yet political thought of this period also exhibited the desire to reach back to ideas that pre-dated the European turn towards the nation state or responded to the need to deal with new problems, whether induced by the very success of the *Sozialstaat* or the crisis of ungovernability and the emergence of new forms of risk. It also had to respond to increasing difficulty that the Federal Republic's key institutions, political parties, experienced in managing these problems. In all this, consensus proved elusive, being invoked most readily when it was said to be under attack.

Notes

1. See Edgar Wolfrum, '"1968" in der gegenwärtigen deutschen Geschichtspolitik', *Aus Politik und Zeitgeschichte* 22–3 (2001), pp. 28–36.
2. Quoted in Kurt Sontheimer, *So war Deutschland nie* (Munich: Beck, 1999), p. 93.
3. See Frieder Günther, *Denken vom Staat her* (Munich: Oldenbourg, 2004), p. 308.
4. Jürgen Habermas, 'On morality, law, civil disobedience and modernity' [1986], in Peter Dews (ed.), *Autonomy and Solidarity* (London: Verso, 1992), p. 233.
5. Horst Ehmke, *Politik als Herausforderung* (Karlsruhe: Müller, 1979), p. 80.
6. Jürgen Habermas, 'Critical theory and Frankfurt University' [1985], in Dews (ed.), *Autonomy and Solidarity*, p. 221.
7. Rüdiger Altmann, 'Vorüberlegungen zum Ernstfall' [1979], in Rüdiger Altmann, *Abschied vom Staat* (Frankfurt am Main: Campus, 1998), p. 193.
8. Jürgen Habermas (ed.), *Observations on 'The Spiritual Situation of the Age'* [1979] (Cambridge, MA: MIT, 1984), p. 6.
9. See John H. Herz, 'Stagnationsfaktoren der modernen Gesellschaft', in Heinz Maus (ed.), *Gesellschaft, Recht und Politik* (Neuwied: Luchterhand, 1968), pp. 147–8.
10. Quoted in Helmut Dubiel, *Niemand ist frei von der Geschichte* (Munich: Hanser, 1999), p. 133.
11. See Ernst Nolte, *Der Europäische Bürgerkrieg* (Munich: Herbig, 1997). The first edition appeared in 1987.
12. See the survey by Volker Rittberger and Hartwig Hummel, 'Die Disziplin "Internationale Beziehungen" im deutschsprachigen Raum auf der Suche nach ihrer Identität', *Politische Vierteljahresschrift* Special Issue 21 (1990), pp. 17–47.
13. Hans-Peter Schwarz, *Die gezähmten Deutschen. Von der Machtbesessenheit zur Machtvergessenheit* (Stuttgart: DVA, 1985).
14. Robert Spaemann, 'Die Utopie der Herrschaftsfreiheit' [1972], in Robert Spaemann, *Zur Kritik der politischen Utopie* (Stuttgart: Klett, 1977), p. 104. On Spaemann, see Claus Leggewie, *Der Geist steht Rechts* (Berlin: Rotbuch, 1987), pp. 145–72.

15. Spaemann, 'Die Utopie der Herrschaftsfreiheit', p. 104.
16. Ibid., p. 123.
17. Helmut Schelsky, *Die Arbeit tun die anderen* (Opladen: Westdeutscher Verlag, 1975), p. 39.
18. In Spaemann, *Zur Kritik der politischen Utopie*, p. 135.
19. Jürgen Habermas, 'Introduction: Some difficulties in the attempt to link theory and practice' [1971], in Jürgen Habermas, *Theory and Practice* (London: Heinemann, 1974), pp. 32–40.
20. Wilhelm Hennis, 'Legitimität' [1976], in Wilhelm Hennis, *Politikwissenschaft und politisches Denken* (Tübingen: Mohr, 2000), p. 268.
21. Dolf Sternberger, 'Der alte Streit um den Ursprung der Herrschaft' [1977], in Dolf Sternberger, *Herrschaft und Vereinbarung* (Frankfurt am Main: Insel, 1980), pp. 15–17.
22. Wilhelm Hennis, 'Ende der Politik?' [1971], in Hennis, *Politikwissenschaft und politisches Denken*, p. 234.
23. Dolf Sternberger, 'Machiavellis "Principe" und der Begriff des Politischen' [1975], in Sternberger, *Herrschaft und Vereinbarung*, pp. 37–42.
24. Niklas Luhmann, *Legitimation durch Verfahren* [1969] (Frankfurt am Main: Suhrkamp, 1983), p. 28.
25. Ibid., p. 30.
26. Helmut Schelsky, 'Der "Begriff des Politischen" und die politische Erfahrung der Gegenwart', *Der Staat* 22 (1982), p. 331.
27. Ibid., p. 341.
28. Jürgen Habermas, *The Theory of Communicative Action*, vol. 1 [1981] (London: Heinemann, 1984), p. 99.
29. Ibid., pp. 341–2.
30. Hennis, 'Legitimität', p. 251.
31. Christian Graf von Krockow, 'Staat, Gesellschaft, Freiheitswahrung', *Aus Politik und Zeitgeschichte* 7 (1972), p. 12.
32. Dieter Grimm, 'Die politischen Parteien' [1983], in Dieter Grimm, *Die Zukunft der Verfassung*, 2nd edn (Frankfurt am Main: Suhrkamp, 1994), p. 273.
33. Hans Herbert von Arnim, *Staatslehre der Bundesrepublik Deutschland* (Munich: Franz Vahlen, 1984), p. 207.
34. Ernst-Wolfgang Böckenförde, 'Die Bedeutung der Unterscheidung von Staat und Gesellschaft im demokratischen Sozialstaat der Gegenwart' [1972], in Ernst-Wolfgang Böckenförde, *Recht, Staat, Freiheit* (Frankfurt am Main: Suhrkamp, 1991), p. 221.
35. Ibid., pp. 229–31.
36. Ernst-Wolfgang Böckenförde, 'Die politische Funktion wirtschaftlich-sozialer Verbände und Interessenträger in der sozialstaatlichen Demokratie' [1976], in Ernst-Wolfgang Böckenförde, *Staat, Verfassung, Demokratie* (Frankfurt am Main: Suhrkamp, 1991), p. 408.

37. Dieter Grimm, 'Die Zukunft der Verfassung' [1990], in Grimm, *Die Zukunft der Verfassung*, pp. 420–1.
38. Schelsky, *Die Arbeit tun die anderen*, p. 158.
39. Grimm, 'Die Zukunft der Verfassung', p. 422.
40. Böckenförde, 'Die politische Funktion wirtschaftlich-sozialer Verbände und Interessenträger in der sozialstaatlichen Demokratie', pp. 430–3.
41. Ibid., p. 418.
42. Jürgen Habermas, *Legitimation Crisis* [1973] (London: Heinemann, 1976), p. 63.
43. Ibid., p. 75.
44. Thus the title of his book *Risk Society* [1986] (London: Sage, 1992).
45. Ibid., pp. 47–9.
46. Thus Grimm, 'Die Zukunft der Verfassung', pp. 417–20.
47. See Gunnar Folke Schuppert, 'Zur Neubelebung der Staatsdiskussion: Entzauberung des Staates oder "Bringing the State Back In" ', *Der Staat* 28 (1989), pp. 91–104.
48. Gerhard A. Ritter, 'Der Antiparlamentarismus und Antipluralismus der Rechts- und Linksradikalen', *Aus Politik und Zeitgeschichte* 34 (1969), pp. 3–27.
49. Martin Kriele, *Einführung in die Staatslehre*, 5th edn (Opladen: Westdeutscher Verlag, 1994), pp. 292–4. The first edition appeared in 1975. For the abiding significance of the 'years following 1968', see the Preface, p. 9.
50. Martin Kriele, 'Das demokratische Prinzip im Grundgesetz', *Veröffentlichungen der Vereinigung der deutschen Staatsrechtslehrer* 29 (1971), p. 49.
51. Ibid., pp. 56–8.
52. Wilhelm Hennis, 'Regierbarkeit' [1977], in Wilhelm Hennis, *Regieren im modernen Staat* (Tübingen: Mohr, 1999), pp. 308–9.
53. Ernst-Wolfgang Böckenförde, 'Demokratie und Repräsentation' [1983], in Böckenförde, *Staat, Verfassung, Demokratie*, pp. 388–90.
54. Michael Stolleis, 'Parteienstaatlichkeit – Krisensymptome des demokratischen Verfassungsstaats?', *Veröffentlichungen der Vereinigung der deutschen Staatsrechtslehrer* 44 (1986), p. 18.
55. Ibid., p. 38.
56. Jürgen Habermas, 'Recht und Gewalt – ein deutsches Trauma' [1984], in Jürgen Habermas, *Die neue Unübersichtlichkeit* (Frankfurt am Main: Suhrkamp, 1985), pp. 100–17.
57. Ernst-Wolfgang Böckenförde, 'Der verdrängte Ausnahmezustand', *Neue juristische Wochenschrift* 38 (1977), pp. 1,881–90.
58. Ernst-Wolfgang Böckenförde, 'Verhaltensgewähr oder Gesinnungstreue?' [1978], in Böckenförde, *Staat, Verfassung, Demokratie*, pp. 277–85.
59. Jürgen Habermas, 'Zivil Ungehorsam – Testfall für den demokratischen Rechtsstaat' [1983], in Habermas, *Die neue Unübersichtlichkeit*, p. 97.

60. Ibid., pp. 83–4, 90.
61. Wilhelm Hennis, 'Verfassung und Verfassungswirklichkeit. Ein deutsches Problem' [1968], in Hennis, *Regieren im modernen Staat*, p. 195.
62. Ibid., p. 197.
63. Ernst-Wolfgang Böckenförde, 'Die verfassungsgebende Gewalt des Volkes' [1986], in Böckenförde, *Staat, Verfassung, Demokratie*, pp. 90–112.
64. Peter Häberle, 'Die offene Gesellschaft der Verfassungsinterpretation' [1975], in Peter Häberle, *Verfassung als öffentlicher Prozess* (Berlin: Duncker & Humblot, 1998), p. 171.
65. Dolf Sternberger, 'Die neue Politie' [1985], in Dolf Sternberger, *Verfassungspatriotismus* (Frankfurt am Main: Insel, 1990), p. 227.
66. Thus Konrad Larenz quoted in Robert Alexy, *A Theory of Legal Argumentation* [1978] (Oxford: Clarendon, 1989), p. 1. For Herbert Krüger's assertion, see 'Die deutsche Staatlichkeit im Jahre 1971', *Der Staat* 10 (1971), p. 18.
67. Alexy, *A Theory of Legal Argumentation*, passim.
68. Robert Alexy, *A Theory of Constitutional Rights* [1986] (Oxford: Oxford University Press, 2002), pp. 47–56.
69. Häberle, 'Die offene Gesellschaft der Verfassungsinterpretation', pp. 174–5.
70. Ulrich K. Preuss, 'Legalität – Loyalität – Legitimität', *Leviathan* 5 (1977), p. 465. For the concerns of Ingeborg Maus, see 'Entwicklung und Funktionswandel der Theorie des bürgerlichen Rechtsstaates' [1978], in Ingeborg Maus, *Rechtstheorie und politische Theorie im Industriekapitalismus* (Munich: Fink, 1986), p. 46.
71. Thus Jürgen Seifert, 'Haus oder Forum', in Jürgen Habermas (ed.), *Stichworte zur 'Geistigen Situation der Zeit'*, vol. 1 (Frankfurt am Main: Suhrkamp, 1979), p. 335.
72. Dieter Grimm, 'Verfassungsrechtlicher Konsens und politische Polarisierung in der Bundesrepublik Deutschland' [1984], in Grimm, *Die Zukunft der Verfassung*, pp. 307–8.
73. See, for example, Ernst-Wolfgang Böckenförde, 'Die sozialen Grundrechte im Verfassungsgefüge' [1986], in Böckenförde, *Staat, Verfassung, Demokratie*, pp. 146–58.
74. Ingeborg Maus, 'Verrechtlichung, Entrechtlichung und der Funktionswandel von Institutionen' [1986], in Maus, *Rechtstheorie und politische Theorie im Industriekapitalismus*, pp. 287–9.
75. Jürgen Habermas, *The Theory of Communicative Action*, vol. 2 [1981] (Cambridge: Polity, 1987), p. 364.
76. Waldemar Besson, *Die Aussenpolitik der Bundesrepublik* (Frankfurt am Main: Ullstein, 1973), pp. 425–6.
77. Alfred Verdross and Bruno Simma, *Universelles Völkerrecht*, 3rd edn (Berlin: Duncker & Humblot, 1984), pp. 232–3.

78. Ulrich Scheuner, 'Die internationalen Probleme der Gegenwart und die nationale Entscheidungsstruktur' [1977], in Ulrich Scheuner, *Schriften zum Völkerrecht* (Berlin: Duncker & Humblot, 1984), pp. 309–10.
79. See Hans Peter Ipsen, 'Über Supranationalität', in Horst Ehmke et al. (eds), *Festschrift für Ulrich Scheuner* (Berlin: Duncker & Humblot, 1973), p. 225.
80. Ibid., pp. 214–15.
81. Arnold Gehlen, *Moral und Hypermoral* [1969] (Frankfurt am Main: Klostermann, 2004), pp. 112, 117.
82. Ibid., p. 118.
83. Bernhard Willms, *Idealismus und Nation* (Paderborn: Schöningh, 1986), p. 14.
84. Michael Stürmer, 'History in a land without history' [1986], in James Knowlton and Truett Cates (eds), *Forever in the Shadow of Hitler?* (New Jersey: Humanities Press, 1993), pp. 16–17.
85. Jürgen Habermas, 'Apologetic tendencies' [1986], in Jürgen Habermas, *The New Conservatism* (Cambridge: Polity, 1989), p. 227.
86. Kurt Sontheimer, 'Makeup artists are creating a new identity' [1986], in Knowlton and Cates (eds), *Forever in the Shadow of Hitler?*, p. 187.
87. Dolf Sternberger, 'Verfassungspatriotismus' [1979], in Sternberger, *Verfassungspatriotismus*, p. 13, and 'Verfassungspatriotismus: Rede bei der 25-Jahr-Feier der "Akademie für Politische Bildung"' [1982], in ibid., p. 31.
88. Ibid. [1982], p. 26.
89. Ibid., p. 20.
90. Dolf Sternberger, 'Anmerkungen beim Colloquium über "Patriotismus" in Heidelberg am 6. November 1987', in Sternberger, *Verfassungspatriotismus*, p. 32.

7

Reunification and Globalisation

'German unity came like a thief in the night – no one had expected it.'[1] This was, of course, not the first time in German history that the unexpected had happened. The apparent stability and permanence of the Cold War division of Germany turned out to be no more firmly rooted than the monarchical principle that had dominated the lands of the Germans until defeat at the end of the First World War. There were, however, enormous differences between the two transitions. After 1918, new constitutions had to be written and implemented against a background of political turbulence, including violence, and the shock of defeat and a detested peace settlement. After 1989, it proved possible to incorporate East Germany into the constitutional order of the Federal Republic without the formation of a new constitution despite the fact that the latter had clearly been envisaged by the Basic Law.

The apparent ease of reunification was deceptive in several senses. In the first place, the rapid process of reunification unsettled some observers. Indeed, the prospect of reunification had not seemed attractive at all to those who still saw the *kleindeutsch* Germany of Bismarck as a more or less unmitigated disaster. Thus, Joschka Fischer warned that 'The German national state of Bismarck, the German *Reich*, had twice overrun the world with wars, which brought with them unspeakable suffering'.[2] The fact that it took place without a fundamental debate about the future state of the Germans compounded the reservations of those with strong attachments to the achievements of the Federal Republic. The politician Fischer was not the only one from the generation of 1968 whose critical pedigree turned out to be mixed with such positive sentiments for the Bonn Republic.[3] In the second place, the extent of the changes that reunification brought soon proved to be greater and more problematic than the optimists had suggested amid the rush to unity. So much did this seem to be the case to Wilhelm Hennis that he complained that 'We are not managing the radical *transformation of circumstances* since 1990, we still do not want to take them into account. The

Federal Republic of 1997 is in fact a completely different Republic from that of 1987.'[4]

The difficulty in dealing with the blend of continuity and discontinuity surrounding reunification was aggravated by the continuing echoes of the past in a country in which, as the conservative Günter Rohrmoser put it, 'Whoever interprets history, so one could say, also determines the politics'.[5] The concept of the political and the profession of politics were on the agenda again as they had been at the beginning of the Weimar Republic when Max Weber gave his influential lecture on the profession of politics. Yet, for all the contemporary relevance of Weber's account, the resurgence of interest in the concept of the political and the professionalisation of politics took place in a context in which the figure of the politician who acted on the ethics of conviction seemed a less plausible case. Towards the end of the twentieth century, it was not so much an excess of conviction that seemed the problem as, to use the title of one book, *Politik ohne Projekt* (Politics without a Project) and the general sense of malaise that surrounded political activity and what was seen as a self-serving political class.[6]

An even more complex entwining of continuity and discontinuity surrounded the idea of the state. The Federal Republic had finally been freed from the residual restraints upon its sovereignty and thus seemed to be, as some put it, a 'normal state' – a characterisation that Jürgen Habermas dismissed as 'The Second Life-Giving Lie of the Federal Republic'.[7] For the advocates of the return to 'normality', the restoration of national unity and state sovereignty had finally put an end to the German *Sonderweg*, though it seemed that Germany's 'special road' now referred less to the circumstances that led to the Third Reich and more to the division of Germany and the presumption that Germans still had to 'come to terms with the past'. Whatever the appropriate interpretation of the past is, it is not clear what counted as normal at the end of the twentieth century. Domestically, the welfare state, which formed the common basis for post-war European states, was under strain. In Germany, that strain was compounded by the difficulty of integrating the new eastern *Länder*, but the basic problem was European-wide. Internationally, the end of the Cold War seemed to enhance room for manoeuvre at the same time as American hegemony restricted it. The rhetoric of sovereignty was challenged by the rhetoric of humanitarian intervention that seemed to some little more than a pretext for imperial ambitions. For Germany, sovereignty had indeed been regained, but this was the sovereignty of a normal member of the European Union. It was the sovereignty of a state enmeshed in innumerable international agreements and subject to the actions of multi-national corporations. Normality, supposing it to have been regained, was not what had been normal.

The state and the constitution

Those who wished to defend the concept of the state as part of the political vocabulary had to fight on two fronts. On the one hand, they had to deflect the accusations that they were in thrall to a tainted tradition that fed into the Third Reich. On the other hand, they had to demonstrate the continuing utility of the idea of the state in the context of a European Union often described in terms of multi-level government and an increasingly complex and interdependent world that made the autarkic state seem even more fictitious than it had seemed to Georg Jellinek a century earlier.

Udo di Fabio acknowledged the second of these challenges but sought to sweep aside the first. It is, he claimed, based upon a tendentious history that swallowed 'one of the greatest lies of Hitler's rule', namely that there was a direct line of continuity from the state of Frederick the Great through to the Third Reich. He pointed, quite plausibly, to the antipathy exhibited by the National Socialist 'movement' towards the concept of the state as further evidence of the questionable nature of the supposed linkage.[8] Di Fabio knew, however, that the advocates of the concept of the state were on the defensive. It is consistent with this that Josef Isensee, who is often identified as the spokesman of the étatists, wrote, under the heading 'Suppression of the "State" by the "Constitution"', of a change of paradigm that had begun in the 1960s and had reached completion after 1990.[9] With explicit reference to Horst Ehmke's work Isensee complained of the resort to 'verbal surrogates for the unspeakable "state": such as "society", "political system", "government", "governance", "democracy"'.[10] He found little comfort in the sentiments that he ascribed to his fellow Germans. Nor did his ally, Paul Kirchhof. He claimed to discern in German history a 'consciously cultivated gesture of demonstrative scepticism and hypercritical protest', which predisposed Germans to resistance rather than loyalty towards the state.[11] Isensee was even more scathing about contemporary attitudes towards the constitution:

> The constitution may be able to ignite moral emphasis and civil-religious edification. A secular literary cult makes a political bible out of it.

This-worldly promises of salvation and political hopes of redemption are read into it. It inspires anarchistic idealism and the utopia of discourse free from domination.[12]

Isensee's critics responded in like kind, emphasising what they took to be the persistence of conceptions dating back to the nineteenth century, at least in the ranks of the teachers of the legal theory of the state. Some acknowledged that a revival of interest in the state had an empirical foundation in the sheer range of activity of modern states but claimed that this 'new fascination' with the state 'draws from the empirical [material] regressive, mythical conclusions'.[13] Similarly, a 'state metaphysics and mysticism' was said to lie behind that 'vision in which the intact, but hollowed-out state shell of the Federal Republic would change into a quasi-undead in a shadowy intermediate realm . . . in which it exhibits too little statehood to live and too much statehood to die'.[14]

Yet Isensee was not engaged in an uncritical perpetuation of an obsolete tradition. He too criticised a German tradition of political thought which had construed the state and the constitution as opposing forces, as a contrast between is and ought, power and law, facticity and normativity and which culminated in either a normativism blind to the state or a decisionism blind to the constitution.[15] He did insist that the state cannot be equated with the constitution in the sense that the constitution deals with 'not the state as such, but the form of the state and government; not the monopoly of violence [*Gewaltmonopol*] but certainly the separation of powers [*Gewaltenteilung*]; not the power of the state, but rather the conditions of its legitimate exercise'.[16] There is, however, some truth in the charge that Isensse was worried by the prospect of the state being 'hollowed out' in at least two senses. The first was the fear that it would lose its tie to a more or less homogeneous population as the prospect of dual citizenship came closer, though this issued in Isensee's exaggerated protest that a state cannot arbitrarily change its population.[17] No-one was proposing that a state could, let alone should, arbitrarily change its population. The second was the prospect that while, according to the constitution, state power could be transferred to international institutions, there is some point at which this would amount to the emergence of a non-sovereign state.[18] In effect, it was less the concept of the state as such and more the concepts of national identity and sovereignty that formed the basis of Isensee's concerns.

Ernst-Wolfgang Böckenförde was another prominent member of the étatist camp, though his estimation of the fate of the concept of the state was ambiguous. He conceded that within the constitutional state only the constitution itself could count as sovereign. Every constitutional organ is no more than a *pouvoir constitué*, and not even the people can dispose of the constitution as they deem fit.[19] He insisted that the question of sovereignty had not, however, disappeared from the world. It recurred wherever revolutionary transformation took place. Here the precedence of the state before the constitution becomes evident, and here the people appear as the *pouvoir constituant*. Evidence of this was, he argued, close at hand in the experiences of the transitions from the old Soviet bloc.[20] Yet Ulrich Preuss drew a diametrically opposed conclusion from exactly the same events. According to Preuss, the striking feature of those transformations was the way in which the existing constitutions had been used to bring about the changes. The real significance of 1989 lay 'in its rejection of the concept of a people existing prior to and above the constitution, which as a *pouvoir constituant* has the quasi-natural right to exercise a *potesta absoluta* . . . to create any kind of new order it desires, and to impose its will on society'.[21] Preuss drew wider conclusions from this, arguing that the model of the people creating a constitution from nothing was misguided. The appropriate model is, rather, 'the transfer of limited authority of an already constituted and reciprocal kind to a government'.[22]

Although Böckenförde reasserted the vitality of the concept of the state and the capacity of the *pouvoir constituant*, he also suggested that the effectiveness of the state as a form of political community rested upon the coincidence of the territorially defined realm of the state with the relevant economic and social realms. Precisely that coincidence could no longer be guaranteed, and indeed contemporary states, especially in Europe, had willingly entered into agreements that made the disjuncture between these various realms possible.[23] The problem is compounded by the fact that citizens of states still expect the state to bear responsibility for their well-being despite its increasing incapacity to do so.[24] Invoking Hobbes's assertion of the linkage between protection and obedience, Böckenförde concluded that this was in danger of unravelling. The Leviathan, the state, was collapsing without a new one emerging at a different level to take its place.[25]

Again it was possible to draw significantly different conclusions from much the same problems. Thus, Juliane Kokott also took up the Hobbesian theme of protection and obedience and the inability of the state to provide the requisite protection, in the context of a wider account of the changing nature and function of the state. Here, she suggested that there had been a '*deterritorialisation*' of military force, in the sense that the military force of the state no longer sufficed to meet such threats as terrorism, and its use for the acquisition of territory was no longer acceptable. Similarly, state boundaries only served as '*relative jurisdictional borders*' in a world in which the state had become the '*executor*' of international and supra-national law.[26] The conclusion which she drew from this was not that the concept of the state is obsolete but that the concept of the sovereign state is obsolete. As she pointed out, Jellinek had noted that the ideas of state power and sovereignty are not inextricably linked.[27] Although Kokott had not in fact suggested that the concept of the state should be discarded, Isensee introduced his response to her observations with the remark: 'Death of the state – but what then?'[28]

The concept of politics

Despite the recurrent prophesies of the imminent death of the state and laments or celebrations for the perceived decline in the study of the state, Ernst Vollrath was not convinced that the grip of the concept of the state had been shaken off. Indeed, he claimed that although Germany had taken over western political institutions, the 'political-cultural perception' of the political remained tied to the concept of the state understood in terms of domination.[29] The consequence is that German political thought tended either to become a lament for insufficient statehood, as exemplified among others by Isensee, or the desire for a domination-free communicative community, as exemplified primarily by Habermas.[30] Similarly, he complained that in relation to the concept of power there was an oscillation between an 'unpolitical obsession with power [*Machtbesessenheit*] and an equally unpolitical neglect of power [*Machtvergessenheit*]'.[31]

Vollrath insisted, however, that there was an alternative approach within the tradition of German political thought. In fact, Vollrath was deeply influenced by Hannah Arendt, whom he quoted in order to indicate this alternative: 'The meaning of politics is freedom'.[32] That in turn presupposes plurality and hence the need for consent. It further presupposes acceptance of the fact that people will have different opinions and that government rests upon opinion, not upon command or truth. Politics, then, appears as an activity in a contingent world, the only antidote to which is the inevitably imperfect attempt to try to think from the standpoint of others, without automatically adopting the actual judgement of those others.

Vollrath's categorisation did not, however, capture the range of approaches towards the end of the twentieth century. Hermann Lübbe, who remained influenced by Carl Schmitt's decisionism, continued to attack the technocratic vision of replacing the domination of men over men by a scientifically informed administration of things. Yet he also saw the centralised state as an appropriate organisational form for essentially agrarian states, not for the complex societies of the modern world. Here, the predictability of the consequences of political decisions renders the technocratic vision even more illusory than it had previously been. One consequence of this, he continued, is that political acts frequently become largely symbolic, lacking any plausible causative impact. Yet Lübbe warned against a precipitate criticism of symbolic politics. Symbolic politics, he claimed, can generate trust that is more essential in a more unpredictable world.[33]

Unpredictability and the need for decisions, increasingly rapid decisions, also played a prominent role in Niklas Luhmann's approach to politics. The state here appears as an historically transient reference point for political organisation and the concept of domination, understood as the successful assertion of a unified will, as inappropriate in the fluctuating environment inhabited by the modern politician.[34] Luhmann cast aside one reference point after another. Decisionism presupposed a purposive goal-orientated understanding of politics that cannot do justice to the speed, flexibility and readiness to compromise that characterise the modern political tradition. Stable interests fare no better in Luhmann's eyes, for these are subject to the impact of unpredictable consequences.[35] According to Luhmann, it follows from this that it becomes meaningless to expect promises, for example, promises made in elections, to be kept – though he did not deny that people would counterfactually have such expectations.[36] Politics appears as a form of activity constituted within a specialised sub-system of society that has tenuous links with its chaotic environment.

Ulrich Beck responded to similar phenomena not by reducing politics to a specialised sub-system but by discerning politics everywhere. Again, however, the starting point was the idea that '*the equation of politics and state*' amounts to a 'category error'.[37] The prime task of politics, namely to establish the social, environmental and legal conditions under which economic activity can take place, is taken over by other actors. For Beck, this is sufficient justification for speaking of 'sub-politics', that is, a politics that takes place underneath or alongside the formal machinery of state and government. In its negative form, it signifies the triumph of globalisation in which economic interests rewrite 'the social rules of the game'.[38] In its positive form, it amounts to a veritable celebration of the capacity of ordinary citizens: 'it is no exaggeration to say that citizen initiative groups have taken power politically'.[39] Beck's enthusiasm for the power of politics from below is far removed from Luhmann's attempt to insulate the political system from an environment perceived as chaotic and from moral judgements perceived as inappropriate to it. Nevertheless, both constitute attempts to reformulate the concept of politics away from what their authors viewed as state-centric approaches.

Nor did Habermas's approach fully fit into the category to which Vollrath assigned it. Habermas sought to side-step and integrate both republican and liberal conceptions of politics. The former, he argued, relies on the assumption of 'a citizenry capable of collective action' and issues in an 'offensive *understanding of politics directed against the state apparatus*'.[40] The liberal conception accepts the separation of state from society and sees citizens as divided by interests which have to be filtered through legal and political process to reach binding decisions. The result is a '*state-centred understanding of politics*'.[41] Habermas's aim was to retain as much of the republican conception as possible without subscribing to the idea of a citizenry bound together by a general will. He sought to do this by adopting a version of Hannah Arendt's concept of political power as something distinct from the pursuit of interests or the pursuit of collective goals, that is, as 'an *authorizing* force expressed in "jurisgenesis" – the creation of legitimate law – and the founding of institutions'.[42] This concept of political power, however, does not extend to the exercise of political power by duly established institutions. Consequently, he distinguished between 'communicative power and administrative power'.[43] Since he was unwilling to allow this distinction to become rigid, he had to explain how communicative power could exercise some influence over administrative power without relapsing into the implausible assumptions of a full-blown republican model. His answer was to suggest that communicative power is properly located not in the citizenry as a whole but in a plurality of associations existing outside the formal machinery of government which nevertheless exert influence upon that machine. Hence, as Habermas put it, 'The idea of popular sovereignty is thereby desubstantialized. Even the notion that a network of associations could replace the dismissed "body" of the people

– that it could occupy the vacant seat of the sovereign, so to speak – is too concrete.'[44]

While Vollrath still saw the baleful shadow of the state looming over the concept of politics, the contingency that had been associated with politics at the beginning of the twentieth century had returned, now compounded by a sense of the accelerated pace of development. Yet it makes a great of difference whether, even in this condition, one holds onto politics as something related to communicative power or allows it to retreat into symbolic politics or a sub-system in which promising, and hence communication, is no longer possible.

Parliamentary democracy and its discontents

Habermas's understanding of politics was at the same time a conception of democracy that sought to promote an understanding of radical democracy as the guarantor of political autonomy supported by rights, for: 'In the final analysis, private legal subjects cannot come to enjoy equal individual liberties if they do not *themselves*, in the common exercise of their political autonomy, achieve clarity about justified interests and standards'.[45] This presupposes that the citizenry, or at least enough of them, share this understanding and that the formal political institutions, including parliamentary bodies and political parties, are responsive to citizens. Yet both the attitude of citizens and the political institutions of the Federal Republic came under considerable criticism.

Just as Vollrath denounced what he saw as the persistence of a state-centric conception of politics rooted in the nineteenth century, so Werner J. Patzelt denounced the persistence of attitudes to political institutions rooted in the same era. The result of this 'latent constitutional conflict' was a widespread distrust of these institutions. Worse still, the citizens seemed to exhibit more confidence in 'those institutions with which even a well-intentioned authoritarian *Obrigkeitsstaat* is ruled: the courts and the police'.[46] Patzelt rehearsed the arguments of Ernst Fraenkel, emphasising that the reality of parliamentary government was characterised by the fact that ministers are also parliamentarians, that governments are supported by more or less loyal disciplined factions in parliament and that the old dualism of executive versus legislative had been displaced by the dualism of government and opposition.[47] The problem, so Patzelt argued, was that this reality was either not understood or positively opposed by many of the citizens and even by some parliamentarians. Such misunderstandings were taken up by others who rooted the failure to grasp the reality of modern parliamentary government in an obsolete conception of the doctrine of the separation of powers, understood as entailing a separation of legislative and executive.[48]

While Patzelt lamented the failure to grasp the reality of parliamentary government, Hans Herbert von Arnim denounced what he saw as its exploitation by a class of professional politicians who are less concerned with the common good than with power, positions and money.[49] Under the heading 'The fictitious democracy', he complained of the formulaic repetition of the Basic Law's provision that all state authority arises from the people combined with a neglect of how much actual interests the people have.[50] There was, he added, a veritable flight from responsibility as the political class sought to spread responsibility so thinly that none of them could be held responsible. Wider public interests remained neglected while special interests benefited from the strategic advantage of being easier to organise.[51] Within parliament, the 'genuine separation of powers between the legislative and executive' had evaporated as governing majorities lacked the will to control the executive, and the opposition had the will but not the power to control it.[52] Von Arnim saw anything from the federal structure of the Republic through to the pensions of parliamentarians as being instrumentalised by a self-serving political class. The intellectual backbone of this parlous condition he found in Gerhard Leibholz's theory of the party state, though he conceded that Leibholz had presumed that the parties would be firmly rooted in the people.[53] Against these vices, he held out two main types of reform that might give more substance to the democratic order: direct democracy and the establishment of independent agencies. Resistance to direct democracy, he argued, was based on a historically rooted 'fear of the people'.[54] Yet, for von Arnim, ordinary citizens can be more trusted to consider the common good than their politicians.[55]

It was inevitable that the shrillness of von Arnim's criticisms would eventually provoke a sharp response. A comparison was drawn between von Arnim's criticisms and assumptions and those of Carl Schmitt and other critics of parliamentary party democracy. The presupposition of a common good, of the idea that parties ought to embody the will of the people, the reference to independent agencies standing above the parties, all invited comparison either with the perceived residues of a political tradition rooted in the *Obrigkeitsstaat* or with the critics of parliamentary democracy who supposedly spoke in the name of a true democracy.[56] Yet the idea of a political class composed of people who live off politics was more widely accepted as a reality. Indeed, Jens Borchert presented it as an unstoppable social trend analogous to industrialisation or democratisation, exactly as predicted by Max Weber.[57] Surveying the various criticisms and suggested reforms in response to this phenomenon, Borchert also suggested that analogies with past arguments could be deceptive. Thus, advocacy of direct democracy at the end of the twentieth century was not intended to point to an alternative to representative democracy but as an attempt to remedy some of its weakness. Similarly, there was less concern with measures that might strengthen the prospects of the formation of parliamentary majorities and more concern with the responsibility of parliamentarians to their electors. The choice appeared to be less one between governability and representativeness and more between party autonomy and democratic control.[58]

The Rechtsstaat *and the* Sozialstaat

The relationship between law and the state embodied in the concept of the *Rechtsstaat* conjured up more than one problem. The image of a substantive concept of the state only subsequently limited by law, and the associated interpretation of the purpose of the *Rechtsstaat* as preservation of liberties against the state, continued to haunt discussion. Konrad Hesse suggested that such a view of the *Rechtsstaat* is based on a reductionist understanding of the concept which should more properly be interpreted as constituting an entire legal structure that defines the political existence of a people.[59] At the same time, there were concerns about preserving the autonomy of law, both in the sense of central legal principles and as a system of law or adjudication, against its political instrumentalisation, even where the driving political principle behind that instrumentalisation is itself a democratic principle. To some, it seemed that the establishment of the principle of the *Rechtsstaat* for all Germans had increased the tendency to see law as the solution for all problems and consequently had increased the disillusion that arose when this proved not to be the case. From this perspective, 'distance' and 'differentiation' seemed to be required: distance in the sense of a separation of state and society, or the idea that the concept of human dignity inscribed in the Basic Law set a limit to the activity of the state, and differentiation in the sense that both state competencies and basic rights had to be separated out into distinctive packages and provided with distinctive guarantees.[60]

A more radical approach was adopted by Luhmann as he continued to refine his attempt to use the idea of differentiation not just as a barrier to pressure on an overburdened legal system but as an overarching principle of social evolution. For Luhmann, the concept of the *Rechtsstaat* embodies a 'civilizational achievement', namely 'the juristic fettering of political power and the political instrumentalisation of law'.[61] He intended the idea of 'the political instrumentalisation of law' to be understood not as something lamentable but as signifying the point at which law, as positive law, became available to a legislator who uses law to achieve political goals. Law and money are the mechanisms that make possible, and require, the enormous apparatus, including political parties, lobbying and so on, with which we associate the political system. None of this, Luhmann argued, would be necessary if the only decisions that had to be taken were about where and when to exert physical force.[62] Yet the fact that force could be deployed by the political system provided the basis for the expansion of the legal system that no longer had to concern itself with the establishment of a peaceful order within which it could operate. The mutually reinforcing roles of the political and legal systems provided the basis for their increasing autonomy as well as their expansion. Indeed, both systems appear in Luhmann's account as self-enclosed, self-referential systems.

Among the differences which Luhmann drew between the two systems is the fact that the political system is not compelled to issue laws, save in limited cases where this is constitutionally prescribed, any more than the state is obliged to conclude treaties; but courts are required to come to judgements in cases put before them. Again, Luhmann swept aside the technical possibility of refusing a definite verdict. The general principle of a compulsion to reach a judgement, that is, not to refuse justice, is, he argued, a driving force in the expansion of the legal system. It also, inevitably, issued in the complaints about judicial interpretation as courts are presented with hard cases.[63] Luhmann readily conceded that in terms of the arguments available even to well-trained judges the law can effectively be indeterminate, but insisted that the key fact is that a decision has to be reached. Decision rather than force of argument defines the law.[64]

For Habermas, against whom Luhmann's point was specifically directed, this amounted to a case of the 'sociological disenchantment of law' in which ' "law" is reduced to the special function of the administration of law. One thereby loses sight of the constitutional organization of the origin, acquisition, and use of political power . . . [and] . . . legal communication is robbed of its *socially integrative* meaning.'[65] Habermas's alternative was to try to formulate a system of rights that would guarantee both private and public autonomy in such a way that citizens can understand themselves as the authors of the law by which they guarantee each other that autonomy. This entails, he claimed, first '*the right to the greatest possible measure of equal individual liberties*', second, 'the *status of a member* in a voluntary association of consociates under law', and third, 'the *actionability* of rights and . . . individual *legal protection*'.[66] Although the necessary elaboration of these rights is reserved to the citizens as legislators, rights of these types define the private autonomy of the citizens and are not at their disposal. Without such rights, the legal medium and hence the *Rechtsstaat* simply does not exist. The fourth category of rights is 'rights to equal opportunities to participate in processes of opinion- and will-formation in which citizens exercise their *political autonomy* and through which they generate legitimate law'.[67] Habermas acknowledged that the *Rechtsstaat* thus understood is viable only if citizens make use of those rights. The fate of democratic institutions which lacked such active support served to refute, he suggested, the image of the legal system as a self-enclosed system. That the *Rechtsstaat* is endangered where citizens do not have a sense of being members of an association governed by law is a point with which Gustav Radbruch had agreed in the Weimar Republic.[68]

Habermas responded to the problems posed by the welfare state with the same emphasis upon the principle of autonomy. Here, Luhmann saw the same problem of the obligation to come to a judgement sucking the courts into an ever-expanding social agenda and turning them into promoters of ever-greater state expenditure. He turned not to the legal system to restrain itself but to other institutions, namely an autonomous central bank, operating according to its own distinct set of principles to counteract this effect.[69] In contrast, Habermas argued for both a less expansive self-understanding by the courts and a change in the understanding of the welfare state. In terms of the courts, the problem, he argued, lay in the fact that the Federal Constitutional Court 'assimilates legal principles to values'. Values here refer to the goals shared by a specific community that can be more or less vigorously pursued and can legitimately conflict. In contrast, legal principles should be construed as universally applicable, are either valid in a specific case or not, and cannot be construed as inconsistent if the legal order is to retain its integrity.[70] Conflating values with principles in this sense increases the risk of arbitrary adjudication that feeds back into the retreat into decisionism of the kind favoured by Luhmann. For Habermas, it also means that the court usurps the decisions of the citizens whose autonomy, guaranteed by legal principles, it is supposed to support.

Yet Habermas did not sanction a retreat to a liberal understanding of the *Rechtsstaat*, nor did he defend what he saw as the existing logic of the *Sozialstaat*. In fact, both were said to suffer from the same structural defect, that is, they are 'fixated on the question of whether it suffices to guarantee private autonomy through individual liberties, or whether on the contrary the *conditions for the genesis* of private autonomy must be secured by granting welfare entitlements'.[71] Neither the old slogan of freedom from the state, secured by rights against the state, nor the new slogan of provision by the state, in the form of a redistribution of goods, addresses the link between private and political autonomy. It is autonomy in this full sense, not well-being, which Habermas put at the centre of his argument.

Habermas's defence of the welfare state was put forward at the same time as it was coming under increasing strain. Escalating costs, changes in societal expectations and above all the growing dependence of national economies on international markets induced reflection on the welfare-state project. It was possible to respond to these challenges by condemning the entire intellectual trajectory that led to the modern welfare state.[72] For Franz-Xaver Kaufmann, however, the undeniable challenges meant that the idea of the *Sozialstaat* had to be reformulated rather than abandoned. In Germany, as elsewhere in Europe, the welfare state had played too great a role in the generation of social solidarity to be cast aside. Others went so far as to suggest that the *Sozialstaat*, together with a competitive economy, was constitutive of German identity.[73] Kaufmann did not, but he did claim that it could play a significant role in integrating the immigrant labour on which European states, especially Germany, were increasingly dependent.[74] Following the English sociologist T. H. Marshall, he invoked recognition of social rights as a necessary supplement to legal and political rights.[75] Consistent with this wider perspective, Kaufmann set the debate about the *Sozialstaat* in the context of a concept of the good life that, he suggested, had been too narrowly focused on work and consumption. The *Sozialstaat* has to be refocused on the development of the competencies required by individuals and has to be perceived as a resource rather than a burden in an increasingly competitive global market.[76]

Globalisation, integration and national identity

The pressures of globalisation and European integration mounted as reunification seemed to promise the reaffirmation of national identity and a role on the international stage for Germany that was consonant with its size. Advocates of a strong sense of national identity promised a cool assessment of Germany's ties to the west. The editors of a volume with that title, *Westbindung*, presented themselves as part of a younger generation unaffected by the trauma of the Third Reich or the events of 1968, who were 'free from the almost mystical glorification of "the west", as it had come to be a confession of faith for many left-liberals and conservatives after 1945'.[77] Yet finding an adequate formulation of national identity proved more difficult than asserting the principle and need for a strong sense of identity. Among the older generation, Böckenförde clung to an ethnic definition of citizenship, though he conceded dual citizenship for most of the resident minorities in Germany precisely on the grounds that they should not be compelled to cast aside their ties to their original homelands, at least not in the short run.[78] The principle of ethnic identity combined with the reality of and need for the immigrants left him with no consistent alternative. Isensee resorted to an old argument, namely that 'Autocratic systems can satisfy themselves with a legal definition of citizenship, because unity is guaranteed by authoritarian compulsion [*obrigkeitlichen Zwang*]'.[79] Democracies require, he suggested, greater internal 'consistency'. That was an exaggeration of the integrative power of authoritarian systems, as the critics of the *Obrigkeitsstaat* such as Hugo Preuss, himself a fervent nationalist, had known all too well. Among the younger generation, Tilman Meyer, a contributor to *Westbindung*, also invoked the past, in the shape of Friedrich Meinecke's *Weltbürgertum und Nationalstaat* (Cosmopolitanism and the Nation State), but only in order to reject Meinecke's concept of a 'cultural nation'. The problem, he explained, is that if one accepts culture as the defining feature of nationality, then one will have to count the nations of the world in thousands instead of hundreds.[80] Instead, Mayer suggested, Germany should indeed learn from the west and accept the idea of the nation state construed as a community based on will and solidarity. From this perspective, he continued, both ethnically homogeneous and ethnically diverse nation states enjoy the same legitimacy. That concession, however, sat uncomfortably with his warning about a 'relapse into the stage of multi-national state, which, so to speak, would undermine the statehood of the nation states and thus lead back to the [concept of the] cultural nations'.[81]

While Tilman lamented uncertainty, Peter Sloterdijk transfigured it into a kind of virtue or at least an inevitability. Sloterdijk built on a speculative account of primeval societies to which he ascribed a 'paleo-politics'. He defined the latter in terms of the horde's need to reproduce itself biologically and to maintain its cohesion through sound and ritual. Perpetuation of the species within small communities requires the cohesion of the group.[82] Although he allowed for subsequent forms of politics, the core of the argument returned in his affirmation of national cohesion. The nation, according to Sloterdijk, is a 'hysterical and panicky information system' that requires constant stimulation and stress in order to convince itself of its own existence. The source of the fear matters little. Sloterdijk invoked global competition as readily as the Cold War. Along with the emphasis on the irrational and manipulative dimensions of national identity, he picked out the underlying biological core of the idea of nationality, that is, the idea that collective identity, whether of an ethnic group, tribe or people, is 'a biological line of investment, which must constantly complete itself through ritual and linguistic practices' in order to survive.[83]

In contrast to the reassertion of what was taken to be established historical precedent or flight into the mythical origins of the human species, Habermas and Ingeborg Maus turned to the historical origins of the nation state in order to understand the challenges that confront it in the post-Cold War world. Maus was sceptical of advocacy of a global state that arose from the supposition that globalisation was consigning the nation state to the past. The error, Maus claimed, arose from a misunderstanding of the original significance of the nation state and a misguided projection of assumptions of ethnic homogeneity that had gained predominance only later back into the origins of the modern nation state. The challenge of globalisation, she suggested, gained part of its force from the belief that territorial borders are crucial to the nation state. The advocates of the sovereignty of the people, that is, of the modern democratic nation state had seen it not primarily as territorially defined but as an association of people. Borders were seen as permeable insofar as immigrants who accepted the constitutional principles of the state presented little problem.[84]

Borders do, however, have some significance in that they are justifiable in terms of their defensive function, not because territory is decisive but because foreign intervention undermines the freedom and right to self-determination of the people. Maus saw these insights as being challenged not only by an erroneous emphasis upon territory but also by the emerging practice of intervention in the name of human rights and a resurgence of ethnic nationalism that claimed to justify secession in the name of self-determination. For Maus, that amounted to the transformation of a right to democratic autonomy into a justification of the priority of pre-political identity.[85]

Habermas had also revisited the 'unexpected topicality' of the nation state.[86] For Germany, reunification had, he noted, put both elements back on the agenda. For some people, reunification was primarily a reassertion of 'the pre-political unity of a community with a shared historical destiny'. For others, it was primarily a restoration of 'democracy and the rule of law in a territory where civil rights had been suspended in one form or another since 1933'.[87] Both in terms of the present and in terms of the historical formation of the concepts of the democratic state and the nation, Habermas argued that the link between them, though historically important, was not conceptually necessary. The concept of the democratic state as a community of free citizens as it emerged at the end of the eighteenth century was not presaged on the existence of a national community. Habermas acknowledged that national identity had played an important functional role in establishing a sense of solidarity in the emerging democratic states.[88] Its significance was, however, ambiguous. The idea of collective identity could be coupled with a range of ideas, including the idea of freedom in a specific sense, that is, as the freedom of the collectivity alongside the freedom of the private individual or the freedom of the autonomous citizen.[89] This freedom found expression in the idea of self-determination, but that raised the problem of what this self was. The reality was that borders, and hence the citizenship of states, were historically contingent products, usually of wars. From this, Habermas concluded that there is no automatic right to self-determination in the sense of secession from an existing state purely on the basis of national self-determination. Revolt against, for example, foreign domination is justified only on the basis of violation of the basic rights of individuals, and secession is justified only where the central power refuses to acknowledge such rights.[90]

The attempt to move the focus of freedom and self-determination away from collective concepts towards the individual was also evident in Ingolf Pernice's assessment of European and national constitutional law. There, even the constitution was said to be 'no longer centred on state and nation, but rather on the self-determination of the individual'.[91] From the existence of a 'multi-level constitutionalism' within the European Union, Pernice further concluded that the member states were not, contrary to the opinion of the Federal Constitutional Court, 'lords of the treaties': 'they are neither lords, nor lords of the treaties, indeed they are . . . not even lords of their own constitutions'.[92] Pernice's judgements met with resistance from other constitutional lawyers, yet they were evidence of a conviction that the traditional concepts, of the state and even the national constitution, were simply no longer relevant as Germany and Europe moved into the twenty-first century. That sense of a fundamental break with the conceptual world of the twentieth and nineteenth centuries was also evident in an attempt to provide an orientation for foreign policy in the twenty-first century by Otto Czempiel. Although he noted that realist doctrines were still highly influential, Czempiel proclaimed their irrelevance. The world was witnessing the transition from a world of state to a world society. States, at least the modern welfare states, can no longer expect their citizens to risk their lives in foreign adventures, and they can no longer control economic flows or even public opinion within their own borders. Sovereignty, he continued, has to be ascribed to society even if such a notion is difficult for the German theory of the state to accept.[93]

The triumph of the idea of society over that of the state that the étatists had always feared was being proclaimed as a feature of the international realm, one regarded as the proper domain of the state alone in terms of both political reality and international law. This sense of radical departure stood in stark contrast to the persistence of the image of the world of states, in which the historian Gregor Schöllgen believed Germany was returning to its normal and appropriate place. Schöllgen proclaimed the 'birth of a German great power' and 'Germany's return to the world stage'.[94] The basis of this power lay, he claimed, in the fact that the Federal Republic has 'the potential to "sabotage" the functions of the international system, by means of non-cooperation'.[95] Critics such as Günther Hellmann warned of the dangers of a 'power political resocialisation' of Germany and of German pursuit of a privileged position in the world, in violation of its own constitutional provisions.[96]

The apparent return of a political vocabulary more appropriate to the beginning of the twentieth century than the beginning of the twenty-first century was, however, deceptive. Unity had been achieved peacefully, not by war. Schöllgen invoked the possibility of non-cooperation, not of the resort to violence, and even the former was not really plausible insofar as Germany was as vulnerable to any sabotage of the international system as any other state. Yet the contrast between Schöllgen's vocabulary and that of Czempiel was but one of several apparent paradoxes. There had been revolutions that appeared to substantiate the idea of the nation as the pre-political *pouvoir constituant* or to be constitutional processes that dispensed with such elevated concepts. The concept of the state seemed still to exert a baleful influence or was actively reaffirmed, yet to others the concept seemed to have been subverted by competing principles at several levels. Reunification had brought with it a complex blend of continuity and discontinuity.

Notes

1. Michael Killian, 'Der Vorgang der deutschen Einheit', in Josef Isensee and Paul Kirchhof (eds), *Handbuch des Staatsrechts der Bundesrepublik Deutschland*, vol. 1 (Heidelberg: Müller, 2003), p. 599.
2. Quoted in Heinrich August Winkler, *Der lange Weg nach Westen*, vol. 2 (Munich: Beck, 2002, p. 521.
3. See Jan-Werner Müller, *Another Country* (New Haven, CT: Yale University Press, 2000), pp. 129–31.
4. Wilhelm Hennis, 'Totenrede des Perikles auf ein blühendes Land' [1997], in Wilhelm Hennis, *Auf dem Weg in den Parteienstaat* (Stuttgart: Reclam, 1998), pp. 155–6.
5. Günter Rohrmoser, *Kampf um die Mitte* (Munich: Olzog, 1999), p. 187.
6. Siegfried Unseld (ed.), *Politik ohne Projekt* (Frankfurt am Main: Suhrkamp, 1993).
7. Jürgen Habermas, 'Die zweite Lebenslüge der Bundesrepublik', in ibid., pp. 283–97. The first was 'We are *all* democrats': ibid., p. 291.
8. Udo di Fabio, *Die Staatsrechtslehre und der Staat* (Paderborn: Schöningh, 2003), p. 64.
9. Josef Isensee, 'Staat und Verfassung', in Isensee and Kirchhof (eds), *Handbuch des Staatsrechts der Bundesrepublik Deutschland*, vol. 2 (Heidelberg: Müller, 2004), p. 7. For Isensee as spokesman of the étatists, see Helmut Quaritsch, 'Standort und Aufgaben der Staatslehre heute', in N. Neuhaus (ed.), *Verfassung und Verwaltung* (Cologne: Bohlua, 1994), pp. 367–8.
10. Isensee, 'Staat und Verfassung', p. 8.
11. Paul Kirchhof, 'Europäische Einigung und der Verfassungsstaat der Bundesrepublik Deutschland', in Josef Isensee (ed.), *Europa als*

politische Idee und als rechtliche Form (Berlin: Duncker & Humblot, 1994), p. 75.

12. Isensee, 'Staat und Verfassung', pp. 15–16.

13. Thus Hans J. Lietzmann, 'Staatswissenschaftliche Abendröte', in Jürgen Gebhardt et al. (eds), *Demokratie, Verfassung und Nation* (Baden-Baden: Nomos, 1994), p. 75.

14. Roland Lhotta, 'Der Staat als Wille und Vorstellung', *Der Staat* 36 (1997), p. 195.

15. Isensee, 'Staat und Verfassung', p. 98.

16. Ibid., p. 20.

17. Ibid., p. 66.

18. Ibid., p. 102.

19. Ernst-Wolfgang Böckenförde, 'Begriff und Probleme des Verfassungs-staates' [1997], in Ernst-Wolfgang Böckenförde, *Staat, Nation, Europa* (Frankfurt am Main: Suhrkamp, 1999), pp. 129–30.

20. Ibid. pp. 136–8.

21. Ulrich K. Preuss, *Constitutional Revolution* [1990] (New Jersey: Humanities Press, 1995), p. 75.

22. Ibid., p. 53.

23. Ernst-Wolfgang Böckenförde, 'Die Zukunft politischer Autonomie' [1997], in Böckenförde, *Staat, Nation, Europa*, pp. 105–6.

24. Ernst-Wolfgang Böckenförde, 'Welchen Weg geht Europa?', in ibid., p. 80.

25. Böckenförde, 'Die Zukunft politischer Autonomie', pp. 118–19.

26. Juliane Kokott, 'Die Staatsrechtslehre und die Veränderung ihres Gegenstandes', *Veröffentlichungen der Vereinigung der deutschen Staatsrechtslehrer* 63 (2004), pp. 14, 22.

27. Ibid., p. 24.

28. Josef Isensee, 'Aussprache und Schlussworte', *Veröffentlichungen der Vereinigung der deutschen Staatsrechtslehrer* 63 (2004), p. 90.

29. Ernst Vollrath, *Was ist das Politische?* (Würzburg: Königshausen & Neumann, 2003), pp. 50, 120, 154. For a survey of the spectrum of debate, see Jan Mueller, 'Preparing for the Political', in Howard Williams, Colin Wight and Norbert Kapferer (eds), *Political Thought and German Unification* (Houndmills: Palgrave, 2000), pp. 209–35.

30. Vollrath, *Was ist das Politische?*, pp. 45–53.

31. Ibid., p. 83.

32. Ibid., p. 203.

33. Hermann Lübbe, *Politik nach der Aufklärung* (Munich: Fink, 2001), pp. 33–7, 151–71.

34. Niklas Luhmann, *Die Politik der Gesellschaft* (Frankfurt am Main: Suhrkamp, 2000), pp. 228, 429.

35. Ibid., pp. 141–3.

36. Ibid., p. 149.

37. Ulrich Beck, *The Reinvention of Politics* [1993] (Cambridge: Polity, 1997), p. 98.
38. Ulrich Beck, *What is Globalization?* [1997] (Cambridge: Polity, 2000), p. 4.
39. Beck, *The Reinvention of Politics*, p. 100.
40. Jürgen Habermas, *Between Facts and Norms* [1992] (Cambridge: Polity, 1996), pp. 297–8.
41. Ibid., p. 298.
42. Ibid., p. 148.
43. Ibid., p. 136.
44. Jürgen Habermas, 'Popular sovereignty as procedure' [1988], in Habermas, *Between Facts and Norms*, p. 486.
45. Habermas, *Between Facts and Norms*, p. xlii.
46. Werner J. Patzelt, 'Reformwünsche in Deutschlands latentem Verfassungskonflikt', *Aus Politik und Zeitgeschichte* 28 (2000), p. 4.
47. Werner J. Patzelt, 'Ein latenter Verfassungskonflikt?', *Politische Vierteljahresschrift* 39 (1998), pp. 725–31.
48. Eberhard Schütt-Wetschky, 'Gewaltenteilung zwischen Legislative und Exekutive?', *Aus Politik und Zeitgeschichte* 28 (2000), pp. 5–12.
49. Hans Herbert von Arnim, *Das System* (Munich: Knaur, 2001), p. 34.
50. Hans Herbert von Arnim, *Vom schönen Schein der Demokratie* (Munich: Knaur, 2002), p. 32.
51. Von Arnim, *Das System*, pp. 68–9.
52. Ibid., p. 304.
53. Ibid., pp. 250–5.
54. Von Arnim, *Vom schönen Schein der Demokratie*, pp. 198–202.
55. Von Arnim, *Das System*, p. 373.
56. See, for example, Peter Lösche, 'Parteienverdrossenheit ohne Ende?', *Zeitschrift für Parlamentsfragen* 26 (1995), pp. 149–59, or Andrea Withensohn, 'Dem "ewigen Gespräch" ein Ende setzen', *Zeitschrift für Parlamentsfragen* 30 (1999), pp. 500–34.
57. Jens Borchert, *Die Professionalisierung der Politik* (Frankfurt am Main: Campus, 2003), p. 206.
58. Ibid. pp. 217–18, 221, 223.
59. Konrad Hesse, *Grundzüge des Verfassungsrechts der Bundesrepublik Deutschland* (Heidelberg: Müller, 1999), p. 84.
60. Thus Eberhard Schmidt-Assmann, 'Der Rechtsstaat', in Isensee and Kirchhof (eds), *Handbuch des Staatsrechts der Bundesrepublik Deutschland*, vol. 2, pp. 556–7, 610–11.
61. Niklas Luhmann, *Das Recht der Gesellschaft* (Frankfurt am Main: Suhrkamp, 1995), p. 422.
62. Ibid., p. 425.
63. Ibid., pp. 310–32.
64. Ibid., p. 402.

65. Habermas, *Between Facts and Norms*, p. 50.
66. Ibid., p. 122.
67. Ibid., p. 123.
68. See above, Chapter 2.
69. Luhmann, *Das Recht der Gesellschaft*, p. 481.
70. Habermas, *Between Facts and Norms*, p. 255.
71. Ibid., p. 408.
72. See Gerd Haberman, *Der Wohlfarhtsstaat. Die Geschichte eines Irrwegs* (Berlin: Ullstein, 1997).
73. Thus Klaus von Dohnanyi, quoted in Lutz Niethammer, *Kollektive Identität* (Hamburg: Rowohlt, 2000), p. 602.
74. Franz-Xaver Kaufmann, *Herausforderungen des Sozialstaates* (Frankfurt am Main: Suhrkamp, 1997), pp. 147–8.
75. Ibid., p. 143.
76. Ibid., pp. 158–9, 192.
77. Michael Grossheim, Karlheinz Weissmann and Rainer Zitlemann, 'Wir Deutschen und der Westen', in Michael Grossheim, Karlheinz Weissmann and Rainer Zitlemann (eds), *Westbindung* (Frankfurt am Main: Ullstein, 1993), p. 15.
78. Ernst-Wolfgang Böckenförde, 'Staatsbürgerschaft und Nationalitäts-konzept' [1994], in Böckenförde, *Staat, Nation, Europa*, pp. 66–7.
79. Isensee, 'Staat und Verfassung', p. 65.
80. Tilman Mayer, 'Fragment zur Bestimmung der deutschen Nationalstaat-lichkeit', in Grossheim et al. (eds), *Westbindung*, p. 502.
81. Ibid., p. 510.
82. Peter Sloterdijk, *Im selben Boot* (Frankfurt am Main: Suhrkamp, 1993), pp. 14–26.
83. Peter Sloterdijk, *Der starke Grund zusammen zu sein* (Frankfurt am Main: Suhrkamp, 1998), p. 46.
84. Ingeborg Maus, 'Vom Nationalstaat zum Globalstaat oder: der Niedergang der Demokratie', in Matthias Lutz-Bechmann and James Bohman (eds), *Weltstaat oder Staatenwelt?* (Frankfurt am Main: Suhrkamp, 2002), p. 231.
85. Ibid., p. 246.
86. Jürgen Habermas, 'Citizenship and national identity' [1990], in Habermas, *Between Facts and Norms*, p. 491.
87. Ibid., p. 492.
88. Jürgen Habermas, 'Der europäische Nationalstaat', in Jürgen Habermas, *Die Einbeziehung des Anderen* (Frankfurt am Main: Suhrkamp, 1997), pp. 136–7.
89. Ibid., pp. 137–8.
90. Jürgen Habermas, 'Inklusion – einbeziehen oder einschliessen?', in Habermas, *Die Einbeziehung des Anderen*, pp. 168–70.
91. Ingolf Pernice, 'Europäisches und nationales Verfassungsrecht',

Veröffentlichungen der Vereinigung der deutschen Staatsrechtslehrer 60 (2001), p. 160.

92. Ibid., pp. 171–2.
93. Otto Czempiel, *Kluge Macht* (Munich: Beck, 1999), p. 17.
94. Gregor Schöllgen, *Die Macht in der Mitte Europas* (Munich: Beck, 1992), p. 186, and *Der Auftritt. Deutschlands Rückkehr auf die Weltbühne* (Berlin: Ullstein, 2004).
95. Ibid., p. 29.
96. Günther Hellmann, 'Wider die machtpolitische Resozialisierung der deutschen Aussenpolitik', *WeltTrends* 12 (2004), pp. 79–88, and 'Ex occidente Lux', *Politische Vierteljahresschrift* 25 (2004), p. 481.

Conclusion

Twentieth-century German political thought was marked by the persistence, or better the recurrence, of certain concepts and by the polemical dispute about what those concepts meant. It appears to be a striking example of the general proposition that the 'possibility of communicative breakdown is an ever-present feature, if not indeed a defining characteristic, of political discourse'.[1] This polemical quality was displayed with greater or lesser skill and greater or lesser consciousness by most German political theorists. Carl Schmitt, one of the most adroit polemicists, was even capable of recognising such skill in his opponents, hence the praise offered by the authoritarian critic of the Weimar Republic for the liberal author of the Weimar constitution, Hugo Preuss.[2] As indicated above, Schmitt saw that polemic was not just a defining quality of political discourse but was the defining quality of the political. Yet Schmitt's polemical practice assumed what his aesthetics of violence denied, namely that, as Max Horkheimer put it, 'To address someone ultimately means to recognise him as the future possible member of an association of free men'.[3]

It is consistent with this insight that the more extreme polemics sought to deny it by excluding their opponents and their opponents' ideas from the national community. Oswald Spengler's denunciation of them as the 'internal England' is one example of such a strategy. It took on even more vicious form in the attempt to eradicate the names of Jewish authors from the literature and discourse of the Third Reich. Yet it was not only those who wanted to metaphorically, or literally, exclude their opponents from the national community who invoked the idea of a distinctively German tradition of political thought. Indeed, from Preuss through to Jürgen Habermas, critics of this tradition, however it has been defined, have invoked it precisely in order to denounce it. The potential difficulty that this entails is illustrated more clearly by Preuss, who had to deploy two arguments which were ultimately inconsistent. On the one hand, he invoked a tradition defined by the *Obrigkeitsstaat* in order to call for reform. On the other hand, he disputed the claim of the critics of Weimar that the

213

liberal and democratic constitution of that republic was un-Germanic. A similar dilemma, albeit one involving far lower stakes, can be seen at the beginning of the twenty-first century in Ernst Vollrath's call for the liberation of the concept of politics from the shackles of a German state-centric tradition at the same time as he appealed to ideas of German provenance for such an alternative.[4]

The only alternative to such dilemmas is to recognise that twentieth-century German political thought was a fragmented tradition, held together as much by polemical dispute as anything else. The inescapable, yet distorting, prism of the Third Reich is proof of that in two ways. First, even among those within the Third Reich who more or less enthusiastically supported the regime, consensus, including consensus about how much of which part of the German intellectual past had to be discarded, proved elusive. Second, and more important, the 'Great Migration' of German intellectuals into exile or emigration proved that only their physical exclusion could even appear to maintain the fiction that they and their ideas were un-Germanic. Their exclusion was the logical consequence of the ideological *Sonderweg* whose roots can be traced back before 1914 but which became a flight into the future only as the structures of the *Obrigkeitsstaat* shattered amid the war and defeat of 1914–1918. At the same time, their continued existence proved that the fiction of a single German concept of the state, the nation and so on, was precisely that. Understanding German political thought as polemically contested, treating assertions about the German tradition, however it is construed, with suspicion, is the best guarantee against lending unintended retrospective justification to those who wanted to exclude their opponents, metaphorically or literally, from that tradition

That does not entail denying the existence of terminology that resists satisfactory translation, such as the *Obrigkeitsstaat* or the *Rechtsstaat*, or of the recurrence of the title, *Allgemeine Staatslehre*, that seems to embody what is peculiar and problematic in German political thought. Nor does it mean concluding that the 'unspeakable "state"' should be expunged from political vocabulary or that the *Allgemeine Staatslehre* is nothing more than the illegitimate projection of specifically German problems and experiences into a universal category.[5] Again, both the Third Reich and the experience of exile suggest that those who invoke the concept of the state, or even the 'state as such', refer to something that at least in the modern era it would be unwise to discard. Its value was evident to those who were driven into a condition of statelessness and who could still see that the state that had exiled them was either a state in decay or possibly not a state at all yet did not amount to the sheer chaos into which Max Horkheimer thought it could descend.

Here, it is at least as arguable that specifically German problems and experiences sharpened awareness of concepts and problems of more general significance as well as provoking the desire to turn away from them as part of a discredited past. Both intellectual polemic and historical experience forced some German theorists to seize on one aspect of these problems to the exclusion of others. Thus, Hans Kelsen was driven by his antipathy to what he saw as state idolatry to construe the state in terms of an hierarchy of norms. Conversely, Hermann Heller insisted on the state as an organisation capable of enforcing decisions when faced with the incipient dissolution of the state in the Weimar Republic. Some hint of what it means when neither law nor organisational unity are present was given by Spengler's effective dissolution of the state into an amorphous atmosphere of command and obedience. The Third Reich provided evidence of what that might look like in reality. The specific context of their approaches is beyond doubt. So too is the broader significance in a world of failed states, rogue states and kleptocracies that look more like the protection rackets that Horkheimer saw as the archetypal form of domination than anything that either Kelsen or Heller would have recognised as a state.

One of the greatest difficulties presented by German political thought in the twentieth century, apart from the obvious one of its sheer range and complexity, is the combination of tradition and modernity, continuity and discontinuity. The dead weight of the past appeared in Franz Josef's celebration of the monarchic principle, in the shape of Preuss's critique of the *Obrigkeitsstaat* and in Helmut Plessner's identification of Germany as the belated nation. Yet, as Wilhelm Hennis observed, 'Germany – at least intellectual Germany – stands for the most radically modern since the beginning of the nineteenth century'.[6] By the beginning of the twentieth century, modernity was manifest in the triumph of positive law and in the criticism of it by the Free Law Movement. The crisis that buried the Weimar Republic has been aptly described as a 'crisis of classical modernity'.[7] At the end of the twentieth century, Jürgen Habermas sought to rejoin law and radical democracy against the background of what he described as a modernity 'now aware of its contingencies'.[8]

Intellectual continuity was ensured by the enduring presence of prominent figures at the beginning of the twentieth century, such as

Max Weber and Georg Jellinek, as well as by the fact that the biographies of many theorists stretched across the political fractures in German political history. Discontinuity was ensured by the socialisation of successive generations in radically different political systems and by the pressure that those systems, including the changing international order, exerted. This also meant that familiar arguments drawn from early periods did not necessarily have the significance they once did. Criticism of political parties or the rhetoric of power politics on the international stage at the end of the twentieth century did not have the same meaning that they did at the beginning of the nineteenth century, in the era of the contested republics or in the Third Reich, even if they sometimes met with responses that implicitly or explicitly drew on analogies with those earlier periods.

It would be inappropriate, of course, to conclude from this that earlier ideas are entirely context-bound. The modernity of German thought at the beginning of the twentieth century makes such a conclusion especially inappropriate. Weber's account of the professionalisation of politics, Jellinek's criticism of sovereignty as *summum imperium, summa potestas* and Kelsen's exposure of the myths of the democratic order retain their relevance because of the more thorough-going professionalisation of politics, because sovereignty no longer has the self-evidence that it once did and because democracy was so successfully re-established in the Federal Republic. Other ideas will recur because they seem to address the anxieties of the twenty-first century. Globalisation and European integration will feed anxiety about national identity. As Josef Isensee's comments indicated, the old myth that democracies require greater social homogeneity than authoritarian states which could guarantee unity through 'authoritarian compulsion' is still in currency.[9] Habermas's fear that concern about foreign intervention in the internal affairs of states could lend some of Schmitt's arguments a 'fatal *Zeitgeist* appeal' has proved all too accurate.[10] Understanding what part of Germany's intellectual history continues to be relevant and what should be discarded or recalled purely as a warning has been a constitutive part of its fragmented tradition of political thought. It will continue to be so.

Notes

1. Terence Ball, 'Conceptual history and the history of political thought', in Iain Hampsher-Monk, Karin Tilmans and Frank von Vree (eds), *History of Concepts: Comparative Perspectives* (Amsterdam: Amsterdam University Press, 1998), p. 79.

2. Carl Schmitt, *Hugo Preuss. Sein Staatsbegriff und seine Stellung in der deutschen Staatslehre* (Tübingen: Mohr, 1930).
3. Max Horkheimer, *Gesammelte Schriften*, vol. 17 (Frankfurt am Main: Fischer, 1996), p. 172.
4. Ernst Vollrath, *Was ist das Politische?* (Würzburg: Konigshausen & Neumann, 2003).
5. As is argued by Christoph Schönberger, 'Der "Staat" der Allgemeinen Staatslehre: Anmerkungen zu einer eigenwilligen deutschen Disziplin im Vergleich mit Frankreich', in Olivier Beaud and Erik Volkmar Heyen (eds), *Eine deutsch–französische Rechtswissenschaft* (Baden-Baden: Nomes, 1999), p. 127.
6. Wilhelm Hennis, 'Zum Problem der deutschen Staatsanschauung', *Vierteljahreshefte für Zeitgeschichte* 7 (1959), p. 4. See also Jürgen Habermas, *The Philosophical Discourse of Modernity* [1985] (Cambridge: Polity, 1987).
7. Thus the subtitle of Detlev Peukert, *The Weimar Republic: The Crisis of Classical Modernity* (Harmondsworth: Penguin, 1993).
8. Jürgen Habermas, *Between Facts and Norms* (Cambridge: Polity, 1996), p. xli.
9. Josef Isensee, 'Staat und Verfassung', in Josef Isensee and Paul Kirchhof (eds), *Handbuch des Staatsrechts der Bundesrepublik Deutschland*, vol. 2 (Heidelberg: Müller, 2004), p. 65.
10. Jürgen Habermas, 'Hat die Konstitutionalisierung des Völkerrechts noch eine Chance?', in Jürgen Habermas, *Der gespaltene Westen* (Frankfurt am Main: Suhrkamp, 2004), p. 192.

Glossary

Beamtentum: officialdom.

Bewegung: movement. It was used by the National Socialists to refer to the SA and other ancillary organisations as well as the National Socialist Party.

Bundestag: Federal Parliament.

Bürger: citizen or bourgeois. The fact that it can mean either has often been seen as a problem.

Führerstaat: leadership state. It is typically associated with Hitler's Germany.

Gefolgschaft: followership, that is, the followers of a leader understood as a collectivity.

Gesetz: law, typically statute law.

Grossraumordnung: order of large spaces. It was used to refer to the order established between continental blocs dominated by hegemonic powers.

Herrschaft: rule or domination. It can be used in contrast to coercive rule or power (*Macht*) but also to emphasise the coercive nature of ruling.

kleindeutsch: 'small German', referring to the German state created in 1871 which embraced only part of the German population.

Macht: power.

Machtstaat: power state, typically a state competing for power with other states.

Obrigkeitsstaat: authoritarian state. It is often associated with pre-1918 German states.

Parteienstaat: a state in which political parties rather than the executive or civil service are predominant.

Parteienverdrossenheit: mood of discontent with political parties.

Polizeistaat: the police or policy state, that is, the state that intervenes extensively in the affairs of its citizens with the purpose of their improvement.

Rechtsstaat: sometimes translated as rule of law, though the concept is often explicitly distinguished from the Anglo-Saxon concept of the rule of law and seen as a concept specific to German constitutional thought.

Reich: empire.

Sonderweg: special road. It is typically used to refer to German departure from the supposedly normal political and constitutional development of Britain and France in the nineteenth century. The concept itself and its chronological reference points are disputed.

Sozialstaat: social state. It often has a broader meaning than welfare state (*Wohlfahrtsstaat*), though some critics have assimilated the two terms.

Verfassung: constitution.

Volk: people or nation. It can have racial connotations, though the concept of the *Volk* can also be explicitly contrasted with the concept of race (*Rasse*).

Völkerrecht: international law.

Biographical Notes

Adler, Max (1873–1937) was an Austrian Marxist and lawyer.

Adorno, Theodor (1900–69) was a member of the Institute for Social Research. He was an exile in England and America but subsequently returned to Germany. His *Minima Moralia* (1951) has the revealing subtitle *Reflections from Damaged Life*.

Alexy, Robert (b. 1945) is a jurist and philosopher.

Altmann, Rüdiger (b. 1922) is a conservative publicist who was influenced by Carl Schmitt.

Anschütz, Gerhard (1867–1948) was a legal positivist who became an advocate of democracy. He was a staunch defender of the Weimar Republic.

Arendt, Hannah (1906–75) was a philosopher who was an exile in France and America. She was stateless for twelve years. Her report on the trial of Adolf Eichmann, *Eichmann in Jerusalem* (1963), caused great controversy.

Arnim, Hans Herbert von (b. 1939) teaches constitutional theory.

Baring, Arnulf (b. 1932) is an historian and political scientist.

Bauer, Otto (1882–1938) was an Austrian Marxist and Foreign Minister of the first Austrian republic (1918–19).

Beck, Ulrich (b. 1944) is a sociologist whose reputation began a meteoric rise with the publication of *Risk Society* in 1986.

Bernhardi, Friedrich von (1849–1930) was a general.

Bernstein, Eduard (1850–1932) was the intellectual leader of revisionism in German socialism.

Besson, Waldemar (1929–71) promoted the development of politics as an academic discipline in the Federal Republic.

Best, Werner (1903–89) was a lawyer and an early National Socialist who rose to high rank in the SS. He was appointed *Reich* Plenipotentiary for Denmark in 1943.

Böckenförde, Ernst-Wolfgang (b. 1930) is a jurist and was a member of the Federal Constitutional Court (1983–96).

Borchert, Jens (b. 1961) is a political scientist.

Bornhak, Conrad (1861–1944) was a constitutional lawyer and pronounced monarchist. In 1933, he proclaimed that he had represented National Socialist ideas before the term was even thought of.

Bracher, Karl-Dietrich (b. 1922) is historian and political scientist. He wrote a pioneering study of the collapse of the Weimar republic.

Bülow, Oskar (1837–1907) was a jurist, colleague and friend of Rudolf von Ihering.

Czempiel, Ernst-Otto (b. 1927) is an emeritus Professor for Foreign and International Politics.

Dehio, Ludwig (1888–1963) was an historian and an early critic of the continuity between the hegemonic ambitions of the Third Reich and Prussia.

Ehmke, Horst (b. 1929) is a jurist. He joined the SPD in 1947 and held high ministerial office in the Federal government (1969–74).

Ehrlich, Eugen (1862–1922) was a leading representative of the Free Law Movement.

Eucken, Rudolf (1846–1926) was a neo-idealist philosopher.

Fabio, Udo di (b. 1954) is a jurist who became a member of the Federal Constitutional Court in 1999.

Forsthoff, Ernst (1902–74) enjoyed a successful career in the Third Reich and the Federal Republic. He was President of the Supreme Court of the Republic of Cyprus (1960–3).

Fraenkel, Ernst (1898–1975) was a lawyer and friend of Franz Neumann. He emigrated in 1938 and subsequently played a major role in promoting pluralist theory and a democratically orientated political science in the Federal Republic.

Friedrich, Carl J. (1901–84) is most well known for his concept of totalitarianism.

Gablentz, Otto-Heinrich von der (1898–1972) was involved in the resistance to the Third Reich. He promoted the development of political science in the Federal Republic.

Gehlen, Arnold (1904–76) was a proponent of an empirically orientated philosophical anthropology.

Gierke, Otto von (1841–1921) was an influential critic of Paul Laband.

Grewe, Wilhelm (1911–2000) specialised in international law and served in the Foreign Office of the Federal Republic.

Grimm, Dieter (b. 1937) is a jurist and was a member of the Federal Constitutional Court (1987–99).

Günther, Hans F.K. (1891–1968) was a prophet of the Nordic idea.

Häberle, Peter (b. 1934) is a jurist who was heavily influenced by Rudolf Smend. He has frequently invoked Karl Popper's idea of the open society.

Habermas, Jürgen (b. 1929) is the most eminent philosopher of the Federal Republic. He has played a highly prominent role in public controversies.

Hayek, Friedrich (1899–1992) was an economist. He had left his native Austria for England before the turn to authoritarianism. Even later in life, he insisted his mind had been shaped by these two countries. His *The Road to Serfdom* has been compared to John Stuart Mill's *On Liberty*, but it also exhibits the influence of Carl Schmitt.

Heckel, Johannes (1889–1963) was a vigorous supporter of the Third Reich.

Heller, Hermann (1891–1933) was a socialist and staunch defender of Weimar. He died in exile in Madrid.

Hellmann, Günther (b. 1960) is a political scientist.

Hennis, Wilhelm (b. 1923) advocated a normative understanding of politics against the dominant behaviouralism of the 1950s and 1960s.

Hermens, Ferdinand A. (1906–98) was exiled in America but subsequently returned to Germany. He was highly critical of proportional representation.

Herz, John J. (b. 1908) was a pupil of Hans Kelsen. He was exiled in Switzerland and America, where he became an influential proponent of a realist approach to international relations.

Hesse, Konrad (1919–2005) was a leading figure in the Freiburg School that included Horst Ehmke, Peter Häberle and Alexander Hollerbach.

Hinze, Otto (1861–1940) applied a comparative and historical approach to politics.

Höhn, Reinhard (1904–2000) was encouraged by Carl Schmitt, against whom he later turned. He joined the NSDAP and the SS. After 1945, he ran a successful management school.

Hollerbach, Alexander (b. 1931) is a jurist.

Holstein, Günther (1892–1931) was a jurist who was influenced by Protestant theology.

Horkheimer, Max (1895–1973) was Director of the Institute for Social Research (1930). He was exiled in America and became an American citizen, but returned to Germany.

Huber, Ernst Rudolf (1903–90) was close to Carl Schmitt and enjoyed a successful career in the Third Reich. Excluded from teaching again until 1952, he wrote a monumental constitutional history of Germany.

Huber, Max (1874–1960) was a Swiss jurist and member of the Permanent Court of International Justice (1922–30). He was an early proponent of the sociology of international relations.

Ihering, Rudolf von (1818–92) was a jurist.

Ipsen, Hans Peter (1907–1998) was close to Carl Schmitt but increasingly distanced himself from Schmitt after 1945.

Isensee, Josef (b. 1937) is a prominent étatist and co-editor of the massive *Handbuch des Staatsrechts*.

Jahrreiss, Hermann (1894–1992) was a jurist.

Jaspers, Karl (1883–1969) was a philosopher. He was forced from his post in 1937. His book, *The Question of German Guilt* (1946), has had an enduring impact on discussion of the theme.

Jellinek, Georg (1851–1911) was a jurist and exerted considerable influence on Max Weber. His theory of the state remains a standard reference point.

Jung, Edgar J. (1894–1934) was an adviser to Chancellor Franz von Papen. He was murdered in 1934 by the National Socialists.

Jünger, Ernst (1895–1998) was a veteran of the First World War, novelist and right-wing publicist.

Kaufmann, Erich (1880–1972) was a jurist and critic of legal positivism in the Weimar years.

Kaufmann, Franz-Xaver (b. 1932) is emeritus Professor of Social Policy and Sociology.

Keller, Hans (b. 1908) was a jurist.

Kelsen, Hans (1881–1973) was a legal positivist. He drafted the constitution of the first Austrian republic. He was later driven into exile in Czechoslovakia, then Switzerland and finally America.

Kirchheimer, Otto (1905–65) wrote his doctorate under the supervision of Carl Schmitt. He was later a member of the Institute for Social Research and worked for the American government (1944–55).

Koellreutter, Otto (1882–1972) was a jurist who competed with Carl Schmitt for influence in the Third Reich.

Kokott, Juliane (b. 1957) is a jurist and Advocate General at the Court of Justice of the European Communities since 2003.

Köttgen, Arnold (1902–67) specialised in administrative law. He continued his academic career after 1945.

Kriele, Martin (b. 1931) is a jurist who called for a clear break with German traditions.

Krockow, Christian Graf von (1927–2000) was a political scientist.

Krüger, Herbert (1905–89) was a pupil of Rudolf Smend but after 1945 was closer to Ernst Forsthoff.

Laband, Paul (1838–1918) was the leading figure in German legal positivism at the end of the nineteenth century.

Landauer, Carl (1887–1945) was co-founder of the Frankfurt Psychoanalytic Institute. He was murdered in Bergen-Belsen.

Langbehn, August Julius (1851–1907) was best known for his *Rembrandt as Educator*.

Laun, Rudolf (1882–1975) was born in Prague. He wrote widely on international law.

Lederer, Emil (1883–1939) was a political economist and sociologist. He went into exile in America in 1933.

Leibholz, Gerhard (1901–82) was a jurist who went into exile in England. He was an influential member of the Federal Constitutional Court (1951–71).

Lenz, Max (1850–1932) was an historian who contributed to the renaissance of the ideas of the nineteenth-century historian and theorist of great-power politics, Leopold von Ranke.

Loewenstein, Karl (1891–1973) was trained as a jurist. He emigrated to America.

Löwenthal, Leo (1900–93) was a sociologist of literature and member of the Institute for Social Research.

Lübbe, Hermann (b. 1926) is an influential philosopher and publicist. He was a member of the SPD and state secretary in the late 1960s.

Luhmann, Niklas (1927–98) became a prolific sociologist after a career in public administration.

Lukács, Georg (1885–1971) became a communist during the First World War and was a minister in the brief Hungarian Soviet Republic.

Mann, Thomas (1875–1955) was a German novelist.

Marcuse, Herbert (1898–1972) was a philosopher and member of the Institute for Social Research. He emigrated to America and subsequently worked for the American government (1942–51). He was popular with radical students in the 1960s.

Maus, Ingeborg (b. 1937) is a political scientist.

Mayer, Otto (1846–1924) wrote pioneering works in administrative law.

Mayer, Tilman (b. 1953) is a political scientist.

Meinecke, Friedrich (1862–1954) was an eminent historian.

Merkl, Adolf Julius (1890–1970) was an Austrian jurist and follower of Hans Kelsen.

Moeller van der Bruck, Arthur (1876–1925) was a young conservative publicist and author of *Das dritte Reich* (The Third Reich).

Morgenthau, Hans J. (1904–80) was a pupil of Hans Kelsen. His *Politics Among Nations* (1948) became a defining text in the realist approach to international relations.

Natorp, Paul (1854–1924) was a philosopher and pedagogue.

Naumann, Friedrich (1861–1919) was a liberal politician and publicist. He was a friend of Max Weber.

Nawiasky, Hans (1880–1961) was a jurist who was driven into exile in Switzerland. He played a role in constitutional deliberations in Germany after 1945.

Neesze, Gottfried (1911–87) played an active role in the Hitler Youth.

Neumann, Franz (1900–54) was a lawyer who acted for German trade unions before emigrating and becoming a member of the Institute for Social Research. He subsequently worked for the American government (1942–7).

Nicolai, Helmut (1895–1955) was a jurist who joined the NSDAP before the seizure of power. He lost influence in 1935 after a dispute with a *Gauleiter*.

Nolte, Ernst (b. 1923) is a controversial historian.

Oncken, Hermann (1869–1945) was a political historian. He was dismissed from his post in 1935.

Patzelt, Werner J. (b. 1953) is a political scientist.

Pernice, Ingolf (b. 1950) is a jurist who has worked for the European Commission.

Piloty, Robert (1863–1926) was a jurist and founding editor of the *Yearbook for Public Law* (1907) along with Georg Jellinek and Paul Laband.

Plessner, Helmut (1892–1985) was a philosophical anthropologist. He was an exile in the Netherlands.

Pollock, Frederick (1894–1970) was a political economist and member of the Institute for Social Research.

Popper, Karl (1902–94) was a philosopher of science. He was born in the Habsburg Empire. His book *The Open Society and its Enemies* (1945) became a standard reference for critics of totalitarianism.

Preuss, Hugo (1860–1925) was a liberal jurist. He drafted the constitution of the Weimar Republic.

Preuss, Ulrich (b. 1939) is a jurist and has been a member of the Bremen State Court of Justice since 1992.

Radbruch, Gustav (1878–1949) was a legal positivist and democrat. His reassessment of positive law in 1946 is referred to simply as Radbruch's formula. He was Minister of Justice in 1923.

Rauchhaupt, Friedrich Wilhelm von (1881–1989) specialised in international and comparative law.

Redslob, Robert (1882–1946) was a jurist.

Renner, Karl (1870–1950) was a Marxist and Chancellor of the Austrian Republic in 1918–20 and President in 1945.

Ridder, Helmut (b. 1919) is a jurist.

Ritter, Gerhard A. (b. 1929) is a political scientist.

Rohrmoser, Günter (b. 1927) is a philosopher and neo-conservative publicist.

Röpke, Wilhelm (1899–1966) was an economist. He went into exile in Turkey and Switzerland.

Rosenberg, Alfred (1893–1946) was a National Socialist and ran the party office for foreign affairs. He was appointed Minister for the Eastern Occupied Territories in 1941. After trial at Nuremberg, he was executed.

Rosenberg, Werner (n.d.) was a justice of the court.

Sauer, Wilhelm (1879–1962) was an eclectic jurist whose enthusiasm for the Third Reich faded.

Schäffle, Albert (1831–1904) was a political economist and sociologist.

Scheler, Max (1874–1928) was a philosopher and pupil of Rudolf Eucken. Scheler developed a materialist ethic of value that influenced some proponents of value-orientated jurisprudence.

Schelsky, Helmut (1912–84) was the most widely read sociologist in Germany in the 1950s and 1960s.

Scheuner, Ulrich (1893–1981) was ambivalent towards the Third Reich. He was a highly respected theorist of the state in the Federal Republic.

Schmitt, Carl (1888–1985) was a jurist and adviser to Chancellors Kurt von Schleicher and Franz von Papen. His prominence among jurists in the Third Reich was undermined by a dispute with the SS.

Schmoller, Gustav (1838–1917) was a political economist and founder of the Association for Social Policy (1872) which promoted social reform.

Schöllgen, Gregor (b. 1952) is an historian and commentator on foreign policy.

Schwarz, Hans-Peter (b. 1934) is an historian and political scientist.

Schwarzenberger, Georg (1908–91) specialised in international law. He emigrated to England.

Simmel, Georg (1858–1918) was a sociologist.

Sloterdijk, Peter (b. 1947) is a highly controversial philosopher and publicist.

Smend, Rudolf (1882–1975) was a jurist whose position in the Weimar years is disputed but who has often been presented as the main protagonist of Carl Schmitt and his students.

Sombart, Werner (1863–1941) was an economist and sociologist, a pupil of Gustav Schmoller and friend of Max Weber.

Sommer, Walter (1893–1946) was a jurist and committed National Socialist.

Sontheimer, Kurt (b. 1928) is a political scientist who was influenced by Ernst Fraenkel. His *Antidemokratisches Denken in der Weimarer Republik* (1962) became the standard work on the topic.

Spaemann, Robert (b. 1927) is a philosopher and a vigorous critic of the stream of thought represented by Jürgen Habermas.

Spann, Othmar (1878–1950) was Austrian corporativist. His main political work is *The True State* (1921).

Spengler, Oswald (1880–1936) was best known for his *Decline of the West* (1918–22).

Sternberger, Dolf (1907–89) played a major role in the development of political science after 1945.

Stier-Somlo, Fritz (1873–1932) was a jurist who welcomed the advent of democracy with the Weimar Republic.

Stolleis, Michael (b. 1941) is a legal historian.

Strauss, Leo (1899–1973) was a political philosopher. He emigrated to America.

Stürmer, Michael (b. 1938) is an historian and was an adviser to Chancellor Helmut Kohl in the 1980s.

Thoma, Richard (1874–1957) was a positivist and defender of the Weimar Republic.

Tönnies, Ferdinand (1861–1936) was a sociologist most widely known for his *Community and Society* (1887).

Treistchke, Heinrich von (1832–96) exerted great influence through his lectures on politics.

Triepel, Heinrich (1861–1946) was a jurist with wide-ranging interests.

Troeltsch, Ernst (1865–1923) was an historian of religion.

Verdross, Alfred (1890–1980) was an Austrian jurist and pupil of Hans Kelsen. He later turned to natural law.

Voegelin, Eric (1899–1973) was sympathetic to the authoritarian government in Austria (1934–8). He narrowly escaped the Gestapo in 1938 and fled to America via Switzerland.

Vollrath, Ernst (1932–2004) was a political theorist strongly influenced by Hannah Arendt.

Wagner, Adolf (1835–1917) was an economist and advocate of state socialism.

Walz, Gustav Adolf (1897–1948) wrote extensively on international law in the Third Reich.

Weber, Alfred (1868–1958) was an economist and sociologist. He was the brother of Max Weber.

Weber, Max (1864–1920) is better known as a sociologist, but his interest in the theory of the state is increasingly recognised.

Weber, Werner (1904–76) was a pupil of Carl Schmitt but distanced himself from Schmitt. He was not related to Max and Alfred Weber.

Willms, Bernhard (1931–91) was heavily influenced by Carl Schmitt.

Zorn, Philipp (1850–1928) was a conservative jurist and member of the delegation to the Hague Peace Conference (1899).

Select Bibliography

This bibliography lists books directly referred to in the notes. It does not include journal articles and other sources or material consulted but not directly referred to.

Adler, Max (1981), *Ausgewählte Schriften*, Vienna: Österreichischer Bundesverlag.

Adorno, Theodor W. (1970), *Erziehung zur Mündigkeit*, Frankfurt am Main: Suhrkamp.

Alexy, Robert (1989) [1978], *A Theory of Legal Argumentation*, Oxford: Clarendon.

Alexy, Robert (2002) [1986], *A Theory of Constitutional Rights*, Oxford: Oxford University Press.

Altmann, Rüdiger (1998), *Abschied vom Staat*, Frankfurt am Main: Campus.

Anschütz, Gerhard et al. (eds) (1920), *Handbuch der Politik*, vol. 1, Berlin: Walther Rothschild.

Anschütz, Gerhard and Richard Thoma (eds) (1930), *Handbuch des deutschen Staatsrechts*, vol. 1, Tübingen: Mohr.

Anter, Max (1995), *Max Webers Theorie des modernen Staates*, Berlin: Duncker & Humblot.

Arato, Andrew and Eike Gebhardt (eds) (1978), *The Essential Frankfurt School Reader*, Oxford: Blackwell.

Arendt, Hannah (1967), *The Origins of Totalitarianism*, 3rd edn, London: Allen & Unwin.

Arendt, Hannah (2000), *Vor Antisemitismus ist man nur noch auf dem Monde sicher*, Munich: Piper.

Arnim, Hans Herbert von (1984), *Staatslehre der Bundesrepublik Deutschland*, Munich: Franz Vahlen.

Arnim, Hans Herbert von (2001), *Das System*, Munich: Knaur.

Arnim, Hans Herbert von (2002), *Vom schönen Schein der Demokratie*, Munich: Knaur.

Asheim, Stephen E. (1994), *The Nietzsche Legacy in Germany 1890–1990*, Berkeley: University of California Press.

Barion, Hans, Ernst Forsthoff and Werner Weber (eds) (1959), *Festschrift für Carl Schmitt*, Berlin: Duncker & Humblot.

229

Bauer, Otto (2000) [1907], *The Question of Nationalities and Social Democracy*, Minneapolis: University of Minnesota Press.

Beaud, Olivier and Erik Volkmar Heyen (eds) (1999), *Eine deutsch–französische Rechtswissenschaft*, Baden-Baden: Nomes.

Beck, Ulrich (1992) [1986], *Risk Society*, London: Sage.

Beck, Ulrich (1997) [1993], *The Reinvention of Politics*, Cambridge: Polity.

Beck, Ulrich (2000) [1997], *What is Globalization?*, Cambridge: Polity.

Becker, F. (2001), *Bilder von Krieg und Nation. Die Einigungskriege in der bürgerlichen Öffentlichkeit Deutschlands 1864–1913*, Munich: Oldenbourg.

Benvenisti, Eyal (1993), *The International Law of Occupation*, Princeton, NJ: Princeton University Press.

Bernhardi, F. von (1914) [1911], *Germany and the Next War*, London: Edward Arnold.

Besson, Waldemar (1973), *Die Aussenpolitik der Bundesrepublik*, Frankfurt am Main: Ullstein.

Bialas, Wolfgang and Manfred Gangl (eds) (2000), *Intellektuelle im Nationalsozialismus*, Frankfurt am Main: Peter Lang.

Bleek, Wilhelm (2001), *Geschichte der Politikwissenschaft in Deutschland*, Munich: Beck.

Böckenförde, Ernst-Wolfgang (1991a), *Recht, Staat, Freiheit*, Frankfurt am Main: Suhrkamp.

Böckenförde, Ernst-Wolfgang (1991b), *Staat, Verfassung, Demokratie*, Frankfurt am Main: Suhrkamp.

Böckenförde, Ernst-Wolfgang (1999), *Staat, Nation, Europa*, Frankfurt am Main: Suhrkamp.

Borchert, Jens (2003), *Die Professionalisierung der Politik*, Frankfurt am Main: Campus.

Bristler, Eduard [John H. Herz] (1938), *Nationalsozialistische Völkerrecht*, Zurich: Europa.

Bronner, Stephen and Douglas Kellner (eds) (1989), *Critical Theory and Society*, London: Routledge.

Bülow, Birgit von (1996), *Die Staatsrechtslehre der Nachkriegszeit (1945–1952)*, Berlin: Berlin Verlag.

Burin, Frederic S. and Kurt L. Shell (eds) (1969), *Politics, Law and Social Change*, New York: Columbia University Press.

Bussche, Raimund von dem (1998), *Konservatismus in der Weimarer Republik*, Heidelberg: Winter.

Caldwell, Peter C. (1997), *Popular Sovereignty and the Crisis of German Constitutional Law*, Durham, NC: Duke University Press.

Canovan, Margaret (1992), *Hannah Arendt*, Cambridge: Cambridge University Press.

Czempiel, Otto (1999), *Kluge Macht*, Munich: Beck.

Dehio, Ludwig (1963) [1948], *The Precarious Balance*, London: Chatto & Windus.

Demm, Eberhard (ed.) (1999), *Politische Theorie und Tagespolitik*, Marburg: Metropolis.

Dews, Peter (ed.) (1992), *Autonomy and Solidarity*, London: Verso.

Dubiel, Helmut (1999), *Niemand ist frei von der Geschichte*, Munich: Hanser.

Dyson, Kenneth H. F. (1980), *The State Tradition in Western Europe*, Oxford: Martin Robertson.

Ehmke, Horst (1979), *Politik als Herausforderung*, Karlsruhe: Müller.

Ehmke, Horst et al. (eds) (1973), *Festschrift für Ulrich Scheuner*, Berlin: Duncker & Humblot.

Ehrlich, Eugen (1962) [1913], *Fundamental Principles of the Sociology of Law*, New York: Russell and Russell.

Elster, L. et al. (eds) (1926), *Handwörterbuch der Staatswissenschaften*, vol. 7, Jena: Fischer.

Fabio, Udo di (2003), *Die Staatsrechtslehre und der Staat*, Paderborn: Schöningh.

Forsthoff, Ernst (1933), *Der totale Staat*, Hamburg: Hanseatische Verlagsanstalt.

Forsthoff, Ernst (1938), *Die Verwaltung als Leistungsträger*, Stuttgart: Kohlhammer.

Fraenkel, Ernst (1979), *Deutschland und die westlichen Demokratien*, 7th edn, Stuttgart: Kohlhammer.

Fraenkel, Ernst (1999), *Gesammelte Schriften*, vols. 1–3, Baden-Baden: Nomos.

Frank, Hans (ed.) (1937), *Deutsches Verwaltungsrecht*, Munich: Eher.

Gebhardt, Jürgen et al. (eds) (1994), *Demokratie, Verfassung und Nation*, Baden-Baden: Nomos.

Gehlen, Arnold (2004a) [1950], *Der Mensch*, Wiebelsheim: Aula.

Gehlen, Arnold (2004) [1969], *Moral und Hypermoral*, Frankfurt am Main: Klostermann.

Göhler, Gerhard, Matthias Iser and Ina Kerner (eds) (2004), *Politische Theorie. 22 umkämpfte Begriffe zur Einführung*, Wiesbaden: VS.

Grimm, Dieter (1994), *Die Zukunft der Verfassung*, 2nd edn, Frankfurt am Main: Suhrkamp.

Groh, Dieter and Peter Brandt (1992), *'Vaterlandslose Gesellen'. Sozialdemokratie und Nation 1860–1990*, Munich: Beck.

Grossheim, Michael, Karlheinz Weissmann and Rainer Zitlemann (eds) (1993), *Westbindung*, Frankfurt am Main: Ullstein.

Günther, Frieder (2004), *Denken vom Staat her*, Munich: Oldenbourg.

Gusy, Christoph (ed.) (2000), *Demokratisches Denken in der Weimarer Republik*, Baden-Baden: Nomos.

Häberle, Peter (1998a), *Verfassung als öffentlicher Prozess*, Berlin: Duncker & Humblot.

Häberle, Peter (1998b), *Verfassungslehre als Kulturwissenschaft*, Berlin: Duncker & Humblot.

Häberle, Peter and Alexander Hollerbach (eds) (1984), *Konrad Hesse. Ausgewählte Schriften*, Heidelberg: Müller.

Haberman, Gerd (1997), *Der Wohlfahrtsstaat. Die Geschichte eines Irrwegs*, Berlin: Ullstein.

Habermas, Jürgen (1974), *Theory and Practice*, London: Heinemann.

Habermas, Jürgen (1976) [1973], *Legitimation Crisis*, London: Heinemann.

Habermas, Jürgen (1981), *Kleine Politische Schriften*, Frankfurt am Main: Suhrkamp.

Habermas, Jürgen (ed.) (1984a) [1979], *Observations on 'The Spiritual Situation of the Age'*, Cambridge, MA: MIT.

Habermas, Jürgen (1984b) [1981], *The Theory of Communicative Action*, vol. 1, London: Heineman.

Habermas, Jürgen (1985), *Die neue Unübersichtlichkeit*, Frankfurt am Main: Suhrkamp.

Habermas, Jürgen (1987a) [1981], *The Theory of Communicative Action*, vol. 2, Cambridge: Polity.

Habermas, Jürgen (1987b) [1985], *The Philosophical Discourse of Modernity*, Cambridge: Polity.

Habermas, Jürgen (1989), *The New Conservatism*, Cambridge: Polity.

Habermas, Jürgen (1992) [1962], *The Structural Transformation of the Public Sphere*, Cambridge: Polity.

Habermas, Jürgen (1996) [1992], *Between Facts and Norms*, Cambridge: Polity.

Habermas, Jürgen (1996), *Die Einbeziehung des Anderen*, Frankfurt am Main: Suhrkamp.

Hamann, Brigitte (1999), *Hitler's Vienna*, Oxford: Oxford University Press.

Hampsher-Monk, Iain, Karin Tilmans and Frank von Vree (eds) (1998), *History of Concepts: Comparative Perspectives*, Amsterdam: Amsterdam University Press.

Hayek, F. A. (1943), *The Road to Serfdom*, London: Routledge.

Heckel, Johannes (1939), *Wehrverfassung und Wehrrecht des Grossdeutschen Reiches*, Hamburg: Hanseatische Verlagsanstalt.

Heller, Hermann (1992), *Gesammelte Schriften*, vols 1–2, Tübingen: Mohr.

Hennis, Wilhelm (1998), *Auf dem Weg in den Parteienstaat*, Stuttgart: Reclam.

Hennis, Wilhelm (1999), *Regieren im modernen Staat*, Tübingen: Mohr.

Hennis, Wilhelm (2000), *Politikwissenschaft und politisches Denken*, Tübingen: Mohr Siebeck.

Hermens, Ferdinand A. (1969), *Zwischen Politik und Vernunft*, Berlin: Duncker & Humblot.

Herz, John H. (1984), *Vom Überleben*, Düsseldorf: Droste.

Hesse, Konrad (1999), *Grundzüge des Verfassungsrechts der Bundesrepublik Deutschland*, Heidelberg: Müller.

Hesse, Konrad, Siegfried Reicke and Ulrich Scheuner (eds) (1962), *Staatsverfassung und Kirchenordnung*, Tübingen: Mohr.

Hilger, Christian (2003), *Rechtsstaatsbegriffe im Dritten Reich*, Tübingen: Mohr.

Hitler, Adolf (1969) [1925–6], *Mein Kampf*, London: Radius.

Horkheimer, Max (1985), *Gesammelte Schriften*, vols 7 and 12, Frankfurt am Main: Fischer.

Horkheimer, Max (1993), *Between Philosophy and Social Science*, Cambridge, MA: MIT.

Horkheimer, Max and Theodor W. Adorno (1973) [1947], *Dialectic of Enlightenment*, London: Allen Lane.

Huber, Ernst Rudolf (1939), *Verfassungsrecht des Grossdeutschen Reiches*, Hamburg: Hanseatische Verlagsanstalt.

Huber, Ernst Rudolf (1965), *Nationalstaat und Verfassungsstaat*, Stuttgart: Kohlhammer.

Hughes, H. Stuart (1987), *Between Commitment and Disillusion*, Middletown, CT: Wesleyan University Press.

Iggers, George (1997), *Deutsche Geschichtswissenschaft*, Vienna: Böhlau.

Ihering, Rudolf von (1968) [1903], *Law as a Means to an End*, South Hackensack, NJ: Rothman.

Ipsen, Hans Peter (1937), *Politik und Justiz*, Hamburg: Hanseatische Verlagsanstalt.

Isensee, Josef and Paul Kirchhof (eds) (2003–4), *Handbuch des Staatsrechts der Bundesrepublik Deutschland*, vols 1–2, Heidelberg: Müller.

Janik, Allan and Stephen Toulmin (1973), *Wittgenstein's Vienna*, New York: Simon and Schuster.

Jansen, Christian (1992), *Professoren und Politik*, Göttingen: Vandenhoeck & Ruprecht.

Jaspers, Karl (2000) [1947], *The Question of German Guilt*, New York: Fordham.

Jellinek, Georg (1929) [1913], *Allgemeine Staatslehre*, 3rd edn, Berlin: Julius Springer.

Jellinek, Georg (1970), *Ausgewählte Schriften und Reden*, 2 vols, Aalen: Scientia.

Jellinek, Georg (1996a) [1882], *Die Lehre von den Staatenverbindungen*, Goldbach: Keip.

Jellinek, Georg (1996b) [1898], *Das Recht der Minoritäten*, Schutterwald: Klaus Fischer.

Jellinek, Georg (1996c) [1906], *Verfassungsänderung und Verfassungswandlung*, Goldbach: Keip.

Jung, Edgar (1995) [1927], *The Rule of the Inferior*, vol. 2, Lewiston: Mellen.

Jünger, Ernst (2001), *Politische Publizistik*, Stuttgart: Klett-Cotta.

Kaufmann, Franz-Xaver (1997), *Herausforderungen des Sozialstaates*, Frankfurt am Main: Suhrkamp.

Keller, Hans (1938), *Das Recht der Völker*, Berlin: Franz Vahlen.
Kelly, Duncan (2003), *The State of the Political*, Oxford: Oxford University Press.
Kelsen, Hans (1925), *Allgemeine Staatslehre*, Berlin: Springer.
Kelsen, Hans (1981a) [1923], *Hauptprobleme der Staatsrechtslehre*, Aalen: Scientia.
Kelsen, Hans (1981b) [1929] *Vom Wesen und Wert der Demokratie*, Aalen: Scientia.
Kelsen, Hans (1994), *Drei Kleine Schriften*, Aalen: Scientia.
Kempter, Klaus (1998), *Die Jellineks 1820–1955*, Düsseldorf: Droste.
Kirchheimer, Otto (1969), *Politics, Law and Social Change*, New York: Columbia University Press.
Knowlton, James and Truett Cates (eds) (1993), *Forever in the Shadow of Hitler?* (New Jersey: Humanities Press.
Koselleck, Reinhard (1973) [1959], *Kritik und Krise*, Frankfurt am Main: Suhrkamp.
Koskenniemi, Martti (2002), *The Gentle Civilizer of Nations*, Cambridge: Cambridge University Press.
Kriele, Martin (1994), *Einführung in die Staatslehre*, 5th edn, Opladen: Westdeutscher Verlag.
Krüger, Herbert (1964), *Allgemeine Staatslehre*, Stuttgart: Kohlhammer.
Lammer, Richard J. (1963), *Der englische Parlamentarismus in der deutschen politischen Theorie im Zeitalter Bismarcks (1857–1890)*, Lübeck: Matthiesen.
Leggewie, Claus (1987), *Der Geist steht Rechts*, Berlin: Rotbuch.
Lehnert, Detlef (1998), *Verfassungsdemokratie als Bürgergenossenschaft*, Baden-Baden: Nomos.
Lehnert, Detlef and Christoph Müller (eds) (2003), *Vom Untertanenverband zur Bürgergenossenschaft*, Baden-Baden: Nomos.
Leibholz, Gerhard (1966) [1929], *Das Wesen der Repräsentation*, 3rd edn, Berlin: de Gruyter.
Leibholz, Gerhard (1967), *Strukturprobleme der modernen Demokratie*, 3rd edn, Karlsruhe: Müller.
Lenk, Kurt (1989), *Deutscher Konservatismus*, Frankfurt am Main: Campus.
Lenz, Max (1922), *Wille, Macht, Schicksal*, Munich: Oldenbourg.
Lessing, H. (1937), *Das Recht der Staatsangehörigkeit und die Aberkennung der Staatsangehörigkeit zu Straf- und Sicherungszwecken*, Leiden: Brill.
Lietzmann, Hans J. (ed.) (2001), *Moderne Politik*, Opladen: Leske & Budrich.
Livingstone, Rodney (ed.) (1972), *Georg Lukács: Political Writings 1919–1929*, London: NLB.
Llanque, Marcus (2000), *Demokratisches Denken im Krieg*, Berlin: Akademie.
Loewenstein, Karl (1944), *Hitler's Germany*, 3rd edn, New York: Macmillan.
Löwenthal, Leo (1980), *Mitmachen wollte ich nie*, Frankfurt am Main: Suhrkamp.

Löwenthal, Leo (1987), *False Prophets*, New Brunswick, NJ: Transaction.

Lübbe, Hermann 1974), *Politische Philosophie in Deutschland*, Munich: DTV.

Lübbe, Hermann (2001a), *Aufklärung anlasshalber*, Gräfeling: Resche.

Lübbe, Hermann (2001b), *Politik nach der Aufklärung*, Munich: Fink.

Luhmann, Niklas (1983) [1969], *Legitimation durch Verfahren*, Frankfurt am Main: Suhrkamp.

Luhmann, Niklas (1995), *Das Recht der Gesellschaft*, Frankfurt am Main: Suhrkamp.

Luhmann, Niklas (2000), *Die Politik der Gesellschaft*, Frankfurt am Main: Suhrkamp.

Lutz-Bechmann, Matthias and James Bohman (eds) (2002), *Weltstaat oder Staatenwelt?*, Frankfurt am Main: Suhrkamp.

McCormick, John P. (ed.) (2002), *Confronting Mass Democracy and Industrial Technology*, Durham, NC: Duke University Press.

Marcuse, Herbert (1955), *Reason and Revolution*, London: Routledge.

Marcuse, Herbert (1968), *Negations*, Harmondsworth: Penguin.

Marcuse, Herbert (1998), *Technology, War and Fascism*, London: Routledge.

Maus, Ingeborg (1986), *Rechtstheorie und politische Theorie im Industriekapitalismus*, Munich: Fink.

Meinecke, Friedrich (1946), *Die deutsche Katastrophe*, Wiesbaden: Brockhaus.

Meinecke, Friedrich (1947), *Strassburg/Freiburg/Berlin 1901–1919. Erinnerungen*, Stuttgart: Koehler.

Meinecke, Friedrich (1979), *Politische Schriften und Reden*, Darmstadt: Toeche-Mittler.

Meinecke, Friedrich (1998) [1924], *Machiavellism: The Doctrine of Raison d'État and its Place in Modern History*, New Brunswick, NJ: Transaction.

Merkl, Adolf (1995), *Gesammelte Schriften*, vol. 1, part 2, Berlin: Duncker & Humblot.

Möllers, Christoph (2000), *Staat als Argument*, Munich: Beck.

Mommsen, Wolfgang J. (1984), *Max Weber and German Politics 1890–1920*, Chicago: Chicago University Press.

Mommsen, Wolfgang J. (ed.) (1987), *Max Weber and his Contemporaries*, London: Allen and Unwin.

Müller, Jan-Werner (2000), *Another Country*, New Haven, CT: Yale University Press.

Nawiasky, Hans (1945, 1952), *Allgemeine Staatslehre*, vols 1 and 2, Einsiedeln: Benziger.

Neumann, Franz (1942), *Behemoth*, London: Gollancz.

Neumann, Franz (1957), *The Democratic and the Authoritarian State*, New York: Free Press.

Neumann, Franz (1986) [1935], *The Rule of Law*, Leamington Spa: Berg.

Niethammer, Lutz (2000), *Kollektive Identität*, Hamburg: Rowohlt.

Noakes, Jeremy and Geoffrey Pridham (eds) (1984), *Nazism*, vol. 2, Exeter: Exeter University Press.

Nolte, Ernst (1997), *Der Europäische Bürgerkrieg*, Munich: Herbig.

Peukert, Detlev (1993), *The Weimar Republic: The Crises of Classical Modernity*, Harmondsworth: Penguin.

Playi, Melchior (ed.) (1923), *Hauptprobleme der Soziologie*, Munich: Duncker & Humblot.

Plessner, Helmuth (1974) [1959], *Die verspätete Nation*, Frankfurt am Main: Suhrkamp.

Plessner, Helmuth (2002) [1924], *Grenzen der Gemeinschaft*, Frankfurt am Main: Suhrkamp.

Popper, Karl (1962), *The Open Society and its Enemies*, vols 1 and 2, 4th edn, London: Routledge & Kegan Paul.

Preuss, Hugo (1885), *Deutschland und sein Reichskanzler*, Berlin: Habel.

Preuss, Hugo (1906), *Die Entwicklung des deutschen Städtewesens*, Leipzig: Teubner.

Preuss, Hugo (1915), *Das deutsche Volk und die Politik*, Jena: Eugen Diederichs.

Preuss, Hugo (1916), *Obrigkeitsstaat und grossdeutsche Gedanke*, Jena: Diederichs.

Preuss, Hugo (1926), *Staat, Recht, Freiheit*, Tübingen: Mohr.

Preuss, Ulrich K. (1995) [1990], *Constitutional Revolution*, New Jersey: Humanities Press.

Radbruch, Gustav (1987, 1990, 1991), *Gesamtaugabe*, vols 1, 3 and 17, Heidelberg: Müller.

Rauchhaupt, Fr. von (1936), *Völkerrecht*, Munich: Voglrieder.

Rebentisch, Dieter and Karl Teppe (eds) (1986), *Verwaltung contra Menschenführung im Staat Hitlers*, Göttingen: Vandenhoeck & Ruprecht.

Redslob, Robert (1918), *Die parlamentarische Regierung in ihrer wahren und in ihrer unechten Form*, Tübingen: Mohr.

Renner, Karl (1949) [1929], *The Institutions of Private Law and Their Social Function*, 2nd edn, London: Routledge & Paul.

Renner, Karl (1994), *Schriften*, Salzburg: Residenz.

Ritter, Gerhard (1948), *Europa und die deutsche Frage*, Munich: Münchner.

Rohrmoser, Günter (1999), *Kampf um die Mitte*, Munich: Olzog.

Rosenberg, Alfred (1934) [1930], *Der Mythus des 20. Jahrhunderts*, Munich: Hohenheichen.

Scaff, Lawrence A. (1989), *Fleeing the Iron Cage*, Berkeley, CA: University of California Press.

Scheler, Max (1979), *Die Zukunft des Kapitalismus und andere Aufsätze*, Munich: Francke.

Schelsky, Helmut (1963), *Die skeptische Generation*, Düsseldorf: Eugen Diederichs.

Schelsky, Helmut (1967), *Ortsbestimmung der deutschen Soziologie*, 3rd edn, Düsseldorf: Eugen Diederichs.

Schelsky, Helmut (1975), *Die Arbeit tun die anderen*, Opladen: Westdeutscher Verlag.

Scheuerman, William (1999), *Carl Schmitt: The End of Law*, Lanham: Rowan & Littlefield.

Scheuner, Ulrich (1978), *Staatstheorie und Staatsrecht*, Berlin: Duncker & Humblot.

Scheuner, Ulrich (1984), *Schriften zum Völkerrecht*, Berlin: Duncker & Humblot.

Schmitt, Carl (1930) *Hugo Preuss. Sein Staatsbegriff und seine Stellung in der deutschen Staatslehre*, Tübingen: Mohr.

Schmitt, Carl (1933), *Staat, Bewegung, Volk*, Hamburg: Hanseatische Verlagsanstalt.

Schmitt, Carl (1934a), *Nationalsozialismus und Völkerrecht*, Berlin: Duncker & Dünnhaupt.

Schmitt, Carl (1934b), *Über die drei Arten des Rechtswissenschaftlichen Denkens*, Hamburg: Hanseatische Verlagsanstalt.

Schmitt, Carl (1938), *Die Wendung zum diskriminierenden Kriegsbegriff*, Berlin: Duncker & Humblot.

Schmitt, Carl (1940), *Positionen und Begriffe im Kampf mit Weimar–Genf–Versailles 1923–1939*, Hamburg: Hanseatische Verlagsanstalt.

Schmitt, Carl (1941), *Völkerrechtliche Grossraumordnung*, 4th edn, Berlin: Deutscher Rechtsverlag.

Schmitt, Carl (1958), *Verfassungsrechtliche Aufsätze aus den Jahren 1924–1954*, Berlin: Duncker & Humblot.

Schmitt, Carl (1963), *Theorie des Partisanen*, Berlin: Duncker & Humblot.

Schmitt, Carl (1985) [1922], *Political Theology*, Cambridge, MA: MIT.

Schmitt, Carl (1988) [1926], *The Crisis of Parliamentary Democracy*, Cambridge, MA: MIT.

Schmitt, Carl (1993) [1928], *Verfassungslehre*, Berlin: Duncker & Humblot.

Schmitt, Carl (1995), *Staat, Grossraum, Nomos*, Berlin: Duncker & Humblot.

Schmitt, Carl (1996) [1932], *The Concept of the Political*, Chicago: University of Chicago Press.

Schmitt, Carl (1997) [1950], *Der Nomos der Erde*, Berlin: Duncker & Humblot.

Schmitt, Carl (1998) [1932], *Legalität und Legitimität*, Berlin: Duncker & Humblot.

Schöllgen, Gregor (1992), *Die Macht in der Mitte Europas*, Munich: Beck.

Schöllgen, Gregor (2004), *Der Auftritt. Deutschlands Rückkehr auf die Weltbühne*, Berlin: Ullstein.

Schönberger, Christoph (1997), *Das Parlament im Anstaltsstaat*, Frankfurt am Main: Klostermann.

Schönwälder, Karen (1992), *Historiker und Politik*, Frankfurt am Main: Campus.

Schwarz, Hans-Peter (1985), *Die gezähmten Deutschen. Von der Macht- besessenheit zur Machtvergessenheit*, Stuttgart: DVA.

Schwarzenberger, Georg (1941), *Power Politics*, London: Cape.

Simmel, Georg (1999), *Gesamtausgabe*, vol. 16, Frankfurt am Main: Suhrkamp.

Simon, Dieter (ed.) (1994), *Rechtswissenschaft in der Bonner Republik*, Frankfurt am Main: Suhrkamp.

Sloterdijk, Peter (1993), *Im selben Boot*, Frankfurt am Main: Suhrkamp.

Sloterdijk, Peter (1998), *Der starke Grund zusammen zu sein*, Frankfurt am Main: Suhrkamp.

Smend, Rudolf (1994), *Staatsrechtliche Abhandlungen*, Berlin: Duncker & Humblot.

Sontheimer, Kurt (1994) [1968], *Antidemokratisches Denken in der Weimarer Republik*, Munich: DTV.

Sontheimer, Kurt (1999), *So war Deutschland nie*, Munich: Beck.

Spaemann, Robert (1977), *Zur Kritik der politischen Utopie*, Stuttgart: Klett.

Spengler, Oswald (1933), *Politische Schriften*, Munich: Beck.

Steger, Manfred B. (1997), *The Quest for Evolutionary Socialism*, Cambridge: Cambridge University Press.

Sternberger, Dolf (1980a), *Herrschaft und Vereinbarung*, Frankfurt am Main: Insel.

Sternberger, Dolf (1980b), *Staatsfreundschaft*, Frankfurt am Main: Insel.

Sternberger, Dolf (1990), *Verfassungspatriotismus*, Frankfurt am Main: Insel.

Stolleis, Michael (1998), *The Law under the Swastika*, Chicago: University of Chicago Press.

Stolleis, Michael (1999), *Geschichte des öffentlichen Rechts in Deutschland*, vol. 3, Munich: C. H. Beck.

Strauss, Leo (1952) [1936], *The Political Philosophy of Hobbes*, Chicago: University of Chicago Press.

Stuckart, Wilhelm et al. (1941), *Festgabe für Heinrich Himmler*, Darmstadt: Wittich.

Thadden, Rudolf von (ed.) (1978), *Die Krise des Liberalismus zwischen den Weltkriegen*, Göttingen: Vandenhoeck & Ruprecht.

Tönnies, Ferdinand (2000), *Gesamtausgabe*, vol. 9, Berlin: de Gruyter.

Treitschke, Heinrich von (1916) [1898], *Politics*, vol. 1, London: Constable.

Triepel, Carl Heinrich (1899), *Völkerrecht und Landesrecht*, Leipzig: Hirschfeld.

Triepel, Carl Heinrich (1943), *Die Hegemonie*, Stuttgart, Kohlhammer.

Tudor, H. and J. M. Tudor (eds) (1988), *Marxism and Social Democracy: The Revisionist Debate 1896–1898*, Cambridge: Cambridge University Press.

Unseld, Siegfried (ed.) (1993), *Politik ohne Projekt*, Frankfurt am Main: Suhrkamp.

Verdross, Alfred (1920), *Die völkerrechtswidrige Kriegshandlung und der Strafanspruch der Staaten*, Berlin: Engelmann.

Verdross, Alfred and Bruno Simma (1984), *Universelles Völkerrecht*, 3rd edn, Berlin: Duncker & Humblot.

Voegelin, Eric (1996) [1938], *Die politischen Religionen*, Munich: Fink.

Vollrath, Ernst (2003), *Was ist das Politische?*, Würzburg: Königshausen & Neumann.

Weber, Max (1924), *Gesammelte Aufsätze zur Soziologie und Sozialpolitik*, Tübingen: Mohr.

Weber, Max (1951), *Gesammelte Aufsätze zur Wissenschaftslehre*, 2nd edn, Tübingen: Mohr.

Weber, Max (1972) [1921], *Wirtschaft und Gesellschaft*, Tübingen: Mohr.

Weber, Max (1994), *Political Writings*, Cambridge: Cambridge University Press.

Wiegandt, Manfred H. (1995), *Norm und Wirklichkeit*, Baden-Baden: Nomos.

Williams, Howard, Colin Wight and Norbert Kapferer (eds) (2000), *Political Thought and German Unification*, Houndmills: Palgrave.

Willms, Bernhard (1986), *Idealismus und Nation*, Paderborn: Schöningh.

Winkler, Heinrich August (2002), *Der lange Weg nach Westen*, vol. 2, Munich: Beck.

Index